Stanley M. Horton
Shaper *of* Pentecostal
Theology

גְּאֻלַּת-יִשְׂרָאֵל

ISRAEL'S REDEMPTION

...so all Israel will be saved...
Romans 11:26a NLT

With heartfelt gratitude for your faithful support of Israel's Redemption and your continued commitment to the salvation of "all Israel."

Stanley M. Horton

Stanley M. Horton, Th.D.

Lois E. Olena

Lois E. Olena, D.Min.

Raymond L. Gannon

Raymond L. Gannon, Ph.D.

Stanley M. Horton
Shaper *of* Pentecostal
Theology

Lois E. Olena
with Raymond L. Gannon

Gospel Publishing House
Springfield, Missouri
02-0564

I dedicate this book to
My Colleague and Friend
Dr. Gary B. McGee
April 22, 1945—December 10, 2008
Person of the Spirit
and
Pentecostal Historian *Par Excellence*

We would like to thank Central Bible College (*The Centralite* and *The CUP)*, the Flower Pentecostal Heritage Center, and especially the Horton family for pictures used in the biography.

Contents

FOREWORD

With echoes from the Azusa Street revival (1906–09) still ringing in their ears, the founding fathers and mothers of the Assemblies of God laid the foundation for what would become one of the largest families of Pentecostal churches in the world. The rough-and-tumble world of early Pentecostalism was marked not only by passionate proclamation of the gospel, but in many quarters by a certain impermanence, impetuosity, and lack of wisdom. Responding to these problems, the Assemblies of God was organized in 1914 by those who recognized the need to provide accountability on doctrine, morals, and finances, and also to establish institutions such as schools, a publishing house, and a missions agency.

Almost one hundred years later, it is imperative that the Assemblies of God reexamine how it arrived at this point on the pilgrimage of faith. The reasons for the existence of the Assemblies of God are every bit as compelling today as they were in the beginning. We must not be distracted by secondary issues and lose sight of these core values.

Few people in the Assemblies of God exemplify its founding ideals better than Dr. Stanley M. Horton. A child of the Azusa Street Mission and revival, he went on to become a bridge linking Pentecostalism's past to its present. Through his dozens of books, hundreds of articles, decades of authoring the *Adult Teacher* Sunday School curriculum, and over sixty years in the classroom, Horton has profoundly shaped and influenced the trajectory of his church. Reflecting the ideals of the Azusa Street revival, he built bridges across racial and denominational lines.

Ironically, this gentle, unassuming scholar became one of the best-recognized names in the Assemblies of God and the broader Pentecostal movement. Graduating with his master's degree in theology from Harvard Divinity School in 1945, his academic credentials initially raised eyebrows among Pentecostals who viewed the academy with suspicion. However, Horton melded academic excellence with pastoral care and quickly proved his commitment to ministry. He has provided an intellectual and theological anchor to countless students and ministers, and has taught us all that Pentecost not only warms the heart, but also energizes the mind.

The Assemblies of God owes a debt of gratitude to Horton. The story of his life and influence, warmly recounted in this volume by Dr. Lois E. Olena and Dr. Raymond L. Gannon, demonstrates how one person, walking humbly and faithful to God's call, can impact generations to come. The Assemblies of God is where it is today in part because of the broad educational and theological foundation that Horton helped to lay. It is my prayer that Horton's example will inspire others to continue to build upon and enlarge this foundation, building a Pentecostal church marked by excellence, a commitment to biblical scholarship, spiritual sensitivity, and service to others.

George O. Wood
General Superintendent
General Council of the Assemblies of God

Endorsements

I am very happy to see in print this tribute to Stanley Horton, one of my esteemed professors, a model of godliness, sacrifice, and scholarship. I am also delighted to learn more about his life, and through it the history of the Pentecostal movement in North America. All who have been touched by this rich heritage will appreciate this work.

—Dr. Craig Keener,
Assemblies of God Theological Seminary alum, author,
Professor of New Testament, Palmer Theological Seminary,
Wynnewood, Pennsylvania

Who has been a greater luminary in the twentieth-century Pentecostal galaxy than Dr. Stanley M. Horton? Many make their mark on but one island of ministry, but heroes impact many. This book shows how this scholar-saint set the standard for Pentecostal scholarship as a model professor, left a unique Gospel witness across the globe, and kept on "getting it right." In a nation of conflicted social policies and in a church of confusing racial standards, he showed how one man's life could clearly reveal Christ's Church. May this volume inform others as much as my teacher Dr. Horton reformed me. Paul said in 1 Timothy 5:17 to give double honor to the elders who rule well; this read is just a portion of such honor.

—Bishop Lemuel Thuston,
Kansas East Ecclesiastical Jurisdiction,
Church of God in Christ

The second half of the twentieth century has seen Pentecostal scholarship emerge and thrive. Out of that emergence, few names are more recognizable than Stanley Horton. Called to teach Bible while a chemistry student at UC Berkeley, Horton did the unthinkable and went to Harvard to prepare for ministry as a Pentecostal scholar. The long shadow of Horton's influence among Pentecostals began humbly and now stretches around the world and into the first decade of the twenty-first century. You may have read his books, but *Stanley M. Horton: Shaper of Pentecostal Theology* will tell you "the rest of the story." As you read, be encouraged and see what a long obedience in the same direction can yield.

—Dr. Byron D. Klaus, President,
Assemblies of God Theological Seminary,
Springfield, Missouri

Wielding an influence that has spanned seven decades, Stanley Horton has been the prince of Pentecostal interpreters—a successor to Myer Pearlman. This book assembles for readers the essentials of his life and influence. Historians will find that the footnotes rival the value of the text itself. The book offers a noble tribute to a revered teacher whose impact in the classroom, in print, and in person has guided and blessed two generations of grateful students.

—Dr. Russell P. Spittler, Provost Emeritus
and Senior Professor of New Testament,
Fuller Theological Seminary,
Pasadena, California

Because of his enormous literary output throughout the latter half of the twentieth century, more Pentecostals know the name Dr. Stanley Horton than any other figure in Assemblies of God history. In a quiet and gentle way, he has shaped both the theology and orthodoxy of modern Pentecostalism. For the first time we are treated to a comprehensive biography of this great man.

—Dr. Stanley M. Burgess,
Distinguished Professor of Christian History,
Regent University,
Virginia Beach, Virginia

At first glance Stanley Horton's life and ministry seem typically Springfieldian, Assemblies of God, and Pentecostal. This comprehensive biography reveals that his life and influence have been far from provincial. The greatest measure of his influence is seen in the thousands of

students educated biblically and shaped theologically under his tutelage, who today serve in posts of ministry around the world. I am one
of those students whose life has been enriched through Dr. Horton's
scholarly skills and theological perspectives, presented so well in this
biographical tribute. I count him a great teacher, an academic colleague,
and a theologian friend, worthy of the tributes displayed in this volume.
At last, this great man will be known to a broader audience.

—Dr. Robert E. Cooley, President Emeritus
and Professor of Biblical Archaeology,
Gordon-Conwell Theological Seminary,
South Hamilton, Massachusetts

Lois Olena's biography of Dr. Stanley Horton provides an example
of Pentecostalism at its best—a spiritual journey replete with powerful
experiences of tongues, healing, prophetic words, and miracles together
with solid biblical scholarship that includes the Christian call to compassion and justice.

—Dr. Margaret M. Poloma,
Professor of Sociological Research and
author of *The Assemblies of God at the Crossroads,*
The University of Akron,
Akron, Ohio

The biography of Stanley M. Horton narrates a convicting and
truthful story that incarnates the deep passion of the Pentecostal movement. It is an account of one who took "the road less traveled," often
forging a third way between competing theological visions. Dr. Horton's steadfast service to the Assemblies of God and his commitment to
the peaceable kingdom serve as a testimony of an authentic spirituality
deeply rooted in the cross of Christ.

—Dr. Cheryl Bridges Johns,
Professor of Christian Formation & Discipleship,
Church of God Theological Seminary,
Cleveland, Tennessee

PREFACE

In 1947 my father left home to get away from his alcoholic father. Saved at twelve, baptized in the Holy Spirit, and called into ministry, my father found his way to Metropolitan Bible Institute in North Bergen, New Jersey, where he was allowed to enroll as a seventeen-year-old and finish his high school requirements. No doubt my father was one of dozens of students who sat under the tutelage of the new Harvard grad, Rev. Stanley Horton, as he taught twenty-one credits per semester at MBI in the 1947–48 academic year.

I, on the other hand, first met Dr. Horton when he was eighty-nine years old. One day at the Assemblies of God Theological Seminary in Springfield, Missouri, I noticed a quiet, unassuming man sitting off by himself. I went and sat by him. Not long into our conversation I experienced his gracious and pleasant spirit, only later realizing who he was.

During a meeting of the Society for Pentecostal Studies in Pasadena a year later, US Missionary and AG National Representative for Jewish Ministries Dr. Ray Gannon proposed a joint project to write Dr. Horton's biography. A former student of Horton's, Ray had recently completed his Hebrew University dissertation, "The Shifting Romance with Israel: American Pentecostal Ideology of Zionism and the Jewish State," which highlighted Horton's Israelology. "Surprised" and "humbled" that we would want to write about his life, Horton agreed, and the project began.

Though demanding ministry responsibilities eventually made it necessary for Dr. Gannon to relinquish a primary role in the authorship of the book, his chapter on Horton's theology of Israel and the Church is a critical component of this biography. I am greatly indebted to Ray for his vision for this book, his counsel and encouragement, and the fine theological contribution contained herein. He has been my teacher, mentor, ministry partner, and friend, for which I will be forever grateful.

Writing about a living person has its limitations as well as its advantages. The temptation exists to withhold critical analysis of a person's life and work out of deference and respect for that individual. At the same time, because of Dr. Horton's longevity and keen mind, I have been privileged to enjoy the pleasure of his good company as he has willingly served as an invaluable source of information. He has patiently answered vital questions, relayed countless stories, and shared valuable insights. I am honored that he now calls me his friend, and frankly, I could not have written this book without him.

The methodology for this book initially involved presenting Dr. Horton with an extensive list of questions from my collection, "Life Chronicles." My arrangement and re-presenting of his answers to those questions—followed by extensive conversations with him by Ray and myself—provide the structure for this book. Some block quotations are taken from those answers or conversations and are not specifically cited. A number of the stories Stanley recounted from his early days are also contained in his book *Reflections of an Early American Pentecostal* and his Fall 1982 *AG Heritage* article "The Pentecostal Explosion: How the Fire Fell in 1906 and Spread throughout the Religious World" (reprinted as "The Azusa Street Revival According to Stanley Horton," *AG Heritage*, Winter 2005–06). In addition to Dr. Horton's personal recollections, this book is the product of extensive secondary source research as well as interviews with Dr. Horton's family, friends, and colleagues.

The bulk of Pentecostal history's first century has played out during the lifetime of this great man. Thus I have at times turned from the straight path of telling his life story to saunter down a few side streets, in order to tell important stories about the lives and events that helped to shape this young Californian and bring him to his place as Pentecostalism's premier theologian.

Producing Stanley Horton's biography has been a community effort. I am thankful for all those who assisted in this project by providing general support, helpful insights, and crucial information, including but not limited to the Horton family (Ed and Diana Horton, Stan Jr. and Linda Horton, Faith and Brent Stilts) and Dr. Horton's sisters Esther Palusko and Ruth Williams for sharing the recollections of family life with me; AG General Superintendent Dr. George O. Wood for his support for the project; Dr. Gary B. McGee, President Byron D. Klaus, Jennifer Hall, and Elizabeth Danalds of the Assemblies of God Theological Seminary for their assistance on various book-related projects; Dr. Darrin Rodgers, Glenn Gohr, Joyce Lee, and the staff of the Flower Pentecostal Heritage Center for being ever-ready and ever-competent sources of information on Pentecostal history; Dr. Jerry Flokstra; Gary and Glenna Flokstra, Jr., of 4 the World Distribution for bibliographic assistance; Dr. Gary Denbow, president of Central Bible College; Lynn Anderson, Alice Harris, and the staff of the CBC library; Dr. Robert Spence, Dr. David Bundrick, Paul Logsdon, and Dr. Martin Mittelstadt of Evangel University; Matthew Paugh (who coauthored an excellent article with Dr. Mittelstadt on Dr. Horton's social justice concerns); Dr. William Menzies; Dr. Robert E. Cooley, president emeritus of Gordon-Conwell Theological Seminary for sharing his insights about AG higher education and the history of AGGS/AGTS; Pastor D. W. (Derreld) Wartenbee; David Drake; Dr. Charles Harris; Rev. Spencer Jones, Bishop Lemuel Thuston, and Rev. Frank Davis for sharing their personal stories relative to Horton's role in their lives in the area of racial healing; Dr. Paul

Elbert; Dr. Stanley Burgess; Dr. Russ Spittler; Russell Wisehart; Dan Betzer; Del and Kay Bonner, and Ray Peters of Maranatha Village; Wanda Grace; Dr. Gary Allen, Rick Knoth, Connie Cross, and the staff of the *Enrichment* journal; Dr. Ken Horn and Kim Hellmer of *Today's Pentecostal Evangel*; Bep Campbell of Calvary Temple in Winnipeg for providing a history of that church; Dr. Don Meyer, Reuben Hartwick, Kathy Terragnoli, Julia Grover, and Kristie Overly of Valley Forge Christian College; Mike O'Brien, missionary to Ireland for information about St. Mark's church in Dublin; Bruce Braithwaite and Beth Kinaf with Bernard Johnson Ministries for providing bibliographic information on Dr. Horton's Brazilian publications; Marilyn Possey for her random act of kindness by returning a long lost picture of Dr. Horton's mother to the Horton family; and the team at GPH for their assistance and support along the way.

Not only through the course of writing this book, but always, my mother, Priscilla Edwards has prayed for me and has served as an example of godly love, Pentecostal passion, and patient perseverance.

Finally, I thank God for my husband, Doug Olena, who believed in me, encouraged me, patiently endured my long hours of time spent on this book in addition to my regular responsibilities at AGTS and Evangel University, and who gave me life's greatest blessing and highest calling—our two wonderful daughters, Arwen and Eden.

Dr. Lois E. Olena
Springfield, Missouri
December 2008

Timeline of Dr. Stanley M. Horton's Life

1916	Born
1922	Saved
1933	Graduated high school (January 1933)
1933–35	Los Angeles Jr. College (A.A.); graduated spring 1935
1935–37	University of California, Berkeley (B.S.); graduated spring 1937
	1936 baptized in the Holy Spirit
	1937 summer—California packing company (Rio Vista ranch)
1937–41	Chemistry lab (starting fall 1937)
1940	Called to teaching ministry
1941–44	Gordon (M.Div.)
	1942 summer—licensed (Northern California-Nevada District); worked in chemistry lab again
	1943 summer—pastored AG church and worked in a slate mill in Monson, ME
	1943 fall/spring—worked in a gas station
	1944 summer—went back to California to work
1944–45	Harvard (S.T.M., Scientiae Theologicae Magistri, the Master of the Knowledge of Theology)
	1945 summer—filled in at Hill Memorial Baptist Church (3 months)
	1945 summer—Lived in Cambridge
	1945 (September 11) Married Evelyn
1945–48	Metropolitan Bible Institute, North Bergen, NJ (taught 21 hours per week)
1945–47	North Bergen
	1945 pastored in Morristown, NJ (10 months)

1946	ordained May 9, 1946 (New York-New Jersey District)
1946	summer to 1948 summer—Pastored at White Plains, NY
1946–47	took courses at Biblical Seminary in New York City
1947	son Stan, Jr., was born
1947–48	Lived in Suffern, NY; commuted to Patterson, NJ, to teach
1948–78	Central Bible College, Springfield, MO
1948	pastored Potter Church and church in Sparta
1949	son Ed was born
1953–59	Central Baptist Theological Seminary, Kansas City, KS (Th.D.)
1956	daughter Faith was born
1962	guest professor, Near East School of Archaeology and Biblical Studies, Jerusalem, Israel
1972	began to be part-time at Assemblies of God Graduate School (changed to Assemblies of God Theological Seminary in 1984); still full-time at CBC
1975	twelve weeks at ICI in Brussels, Belgium
1978–91	Assemblies of God Theological Seminary, Springfield, MO
1978–84	Adjunct professor at CBC
1979–80	President of Society of Pentecostal Studies
1980	Began international travel and teaching
1987	Awarded "Distinguished Professor of Bible and Theology" in recognition of his scholarship and long-term service to the AG
1987, 88, 90	named Chairman of Bible Department at AGTS
1991	named Distinguished Professor Emeritus of Bible and Theology
1991	retired from AGTS
1991	Honorary L.H.D. (Litterarum Humanorum Doctor) from Faraston Theological Seminary
1991–2000	Pentecostal Textbook series/Logion Press (General Editor)
1995–present	Commission on Doctrinal Purity (various terms)
2001–04	Evelyn sick; passed away 2004
2004–present	Speaking/Teaching engagements (Alaska, Singapore, continental U.S. cities)
2008	Moved to Maranatha
	Work with Commission on Doctrinal Purity (on divorce and remarriage)

CHAPTER 1

A Godly Heritage

The message of personal sanctification characteristic of John Wesley's Methodism inspired later generations of Pentecostal Americans to anticipate a grand new encounter with God's Spirit to affect not only private piety but a restoration of primitive New Testament Christianity leading to successful global evangelization immediately preceding the Second Coming. The refreshing revival streams of the Great Awakening continued to irrigate the seeds of redemptive hope planted among the succeeding American generations.[1]

The Hortons in Canada

Stanley Horton's earliest memories, of hearing "songs of joy, shouts of 'Hallelujah!' and much prayer in an upstairs hall on Los Angeles Street"[2] only blocks from the Azusa Street Mission in the early 1900s would not have been a reality were it not for John Wesley's late eighteenth-century revivals. As a result of Wesley's powerful services in Ireland,[3] Horton's Irish ancestors on his father's side had all become Methodists. Thus, his godly heritage runs deep, providing the fertile ground for his own life of service—characterized by Pentecostal fervor, a commitment to biblical scholarship, and Christlike character.

Born in Wexford, Ireland, Horton's great-great-grandfather married and immigrated to Ontario, Canada, around 1800. In 1809, their son Samuel was born in the town of Brockville. At the age of twenty-two, Samuel married Ann Jane Powell (originally from County Cork, Ireland), and in 1843 Stanley Horton's paternal grandfather, Samuel Horton, Jr., was born in Ontario.

After marrying Margaret Amelia Miller, whose father George Miller owned a grocery store in Owen Sound, Samuel, Jr., owned and operated a grain and dairy farm on the edge of Owen Sound, Ontario, Canada. Their son, Harry Samuel Horton (Stanley's father), was born in Owen Sound on March 12, 1880, the next-to-the-youngest child, with one brother and five sisters.

The family grew grass as fodder and had an apple orchard there on the farm. Harry recounted to his son years later how he loved the apples as a boy. One time when Harry and his older brother were cutting down a tree, Harry was in the way of the tree falling. Fortunately for Harry—and for all those who would come to enjoy the life's work of his yet-unborn son Stanley—Harry's brother pulled him away just in time!

The Hortons had a twelve-room house and a summerhouse next to it the same size but with two floors, one open room on each floor where "husking bees" (shucking corn) were great events. The neighbors would get together and all shuck corn at the same time. After Harry's brother George established a real estate business in Winnipeg, Manitoba, his parents moved there.

Harry Horton's Journey

Before his parents moved, however, Harry decided he wanted to travel across Canada with his friend. As a small boy Harry had been baptized in a river, but at the age of twenty-one he rebelled against the strict rules of the old-fashioned Methodists. Attempting to free himself from those restraints, he and another young man worked their way across Canada, stopping in Yellow Grass, Saskatchewan, to help in the wheat harvest on the ranch owned by his oldest sister, Amelia, and her Welsh husband, Stanley Jones (after whom Stanley Horton was named). They then followed surveyors for the Canadian Pacific Railroad and went down the West Coast as far as Los Angeles. Everywhere they stopped to work, a revival would be taking place. Harry's young friend would go to the revival, but Harry was still running from God and so refused.

Ultimately their travels led them to San Francisco. The day before the great 1906 earthquake, Harry was walking in Golden Gate Park. Suddenly a voice came to him: "Get out of this city!" The message came again and again, stronger and stronger. So finally Harry found his friend, and the two young men took a ferry over to Oakland. That night the famous San Francisco earthquake and fire destroyed the place where they had been staying. If they had remained in the city, they would have been killed—and Stanley Monroe Horton would never have been born!

Not long after the earthquake, Harry and his friend returned to Los Angeles. One Wednesday evening, Harry was going by a Nazarene church and felt compelled to enter. The pastor gave a brief altar call at the end of the service, but Harry felt glued to the seat. He left the church and was already a block away when he felt a tap on his shoulder. He turned and looked. It was the pastor, standing there with questioning eyes. "Don't you want to come back to the church and get saved?" he asked. In no time, Harry was crying out, "God, forgive me, a sinner!" Because Harry had been in such a mindset of rebellion, however, God seemed silent to him—until the pastor quoted the Scripture, "Him that cometh to me, I will in no wise cast out." Suddenly Harry felt his burdens lifted and left the place as if walking on air. Not long after, he wrote his mother telling her he'd gotten "saved." A treasured account, his son Stanley has kept the letter to this day.

After his rededication to the Lord, Harry decided to go back to Winnipeg to see his parents and tell them news he was sure would cause them to rejoice. Setting out from San Francisco, he stopped in Oakland on his way east from the city and went by a street meeting where he learned of Holy Spirit baptism—his first exposure to this teaching. Back in Winnipeg, Harry found a prayer meeting in the home of a woman named Helen Rosenblatt; Helen and her mother had traveled to the Azusa Street Mission[4] and received the baptism in the Holy Spirit. On a Tuesday evening not long after his arrival in Winnipeg, Harry too was powerfully baptized in the Spirit, at the Rosenblatts' home.

The next evening Harry went with his parents to the Methodist church.[5] When the pastor asked him to lead in prayer, Harry broke out praying in tongues for half an hour! Given the strong presence of the Lord in that place, the pastor could only acknowledge that what was happening was of God. Many from that Methodist church eventually joined with A. H. Argue.[6] A participant in the Azusa Street Revival in 1906, Argue had heard about the Pentecostal outpouring, and eventually received the baptism in the Holy Spirit after tarrying for nearly three weeks at William H. Durham's mission on North Avenue in Chicago in 1907. Argue's group began Calvary Temple, a Pentecostal Assemblies church in Winnipeg still going strong today.[7]

Harry Horton felt a call to preach; he began working with Pastor Argue, getting to know Argue's son Watson well. Not long after, he went to Levi Lupton's Missionary Training Institute in Alliance, Ohio, and graduated in 1910 expecting to go to Liberia as a missionary. He even mailed a letter to his mother, listing what he would need to take with him—a letter he showed to his son Stanley years later. For some reason, though, the Lord stopped Harry from going. Most of those who did become missionaries in Liberia died of malaria and other tropical fevers. Instead, Harry became an evangelist, traveling through Canada and the Midwest with another graduate of Lupton's school, Franklin Small. On one occasion when Harry came out of the meeting, a group of thugs grabbed him and held him down while they tried to pour whiskey in his mouth. But Harry kept his teeth tightly shut, and they finally gave up after giving him a severe beating. On another occasion, in Arizona, neighbors had Harry thrown in jail for a night because they said his meetings were too loud! Because of his passion for evangelism, Harry always referred to himself as an evangelist, even in later years when serving as pastor of the Upper Room Mission.

Grandma Fisher—Smart *and* Spirit-Filled

Stanley Horton's maternal grandmother, Clara Daisy Sanford, was born in Homer, New York, in 1866. She was the granddaughter of Dr. Stephen William Taylor, who from 1836–1848 served as president of what is now Colgate University. Clara's father, Dr. Heman Howes Sanford (1829-1909),[8] was an ordained Baptist

Stanley Horton's grandmother Clara Daisy, with her children and grandchildren. (Taken in the mid-1930s) Top row l to r: Eugene Fisher (Uncle Harold's son), Donald Horton (Stanley's brother), Wesley Steelberg (Stanley's cousin, Aunt Ruth's son), Uncle Wesley Steelberg (who became AG General Superintendent), Harold Horton (Stanley's brother), Harry Samuel Horton (Stanley's Dad), Robert Fisher (boy–son of Uncle Harold), Uncle Harold Fisher (Stanley's mother's brother), Stanley Horton, Charles Fisher (Uncle Harold's son), Wesley Fisher (Uncle Harold's son). Front row l to r: Eva Horton (Stanley's sister), Juanita Steelberg, Aunt Ruth Fisher Steelberg (sister to Stanley's mother), Marvel Steelberg, Clara Daisy Sanford Fisher (Stanley's grandmother), Esther Steelberg, Myrle Horton (Stanley's mom), Aunt Anna Fisher (Uncle Harold's wife), Joyce Fisher (Uncle Harold's youngest and only girl), Esther Horton (Stanley's youngest sister), Ruth Horton (Stanley's sister)

minister. He had a Doctor of Philology degree, spoke fourteen languages fluently, and was professor of Greek and Latin at Syracuse University. As a child, Clara showed evidence of a great memory. She would visit a nearby nursery, read the Latin names of the plants and flowers, and come back later, still able to repeat them from memory. She was also a bit precocious. One day she took inks into the cupola of their home and mixed something with them, causing a minor explosion.

Because Clara Daisy's father was a professor, Syracuse University let her go through until graduation, but didn't give her a degree, because they weren't giving degrees to women at that time. Though these were days of increasing focus on American women's rights and temperance concerns even in her hometown,[9] Clara did not stop to decry the lack of a degree but focused on persevering in ministry.

Soon Clara Daisy became president of the New York State United Christian Endeavor societies. This group had been founded in 1881 for the purpose of partnering with the local church to equip young people for ministry and a lifestyle of Christian leadership. Because she was president she went to a convention at one point in New York City where she became acquainted with A. B. Simpson[10] and attended his church. There on the scorching brick sidewalks of New York she got sunstroke. She never got over that. Even years later when Stanley went as a boy to see her, the heat of the California summer would go to her head. She used to say that nothing would take it down except ice cream, so she would send Stanley out to buy a quart of chocolate ice cream every day in summer for the two of them to split.

Clara's earliest spiritual experiences took place when Keswick[11] preachers and teachers from England "stirred her heart with a desire to live victoriously by the power of the Holy Spirit."[12] Her involvement with Christian Endeavor societies led her to become a speaker on the Chautauqua, New York, circuit, speaking for camp meetings and Keswick conferences. One day in the mid-1880s after praying earnestly for the service, she stood to speak to a group of women in a Baptist church near Erie, Pennsylvania. She felt the power of the Spirit and suddenly began to speak in a language she had never learned. Years later she told her grandson Stanley that the Holy Spirit had given her an interpretation that was all Scripture and that fitted together to form a message. The women wanted to know what that "funny foreign language" was, but she didn't know and didn't fully understand what had happened. She had had a "pre-Agnes Ozman"[13] experience and only later found out what it was. She continued to pray in tongues when she was alone, but didn't tell anyone about it—not even her husband.

Perhaps it was Clara's example as a capable woman in ministry, as well as the many empowered Pentecostal women surrounding Stanley Horton as a young boy in revival-soaked Los Angeles that spurred him on in later years to serve as an advocate for women in ministry—even when it may not have been popular to do so. With his godly grandmother as living proof that God uses women, Horton's own thorough study of the Scriptures confirmed what he already knew to be true in life. In his article, "Rediscovering the Prophetic Role of Women,"[14] Horton affirmed the prophetic role of women in light of the biblical examples of Miriam, Deborah, Isaiah's wife, Anna, Elizabeth, and Philip's four daughters, as well as the Holy Spirit's outpouring and empowerment on "*all* people . . . sons *and* daughters . . . men *and* women" (Acts 2:17,18, emphasis added).

The Fishers—From the Midwest to California

Stanley's maternal grandfather, Elmer Kirk Fisher,[15] was born in 1866 on a farm in Wintersville, Ohio, to Methodist parents William R. Fisher and Lydia Jane (Kirk) Fisher. Though he grew up in the Methodist Church, Elmer later joined the Baptists. After graduating from college in Ohio he felt called to ministry, so he went through Moody Bible Institute in Chicago, graduating with a two-year certificate in 1894. At that time, students had to carry out certain duties as part of their tuition. Elmer counted it a privilege to clean the bathroom in D. L. Moody's[16] apartment.

During the World's Fair of 1893 in Chicago, a circus opened opposite the entrance to the fair. The circus was closed on Sundays, so Moody rented the circus tent for Sundays and put up a large sign announcing, "Circus Weekdays, Moody on Sunday." After that he sent his students out to hold meetings in tents and rented halls all over Chicago. The result was that the fair closed on Sundays for lack of attendance. Elmer Fisher preached in one of those halls, and his soon-to-be wife, Clara Daisy Sanford, also a student by that time at Moody Bible Institute, went along to play a little pump organ. One day shortly after the fair, Moody and Evangelist R. A. (Reuben Archer) Torrey, who had already been preaching by then that the baptism in the Holy Spirit was an empowering experience available for all people, lined up the students and laid hands on each one, saying, "Receive ye the Holy Ghost!" Though Elmer felt nothing at the time, something began to stir in him to seek more of the Spirit.

Horton's grandfather Elmer Kirk Fisher, pastor of the Upper Room Mission, California (ca. 1910)

After Elmer married Clara in 1894, the two of them went into general evangelistic work for the Congregational Christian Church in portions of the Upper Midwest and later for the Northern Baptists. On one occasion while holding a meeting in a schoolhouse, a frequent venue for their preaching, Elmer heard that a gang was going to try to stop the meeting. He learned the leader's name, and when the gang came in, he called out the leader's name and appointed him to keep order. Fortunately for everyone, Elmer's strategy worked!

Back on the farm near Medina, Ohio, Stanley Horton's mother, Myrle May Fisher, was born in 1895. Two years later her brother Heman Harold Fisher—who became the father of Dr. Robert Fisher, organizer of the Azusa 2006 Centennial celebration of the 1906 Azusa Street Revival—was born.[17] Harold never liked the name Heman and preferred to be called Harold; in his teens he decided to take the name Harold, signing his name "H. Harold Fisher." Because of Harold's health, the family moved to California where Elmer Fisher pastored a Baptist church on the coast north of Los Angeles.

Myrle Fisher, 2 years old[18]

As a young girl, Myrle used to walk down a beautiful double row of trees that shaded the path to her one-room schoolhouse. She would often climb a tree and go from one tree to the other on the way to school. One day she ran down a hill to see a train go by and fell against a barbed wire fence. The barbs pierced her eyes and she was blind, unable to go to school for a year—but God miraculously healed her.

Myrle experienced the power of God in her life numerous times. When she was at school recess in Glendale, California, one day as a girl of twelve, her six-year-old brother, Dwight, fell off an acting bar[19] and broke his arm. His teacher sent for a doctor, but Myrle ran home about a block away and brought back her father. Fisher prayed for his son Dwight, and his arm was instantly healed. When the doctor came he examined Dwight's arm and said it was set better than *he* could have set it! These early miracles in her life were just the beginning for young Myrle

Fisher as she continued to grow up in the midst of the revival of the century.

Grandpa Fisher Discovers the Spirit's Power

Elmer Fisher's first pastorate was a Baptist church in Camarillo, California (1903–1905). In 1905 he went to pastor the First Baptist Church of Glendale, California, but a year later began to sense his need for the Spirit's power. He would spend nights in prayer, sometimes joined by others, and also began reading a series on the Holy Spirit by his former teacher R. A. Torrey. Soon after he preached a series of sermons on the Holy Spirit and His power. The results were too much for the deacons. Some in his congregation began to give "demonstrations of joy."[20] The deacons came to Pastor Fisher and said, "We don't like the excitement you are causing. It is all right for you to preach on courage or on Daniel, but soft-pedal this on the Holy Spirit." So Fisher resigned. No deacon was going to tell him to stop preaching what God had told him to preach!

Soon after, just "two days after the folks at the Bonnie Brae Street prayer meeting decided to begin their quest in earnest, Fisher resigned from his pastorate in Glendale"[21] and quickly made his way to Dr. Joseph Smale's First New Testament Church in Burbank Hall at Sixth and Main Streets in Los Angeles. (While pastoring his previous church, First Baptist Church of Los Angeles, Smale had traveled to Great Britain in 1905 to visit the Welsh revival; he came back wanting to see something like that in his church! God did move, but one of his deacons opposed him, so he left—taking a couple of his deacons with him—and started the New Testament Church.) Smale quickly welcomed Fisher as a part of his staff.

Just days later, on Easter Sunday, April 15, 1906, Jennie Evans Moore (the woman who would eventually become Mrs. William Seymour) came to Smale's church with a group from the Bonnie Brae Street prayer meetings—where seven had been baptized in the Spirit and spoken in tongues a week earlier—and told how the Holy Spirit had been poured out there according to Acts 2:4. That was the key. One woman at Smale's church received the baptism in the Spirit immediately. Others, including Elmer Fisher, received shortly after.

Crowds soon forced Brother Seymour to move to a frame building on Azusa Street where planks on top of empty kegs provided seating space for two or three hundred people. A board walk around the building provided standing room for others who crowded to look in at the low windows. Multitudes came from every denomination to see what God was doing. Meetings continued every night, and the dawn often found a crowd still there praying for those seeking the Baptism.[22]

Every night the little building [at Azusa Street] would be packed with two or three hundred people, with others looking in at the windows. . . . There was no planned program, for they felt that the Holy Spirit was able to protect them from anarchy or wicked spirits, and they believed the Holy Spirit could use any member of the body.

Brother William J. Seymour would come in, kneel, and put his head in one of the boxes that served as a pulpit, and begin to pray. The glory would come down. People would start familiar hymns like "Higher Ground" or "Tis Burning in My Soul." Some would begin to sing spontaneously (in English) in what they called "the heavenly choir." Then Brother Seymour would call everyone to prayer and they would kneel at their seats, crying out to God.

Often letters would be read. One, for example, told of the thrilling revival at Pandita Ramabai's school in Mukti, India. Another, from T. B. Barratt in London, gave news of an Ignatian monk saved and seeking a Pentecostal experience. From D. E. Evans in Swansea, Wales came the report of a number receiving the baptism with the Bible sign of tongues. From Brother Berntsen, in North China, came news of quite a stir. From sisters A. Moomau and L. Phillips, in Shanghai, came word of Chinese filled and a few missionaries pressing in. Other letters came from South America, South Africa, and Germany. These letters brought outbreaks of praise and spontaneous songs.[23]

Though Smale had reservations about some of the events and teachings of the Azusa Street Mission during the early months of the revival, he became a strong ally. In late October 1906, however, First New Testament Church split over issues of order. Smale, called the "Moses" of the movement because he was able to see it but not fully enter into it,[24] eventually dropped his support of the revival and broke with the Apostolic Faith movement. Those who disagreed with him, including Dr. Henry S. Keyes and Elmer Fisher,[25] began the Upper Room Mission, with three hundred in attendance. The Upper Room Mission began at 107½ North Main Street, just four blocks from the Azusa Street Mission. It later moved to 327½ South Spring Street, also about four blocks from the mission. In 1914 Fisher moved the Mission to 203 Mercantile Place and then to Kohler Street and in 1915 to 406½ Los Angeles Street.[26]

After the break with Smale, Fisher forged closer ties with the Azusa Street Mission and soon became a member of the board of elders, working with William J. Seymour. He participated in weekly leadership meetings with Seymour and other Los Angeles area pastors for "prayer, mutual support, counsel, Bible study, and both short- and long-term strategic planning."[27] This partnership was mutually beneficial. For example, following a summer camp meeting in 1907 where a number of local ministries joined together with the Azusa Mission for extended services, Seymour left on evangelistic tours in the South for four months, during which time Fisher helped lead the meetings at the Azusa Street Mission.[28]

Exterior view of Upper Room Mission on Los Angeles Street, ca. 1925, when Harry Horton was pastor

During the early days of the revival in 1906, when Fisher first took his wife, Clara, to the Azusa Street Mission, she looked around, and after observing what was going on, said, "I already have this!" They told her, "You couldn't have. You are a Baptist!" The folks at Azusa were then teaching that the baptism in the Holy Spirit is a third experience after an experience of sanctification. They told her that the experience she had had "could not have been the Pentecostal baptism; because as a good Baptist she had not sought an experience of sanctification first."[29] Clara didn't argue with them. She just got down and began to pray. Soon she was praying in tongues! At the Azusa Street Mission, people were already coming from all over the world. On one occasion when Clara was speaking in tongues, a man from Denmark told her that she was speaking in Danish.

The Fishers also took their children to Azusa. Those ministering at the Mission had the Fishers' eleven-year-old daughter Myrle kneel down to pray "to be sanctified." In about ten minutes

Myrle was speaking in tongues though she didn't observe any intermediate experience of "sanctification." A black woman from one of the French-speaking islands told Myrle she was speaking in French. When Myrle got older she found this woman, who confirmed this experience. More than this confirmation of speaking a known language, the fact that Myrle had spoken in tongues without ever before having seen anyone be filled with the Spirit was a witness and of great comfort to her mother, Clara,[30] who had experienced the Spirit's outpouring in the mid-1880s, also without ever having seen such an experience before in her life.

There was enough of the experience of tongues as recognized languages at the Azusa Street Mission to assure Myrle and others that this was indeed the Pentecost of Acts 2:4. Some misinterpreted these instances of tongues as being known languages, supposing they could go to the mission field and preach the gospel without having to learn the native language. Myrle personally knew three couples who did so but who were all disappointed. As Stanley would later point out, these early Pentecostals did not understand that the Great Commission was a command, not just to preach the gospel, but also

Horton's mother, Myrle Fisher, in a photo taken at the Azusa Street Golden Jubilee, Los Angeles, California, September 1956 (second row, far left)

to make disciples (i.e., "learners"). Missionaries needed to *know* the language and the culture to make people *learners*.

Elmer Fisher was among those who offered instruction from time to time at the Azusa Street Mission about how to receive the baptism in the Holy Spirit. One of his teachings provided the following clear and simple guidelines for seekers:

1. Believe the truth concerning it. Jesus commanded the disciples not to depart from Jerusalem, but to tarry until they were endued with power from on high (Luke 24:49). Be assured that when the early disciples received they were all filled with the Holy Ghost and spake with tongues as the Spirit gave them utterance (Acts 2:4).
2. You must feel your need. Is your life barren of power? Ye shall receive power. Acts 1:8.
3. Tarry until – Cease from your own works and fix your eyes on the exalted Christ. Abandon yourself to God and cut every tie that binds you to the world.
4. Be sure your heart has been cleansed by the blood.
5. Obey quickly every little commandment the Lord gives you (Acts 5:32), with your prejudice given up, your theology submitted, and Christ will be all in all to you.[31]

Expectation for the coming of Christ was another characteristic of early Pentecostalism. This was also evidenced in the Fisher family. Grandpa Fisher believed that the Pentecostal revival they were experiencing was not only an important sign of the Lord's coming, but also perhaps the only real sign. Every day Fisher looked for the Lord to return.[32] He was so convinced of the Lord's soon return that after his daughter Myrle finished the eighth grade her father told her it was no use for her to go to high school because the Lord was coming so soon. Though his hope of Jesus' return remained strong, Grandpa Fisher did let Myrle's younger brothers and her sister go to high school.

Myrle loved to read and loved history. She was a very intelligent woman but unfortunately was not permitted to pursue higher education. She regretted that, and also remained disappointed that she never got to preach. Only after her husband's death did she take college courses and become a librarian for West Coast Bible School in Fresno.

As Myrle continued to grow in God as a young girl, the power of the Spirit was permeating Los Angeles. At Azusa Street, "Sinners were saved and filled with the Holy Spirit. The sick were healed. . . . Cold church members found new dedication and zeal. . . . Hundreds from every denomination, from practically every state, and from every continent came and sought God."[33] In the midst of such an ongoing move of the Spirit that impacted their entire lifestyle, Elmer and Clara often rode the streetcar to the Azusa Street Mission in silence, so as to keep their minds in readiness for what they expected to receive from the Lord. They never missed a meeting there, not even one night in 1907 when young Myrle was very sick. After praying for their eleven-year-old daughter, Elmer and Clara Fisher proceeded to the meeting, leaving Myrle at home in bed.

That evening Myrle had a vision, after which she was completely healed. Standing upon the altar rail at the Azusa Street Mission the next evening, she recounted her vision. The account of her vision reported in the next issue of the Azusa Street paper, *The Apostolic Faith Mission Publication.*

A Little Girl's Vision of Heaven

Our little girl [Myrle] was recently taken with a severe cold and sore throat and had every symptom of scarlet fever. She knows the Lord, having been saved three years ago, has received the Baptism of the Holy Spirit, and speaks in tongues.

During a season of prayer on Tuesday evening, December 18th, all the family, papa, mamma, [Heman], and four-year-old Ruth laid our hands on her head and each one prayed for her healing. A wonderful spirit of song came upon us. The Spirit sang the songs of Zion through our lips. During this season of song, my little girl sat on a chair with her eyes closed; and when the song stopped, she said, "O papa, I have seen Jesus." She then told the following vision:

I came to a city of many streets. There seemed to be a division in the city, there was a narrow street that separated. On one side the streets were clean and paved, the buildings were of marble and strong, and there was a car there with the words on the front, TO ZION. On the side of the car was TO THE BEAUTIFUL CITY OF GOD. On the dirty street was a dirty car, and on the front was TO HELL. On the side was GOING DOWN.

After I got on the clean car, I went to the conductor and asked him if I could go over to the unclean car, and the car was stopped and I went across with others, and we took five apiece off from Satan's car. When they came across the line from the unclean street to the clean, their garments and faces became clean. When we came to the white car, the car expanded to make room for all that came.

I saw the car the devil was on, go down into a dark abyss. Then our car stopped and we all went over to where this car disappeared. Jesus spoke, a great grate of iron came, and then a great stone, and stopped up the mouth of the abyss so that Satan could come out no more.

As the car went on, I saw that everything was beautiful. The mists rolled away. Beautiful flowers appeared.

When we arrived at the beautiful city of God, there were lovely homes given to us. After we were there long enough to be adjusted, we went to visit the Palace of the King. I saw Jesus on a throne made of diamonds and pearls. He was dressed in shining raiment, sparkling in every color.

A beautiful Christmas feast was spread on tables. The cloth on the tables and the food was beautiful. The walls of the room and the carpet on the floor shone with beautiful colors. I looked in a mirror and saw I was clad like the angels. I saw my father, mother, brother, and sister coming in, and their clothes were transformed like the rest. The molding around the room was decorated with holly, most beautiful to behold. Jesus called attention to me and said, 'Do you see that little girl down there?' Their eyes seemed to look clear through me. Then he said, 'This girl was very sick and had faith and I healed her.' All the host sang a most beautiful song of praise. Then Jesus took us and showed us all around. When we came out, He had a beautiful chariot ready to take us all back to earth.[34]

Myrle's vision was one of many dreams and visions recorded in the *Apostolic Faith Mission Publication* throughout the time of the Azusa Street Revival. Such visions were seen as further evidence that believers were experiencing the outpouring of the Spirit foretold by the prophet Joel and further confirmed by the apostle Peter. Using the story of his grandmother as an example, Myrle's son, Stanley Horton, later wrote of how Christians today need to encourage both young and old believers to remain open to these types of visions in order to withstand the pressures of the world against the Church. As believers experience such divine phenomena, they are encouraged to "trust God, believe His Word, and rejoice in the hope of the future that His Word promises."[35] If God could use the young Samuel, the young Zephaniah, and Stanley's own mother when she was at the tender age of eleven, He can use children today,[36] Horton admonished, to speak for God in order to strengthen, encourage, and comfort the body of Christ.

Not only was it clear at Azusa that God was no respecter of age, He was also no respecter of color. The egalitarian spirit that young Myrle experienced at the Mission made a profound impact on her. She would later recount to her children the good things that took place there—about the power of God and the wonderful worship of many different people groups together. As Stanley recalls:

> In the summer of 1907 my grandfather and others who had started their own services in various halls and storefronts closed up to join the Azusa Street Mission in a camp meeting in the Arroyo Seco between Los Angeles and Pasadena. Three or four hundred persons lived in tents on the grounds. No special speakers were advertised, but ministers from all denominations spoke as the Lord led. By this time about two thirds of the congregation were white, but there was no segregation problem in those days. People were so hungry for God they paid no attention to the person sitting next to them. White people who attended the camp meeting still talk of the transports of glory that lifted them into the heavenlies while the [black] people sang, "In Perfect Peace I'll Keep Him."[37]

At least for a time, Azusa was indeed a haven from the prejudice experienced in the greater Los Angeles community at this time—not only for people of other colors, but for Pentecostals as well. The morning after Myrle received the baptism in the Holy Spirit, none of the other school children would let her play with them on the playground—except one little black girl. But at Azusa—as Frank Bartleman, whose firsthand accounts[38] of the Azusa Street revival helped popularize the revival far and wide— would note, "The 'color line' was washed away in the blood."[39]

By 1908, many whites began attending the Upper Room Mission who had earlier been a part of the Azusa Mission.[40] One of those was George Studd, famous Cambridge cricketer and brother of missionary C. T. Studd, who began attending mid-May 1908 and eventually served as a close associate of Fisher's—teaching, preaching, and cowriting the mission's periodical, *The Upper Room*, from 1909 to 1911.[41] In 1910 alone, the Mission sent out 86,000 copies of the periodical.[42]

Heir to a significant fortune, George had helped establish the interdenominational Holiness Mission, Peniel Hall, providing in 1894 a then-anonymous gift to help Manie and Theodore Ferguson expand that ministry. Studd became one of the mission's four superintendents (along with the Fergusons and Phineas Bresee), but defected to Pentecostalism in 1907 to help fund the Azusa Mission and Upper Room Mission, ultimately exhausting his fortune for the work of the ministry.[43]

According to Bartleman, *most* of the whites from Azusa went with the Upper Room Mission when it began in late 1906.[44] In his 1908 report published in the early British Pentecostal periodical, *Confidence*, Studd's comment on the racial makeup of the Azusa Mission seems to imply a predominantly white makeup of the Upper Room Mission in contrast. "The Sunday services [at the Upper Room Mission] are crowded and inspiring. This hall is in a central location on one of the best streets, and is in addition to Azusa Street, which is entirely controlled (humanly speaking) by the coloured people, though white people attend there."[45]

Along with glowing reports of Mission activities throughout Los Angeles, Studd did write in his 1908 diary of some disputes, conflicts, and personality clashes at the missions. Grant Wacker points out that though Studd did not attribute these incidents to racial distrust, "it is reasonable to assume it played a role."[46] Clearly the racial harmony experienced in the early months of the revival was short-lived.

Though the makeup of the missions changed somewhat,[47] Seymour and Fisher maintained a good relationship. In no small part due to Seymour's willingness to work closely with neighboring missions and Fisher's maintaining a partnering relationship with Seymour rather than acting as a competitor,[48] the ministry at the Upper Room Mission flourished in its early years. A powerful anointing of God rested upon Fisher's life both in the pulpit and in his daily pastoral ministry, which also blessed the Upper Room ministry. In his 1908 diary, Studd writes repeatedly of Fisher's "splendid" services and of God's "great power on Bro. Fisher."[49] On one occasion when Studd had sprained his ankle and had such pain that he could not rest well, Fisher stayed by his side all night, rejoicing in God's healing throughout the next day.

Fisher and Studd wrote in January 1911:

> We thank God for His great blessings in the Upper Room Mission, where He has met us day after day, and where with saints from many lands, as well as from all parts of this country, we have enjoyed times of refreshing and power from the presence of the Lord amongst us, and where we have seen many sick healed, sinners saved, believers sanctified and baptized with the Holy Ghost.[50]

On the heels of this great report, however, the Mission suffered a blow in attendance not long after, as a result of the controversy[51] surrounding the preaching of evangelist William H. Durham at the Azusa Street Mission on the "finished work" theory of sanctification. Durham had initially tried to persuade Fisher to allow him to preach this message at the Upper Room Mission, but Fisher refused. Angry, Durham moved on to the Azusa Street Mission where—during Seymour's absence—his "forceful, eloquent preaching won many people over [and] . . . overnight, the 'bottom' simply 'dropped out of the Upper Room' Mission."[52]

Studd resigned from the Upper Room Mission on April 6, 1911, one month before his marriage to Mable L. Preston, though from his personal "Chronology," it appears he returned for ten months in 1917 when the Mission was then in Chinatown. He assisted in the 1913 World Wide Camp Meeting in Arroyo Seco of South Pasadena with Evangelist Maria Woodworth-Etter—a woman much used in a miracle and healing ministry—and was involved in other ministries and world missions. While in Pasadena one day in early 1945, Studd fell on the street and seriously injured himself. He contracted pneumonia not long after while in the hospital; though he recovered from the pneumonia, he became exhausted and weak, and eventually died on February 13, 1945.

In 1913 Harry Horton's cousin, R. J. Scott, also was involved in helping to launch the World Wide Camp Meeting in the Arroyo Seco.[53] Also having been at Azusa, R. J. was a key person to help make arrangements for the revival meetings. He persuaded the then thirty-three-year-old evangelist Harry Horton to come.

When he came to Los Angeles in 1913, Harry's testimony about his salvation, his call to ministry, and the evangelistic work he'd been doing caught the attention of Elmer Fisher. That year, on the basis of Harry's testimony, Fisher asked him to serve as associate pastor at the Upper Room Mission.[54] A year later, Fisher turned over the Mission to Harry. It wasn't long before Fisher's now nineteen-year-old daughter Myrle was intrigued by this new associate and his stories of travel. They fell in love and were married on July 17, 1915.

After turning the Upper Room Mission over to Harry, Elmer Fisher pastored an Armenian congregation in Boyle Heights, Los Angeles (a couple of miles away from the Mission).[55] Stanley Horton believes this congregation in Boyle Heights was the same Armenian congregation that had first begun in 1905 just three miles from Boyle Heights, in the Shakarian home at 919 Boston Street. The Shakarians and seven other Armenian families had immigrated to Los Angeles as a result of a prophecy an eleven-year-old Russian boy had given in 1855:

> For seven days and seven nights he was under the power of God writing prophecy of things to come. He

neither ate, drank, nor slept during the seven days and seven nights. Although he was an illiterate boy, he wrote in beautiful handwriting and drew pictures and maps and charts. He foretold that peace would be taken from the earth and that Armenia would be overrun by the Turks and that the Armenian Christians would be massacred unless they went to a land across the ocean, which the pictures and charts and maps showed to be America.[56]

Myrle May Fisher and Harry Samuel Horton's Wedding Picture—July 21, 1915

Forty-five years later, the Lord reaffirmed this prophecy to the now fifty-six year old man, warning them that the time had come for its fulfillment. The Shakarians, previously Presbyterians, were among the first in Armenia to experience the outpouring of the Holy Spirit there. They came to America in 1905. The last Pentecostal family in their hometown left in 1912, two years before the beginning of World War I. In 1914, the prophecy was fulfilled. In 1906, Demos Shakarian, Sr., and his brother-in-law were walking down a street near the Azusa Street Mission. They heard prayers and singing and shouts of joy similar to what they had experienced in their own services. When they got to the Mission, they heard several people speaking in tongues. They rushed back to their families to tell them the good news of how God was moving in America as He had in Armenia.[57]

In addition to pastoring the Armenian congregation, Fisher also conducted evangelistic services in Seattle and Canada, and then for a short period went to Denver and founded a Pentecostal church there. Eventually he returned to California to minister in the Upper Room Mission.

Stanley remembers very little of his grandfather, since Fisher went to be with the Lord when Stanley was only three. Nonetheless, Fisher had a profound impact on Stanley's young life through the stories that were told to him about his grandfather. One story Stanley's mother recounted to him years later was about how when Stanley was just a little over a year old, God used Fisher to pray for his healing. A friend of Myrle's had come to visit, accompanied by her baby, which happened to have whooping cough. Stanley caught the whooping cough and came down with pneumonia as well. He was close to death. His grandfather walked the floor carrying him and praying fervently. The Lord answered his prayer and healed Stanley.

In 1918 the new pastor of the Upper Room Mission, Harry Horton, was drafted. Because World War I ended soon after Harry was drafted, however, he was immediately released and returned to pastor the Mission.

One year later, the influenza epidemic caused more deaths than World War I. Harry became so sick that he could not keep

Eva Horton (Stanley's sister), Clara Daisy Sanford Fisher (Stanley's grandmother), Myrle Fisher Horton (Stanley's mother), and Ruth Horton (Stanley's sister)

down even a teaspoonful of water. One day when he was alone in bed he saw a "yellow glob" in the corner of the room. There were no horns or anything traditionally pictured as the devil, but Harry knew it was the devil. As he would later tell his son Stanley, he felt Satan spoke to him, saying, "I am Satan. I've got you in my power now." Harry felt himself sinking and heard screams below him. But then suddenly he heard singing, looked up, and saw an angel choir singing "Rock of Ages, cleft for me." He felt himself rising. Suddenly, he felt completely well and very hungry. He called to his sister to bring him something to eat quickly. She broke a raw egg into a cup, which he swallowed and kept down. After that he got up and dressed—fully recovered!

Throughout the flu epidemic, Stanley's grandfather Fisher visited and prayed for many people. Eventually, however, he came down with the flu himself. While sick, he received a message that a dying man wanted to pray with him for salvation. Instead of staying in bed in an attempt to preserve his own health, Fisher got out of bed, went to pray for the man, and then came home. He died not long after, on January 19, 1919. His funeral was held in the Church of the Open Door at the Bible Institute of Los Angeles, with a great crowd attending. Many of those for whom he had prayed were led to the Lord and were healed of the flu.

After Fisher's death, his wife, Clara, was devastated. Not long after, though, a despondent woman wrote to her about a struggle she was having. She confided to Clara in this letter, "I'm going to commit suicide if I don't get help." Clara wrote back, "Do *something* for *somebody*—quick." In Clara's wise counsel to this woman, she realized that serving others rather than focusing on one's own troubles was the healthier choice on the road to recovery. The woman responded with gratitude. Stanley Horton's Uncle Wesley Steelberg, who had married Clara's daughter, Ruth, saw how his mother-in-law's compassion was in itself a ministry to people, especially now in her own time of loss. He had a plaque made for her with the name, "Dr. Sunshine" on it, for her to put on her door. Soon Clara was decorating tracts and poems and sending them out all over the country to people she felt needed help. She also provided many poems and quotations for Charles E. Fuller[58] to use on his radio program and in his magazine. Her ministry of writing encouraging letters to others helped Clara cope with the loss of her husband.

Years later when Stanley was grown and away at Gordon Divinity School, Grandma Fisher told her daughter Myrle (Stanley's mother), "God has sent me a telegram; the angels are about to take me home." She died and was buried with her husband, Elmer Fisher, at Forest Lawn Memorial Park in Glendale, California.

Endnotes

[1] Ray Gannon, "The Shifting Romance with Israel: American Pentecostal Ideology of Zionism and the Jewish State" (Ph.D. diss., Jerusalem: Hebrew University, 2003), 45.

[2] Stanley Horton, "The Pentecostal Explosion: How the Fire Fell in 1906 and Spread," *AG Heritage* (Fall 1982): 2. [Reprinted as "The Azusa Street Revival According to Stanley Horton," *AG Heritage* (Winter 2005-06): 30.] As Stanley recounts in his *Reflections of an Early American Pentecostal* (Baguio City, Philippines: APTS Press, 2001), iii, "People came to Azusa Street from all over the world and from all walks of life. They sought God. They recognized Jesus as the mighty Baptizer, and were filled with the Holy Spirit. Then they took the Pentecostal message to every continent and to the islands of the sea. The revival and its blessings are still spreading in all directions."

[3] A church in Dublin where Wesley preached is now an Assemblies of God church, St. Mark's Family Worship Center. Stanley Horton visited that church around 1997. He remembers, "It was packed with 300-400 people, and the Spirit of the Lord was wonderfully present in the service."

[4] Home of the Azusa Street Revival, "The term given to events that ran from 1906 to 1913 in and around the Apostolic Faith Mission (AFM), located at 312 Azusa Street in Los Angeles, CA." See Cecil ("Mel") Robeck's article, "Azusa Street Revival," in *The New International Dictionary of Pentecostal and Charismatic Movements*, 2nd ed., ed. Stanley M. Burgess and Eduard M. Van Der Maas, 344–350 (Grand Rapids: Zondervan, 2003), 344.

[5] Harry's mother, Margaret Amelia Miller Horton, was born in Cooksville and was brought up as a strict Methodist. She and her husband Samuel, Jr., joined in with A. H. Argue, and that was where she received the baptism in the Spirit in Winnipeg, around 1908.

6 Andrew H. ("A. H.") was a businessman in Winnipeg. After he was filled with the Spirit, he—and his family—became "one of the best-known Pentecostal families dedicated to evangelism" (Gary B. McGee, *People of the Spirit: The Assemblies of God* [Springfield, MO: Gospel Publishing House, 2004], 303). A. H. was the father of Zelma Argue, a woman who at age twenty joined her father in ministry, traveling with him (and sometimes her siblings Watson and Beulah). Also a prolific writer, Zelma served the Lord in the evangelistic field for sixty years. On Zelma Argue, see also Edith L. Blumhofer, *Pentecost in My Soul: Explorations in the Meaning of Pentecostal Experience in the Early Assemblies of God* (Springfield, MO: Gospel Publishing House, 1989), 155–170.

   Dr. Don Argue, currently serving on the United States Commission on International Religious Freedom (USCIRF), is A. H.'s grandson. Don previously served as president of Northwest University (AG) in Kirkland, Washington, president of the National Association of Evangelicals (NAE), and president of North Central University (AG) in Minneapolis, Minnesota. He has also held pastoral and denominational positions.

7 See "100th Anniversary History & Memories: Calvary Temple 1907-2007" (Winnipeg, Manitoba: Calvary Temple Centennial Committee, 2007). The pastor of Calvary Temple at the time of this writing is Bruce Martin.

8 Clara's great-grandfather, William J. Sanford, Jr. (1757–1837), fought in the Revolutionary War, serving in the Rhode Island Militia from 1775–1779, at Taunton, Howland Ferry, Brisol Ferry, Little Compton, Trenton Shore, Fall River Mills, and Newton Harbor. His ancestor (great-grandparent x5) Francis Cooke came over on the Mayflower and died in Plymouth, Massachusetts, in 1663 (Horton family tree, Ancestry.com).

9 One activist who spent her early years (1818–1852) in Clara's home county (Cortland County, New York), was Amelia Jenks Bloomer, who published a bi-weekly paper for women called *The Lily*, dealing with news items and topics of women's rights and reform. Bloomer may be best known for the innovative, less restrictive women's fashion, "Bloomers," named after her.

10 Albert Benjamin (A. B.) Simpson (1843–1919) was a Canadian preacher, theologian, and author. He founded The Christian and Missionary Alliance denomination. In 1882, he began the Missionary Training Institute (now Nyack College and Alliance Theological Seminary). Since many yearly Pentecostal leaders attended this Institute, Simpson and the C&MA had a profound influence on the Pentecostal movement.

11 The Keswick conferences that began in Great Britain in 1875 impacted the thinking of American Holiness thinkers. To Keswick teachers, the baptism in the Holy Spirit brought an "ongoing victorious life (the 'higher,' or 'deeper,' life), characterized by the 'fullness of the Spirit.' This became the interpretation they preferred rather than the Wesleyan concept, which maintained that Spirit baptism brought 'sinless' perfection." Gary B. McGee, "The Pentecostal Movement and Assemblies of

God Theology: Exploring the Historical Background," Part 1, *AG Heritage* (Winter 1993–94): 11.

[12] Horton, *Reflections of an Early American Pentecostal*, 11.

[13] Agnes Ozman was the first person to speak in tongues at the "Topeka Revival" on January 1, 1901. This revival took place at the Bethel Bible School led by Charles Parham. After the Bible School closed that fall, Agnes "returned to city mission work and did not identify with the Pentecostal movement again until 1906" (McGee, *People of the Spirit*, 55–56).

[14] Stanley Horton, "Rediscovering the Prophetic Role of Women," *Enrichment* journal, http://enrichmentjournal.ag.org/200102/080_prophetic_role.cfm (accessed January 4, 2007). AG General Superintendent Dr. George O. Wood, in his article, "Exploring Why We Think the Way We Do About Women in Ministry," *Enrichment* journal, http://enrichment-journal.ag.org/200102/008_exploring.cfm (accessed July 7, 2008) agrees with Horton's "foundational exegetical arguments" regarding his affirmation of the role of women in ministry.

In one of our many interviews while working on this book, I asked Dr. Horton about 1 Timothy 2:12 since he had not dealt with that Scripture in his article on women. At first he answered, "I think he's talking about relationships between the wife and husband. He doesn't want women to take the idea of being the teacher of their unsaved husband. They're not going to win them to the Lord by doing that." I asked him if he meant when one spouse is unsaved, or if he thinks that this applies to a marriage where both are believers. He replied, "I think that's partly cultural." After a long pause, he added, "It's a difficult situation." I mentioned the book *God's Women Then and Now* and the conclusion Gill and Cavaness come to, and asked him about whether it could be referring to one woman Paul didn't want to teach heresy. "Now that I think of it," he said, "that could be it. That's a stronger possibility."

[15] See: "Fisher, Elmer Kirk (1866-1919)," in *The New International Dictionary of Pentecostal and Charismatic Movements*, rev. and expanded edition, ed. Stanley M. Burgess and Eduard M. Van Der Maas (Grand Rapids: Zondervan, 2003), 641.

[16] Dwight Lyman ("D. L.") Moody (1837–1899) was a world-famous international evangelist who founded the Moody Church, Northfield School and Mount Hermon School (now the Northfield Mount Hermon School), the Moody Bible Institute, and Moody Publishers.

[17] At the time of his death on September 28, 2005, Stanley's first cousin Dr. Robert E. Fisher was serving as the executive director of the Center for Spiritual Renewal, an organization dedicated to commemorating world revival. He was in the midst of planning his largest project yet—the April 25–29, 2006, Azusa Street Centennial Celebration, which he had envisioned—when he passed away. A native of the San Joaquin Valley in the central part of California, Robert received undergraduate degrees from West Coast Christian College and California State University (both in Fresno), an M.A. in Educational Psychology from California State

University, and a Ph.D. in Counseling Psychology from the University of Hawaii. A visionary leader, prolific author, and gifted administrator, Robert Fisher served the Lord within the Church of God in many educational, pastoral, and administrative capacities, including state overseer of Hawaii, Maryland/Delaware/DC, Georgia, and W. North Carolina. From 1989–2000, he held various positions with the COG national headquarters in Cleveland, Tennessee, including Director of General Education, General Secretary-Treasurer, Assistant General Overseer, and Director of Ministerial Care. Robert's widow, Mary, carries on the work of promoting revival within the Church of God. "Dr. Robert E. Fisher's Ministry Touched Thousands," Church of God News, Church of God, http://churchofgod. org/articles.cfm?sid=6029 (accessed July 2, 2008). His son Dr. Robert W. Fisher is Professor of Psychology at Lee University.

[18] This picture of Myrle—with her name written in pencil on the back of the original—was found in an antique store by a woman named Marilyn Posey. In 2004, she posted information about the photo on the Internet, seeking the owner. In 2008, Glenn Gohr of the AG's Flower Pentecostal Heritage Center, in a search for information on Myrle in connection with this biography, came across the post and contacted Marilyn, who returned the original to the Horton family. (Read more at: http://ifphc.wordpress.com/2008/07/29/long-lost-photograph-finds-a-home/#more-182). This gift was especially meaningful, since most of what Myrle owned was lost in a fire when she lived in Fresno, California, in her later years. What Myrle had stored in the garage adjacent to the house she rented included many things from her parents and ancestors, even pre-Revolutionary War era letters and a deed to property in Connecticut dated in the reign of King Charles II of England. Stanley remembers seeing all of those things when he was a boy. His sisters believe the renters set the garage on fire because they could not use it.

[19] A round metal pole set between two posts. Children used to play "skin the cat" or just swing back and forth on the pole.

[20] Cecil M. ("Mel") Robeck, Jr. *Azusa Street Mission and Revival: The Birth of the Global Pentecostal Movement* (Nashville: Thomas Nelson, 2006), 66.

[21] Ibid., 67.

[22] Stanley Horton, "The Azusa Street Revival According to Stanley Horton," *AG Heritage* (Winter 2005-06): 30. [Reprinted from *AG Heritage*, (Fall, 1982): 2-3.] In this article, Dr. Horton also describes a typical day at the Azusa Street Mission. This portion of the article has also been reprinted as a stand-alone article. See *Enrichment* journal (Fall 1999): 34.

[23] Horton, *Reflections of an Early American Pentecostal*, 16–17.

[24] Robeck, *Azusa Street Mission*, 190.

[25] Ibid., 190, 198–204.

[26] Ibid., 94, 203.

[27] Ibid., 95.

[28] Ibid., 99.

[29] Horton, "The Azusa Street Revival According to Stanley Horton," 31. The Upper Room Mission also initially included "sanctification, as a second definite work of grace" in its doctrinal statement, since it had been a part of the Azusa teachings. However, before Elmer Fisher died in 1919, the teaching was dropped (Ibid., 42).

[30] Ibid.

[31] Horton, *Reflections of an Early American Pentecostal*, 17–18. Also in Elmer Kirk Fisher's article, "How to Receive the Baptism of the Holy Ghost and Fire," in *The Upper Room*, vol. 1, no. 1 (June, 1909): 4.

[32] This hope was also used as a means of admonishing believers to live consecrated, holy lives.

[33] Horton, "The Azusa Street Revival According to Stanley Horton," 32. From "How to Receive the Baptism of The Holy Ghost and Fire," *The Upper Room*, vol. 1, no. 1 (June, 1909): 4–5.

[34] "A Little Girl's Vision of Heaven," in *Azusa Street Papers*: A Reprint of *The Apostolic Faith Mission Publication*, Los Angeles, CA, 1906–1909, ed. William J. Seymour. (Foley, AL: Together in the Harvest Publications) (public domain), vol. 1 no. 5 (Jan. 1907): 28. Also available from: http://www.evanwiggs.com/revival/history/azusa.html (accessed April 25, 2008). The recorded account of Myrle's vision ends with the following notation: "-E.K. Fisher, Glendale, CA; Lock Box 145 (Brother Fisher is one of the pastors of Pentecostal Missions in Los Angeles, at 327½ S. Spring St.)."

[35] Stanley Horton, "Visions and Dreams" *Enrichment* journal, http://enrichmentjournal.ag.org/200001/086_vision_and_dreams.cfm (accessed July 8, 2008).

[36] Stanley Horton, "Your Sons and Daughters Will Prophesy" *Enrichment* journal, http://enrichmentjournal.ag.org/200103/084_sonsdaughtsproph.cfm (accessed July 8, 2008).

[37] Horton, "The Azusa Street Revival According to Stanley Horton," *AG Heritage* (Winter 2005–06): 31.

[38] Bartleman knew E. K. Fisher both from the Azusa Street Mission and Upper Room Mission. Stanley recalls Frank Bartleman coming to visit his father, Harry Horton, who was then pastor of the Upper Room Mission. He speaks of this visit in his interview portion of the movie, *The Azusa Street Project*, a film by Jessie Ottolini. The film includes interviews with: Maria Doyle; Clay Banks; G. R. Thompson; Charles E. Blake, Sr.; Jack W. Hayford; Marilyn Hickey; Stanley M. Horton; Noel Jones; Larry Martin; Joyce Meyer; Betty R. Price; Frederick K. C. Price; Jim Reeve; Cecil M. Robeck; Vinson Synan; Thomas E. Trask; William M. Wilson; Matt Gibson; and Krista Meadows; Global Godworks Media; Azusa Street Project; Passion River Productions (http://www.azusastreetproject.com/) "I went out to play while he talked with my dad," Horton recounts. "I remember him as tall, straight, and carrying a little satchel." (Stanley Horton, e-mail to author, May 21, 2008).

[39] Frank Bartleman, *Azusa Street: The Roots of Modern-day Pentecost* (S. Plainfield, NJ: Bridge Publishing, Inc., 1980), 54. (Originally published in Los Angeles in 1925).

Bartleman criticized Fisher because he "believed in order and did not allow all to speak who thought they were moved by the Spirit" (Fisher, Elmer Kirk (1866–1919)," in *The New International Dictionary of Pentecostal and Charismatic Movements*, 641). Though Fisher believed in order, he had a "distrust of organized religion and preferred to be 'free.' . . . [not allowing] a membership list and [avoiding] as much of the ritual he was used to as possible. No offerings were taken, but a mailbox nailed up by the door was available for people to deposit tithes and offerings" (Horton, *Reflections*, 52).

[40] Robeck, *Azusa Street Mission & Revival*, 94.

[41] The January 1911 issue was published by Fisher and Studd. Perhaps due to the Durham controversy of February 1911, the next (and last) issue was not published until May of 1911. That issue only lists Fisher as the publisher, since Studd had resigned from the Upper Room Mission on April 6, 1911. (George Studd, "Chronology," a brief overview of his life from 1906–1943, FPHC Archive). In addition to the upheaval of the early part of that year, perhaps the lack of Studd's financial support made it too difficult to continue producing the paper.

[42] "1910–1911," *The Upper Room* vol. 2, no. 4 (January 1911): 1.

[43] Grant Wacker, *Heaven Below: Early Pentecostals and American Culture* (Cambridge: Harvard University Press, 2001), 204.

[44] Bartleman, 84. He notes that the Upper Room Mission for a time was the "strongest mission in town." In Bartleman's opinion, both Smale's New Testament Church and the Azusa Mission had "largely failed God" (85), even by late 1906 when the Upper Room was established.

[45] George Studd, "Los Angeles," *Confidence,* August 15, 1908, 10.

[46] Wacker, 230.

[47] The January, 1911 issue of *The Upper Room* mentions that for many months the Upper Room had a regular attendance of "Mexican brothers and sisters, some of whom already have received their Pentecost." Thus, the mission leadership decided to begin a "Spanish meeting" once a week. Fisher officiated at a wedding at the first Spanish service.

[48] Ibid., 296, 301.

[49] George P. Studd, "Diary," January 19, 1908–December 7, 1908 (FPHC Archive). The one time Studd notes that the service was "not so good" was on August 2, when Fisher had gone to Long Beach.

Wacker calls Studd somewhat of a "mission buff" (135) since "Nearly every day of the year we find him visiting one meeting or another, occasionally speaking, sometimes offering a public prayer, but usually just showing up, singing, and then going on to a member's house afterward for additional prayer, singing, and—not incidentally—victuals."

[50] "1910–1911," *The Upper Room*, 1.

[51] For a thorough account of the "Finished Work" controversy and conflict with Durham, see McGee, *People of the Spirit*, 82–85.

[52] Ibid., 316. Robeck says that after Durham's death in 1912, the Upper Room Mission "went out of business, and Elmer K. Fisher retired from the ministry" (Ibid., 317). However, elsewhere Robeck notes that Fisher pastored the Upper Room Mission until 1914 and that in 1914 it moved to 203 Mercantile Place and in 1915 to 406½ Los Angeles Street, ceasing to exist in 1918 (Ibid., 203). *The New International Dictionary of Pentecostal and Charismatic Movements* (p. 641) lists several ministry endeavors of Fisher's after he turned over the Upper Room Mission to his son-in-law Harry Horton; thus, he did not retire in 1912 from ministry. The Mission continued for many years under Horton, until about 1926. It ceased to exist when Horton stopped preaching there.

[53] See picture of Mr. and Mrs. R. J. Scott in the *Full Gospel Men's Voice*, vol. IV, no. 8, Monterey Park, CA (September 1956): 15. The caption notes that Scott "instigated plans for the great Azusa Street Camp Meeting in Arroyo Seco, August 1907." According to a chronology written by George B. Studd, who also helped organize the event, he was involved with this camp meeting from April 15 to June 1.

[54] Even when Harry Horton was a pastor, he always referred to himself as an evangelist, since he had been an active evangelist in the years before he came to the Upper Room Mission.

[55] "Fisher, Elmer Kirk (1866-1919)," in *The New International Dictionary of Pentecostal and Charismatic Movements*, 641. For more on the Shakarian story and their connection with the Azusa Street Revival, see: *Full Gospel Men's Voice*, vol. IV, no. 8, Monterey Park, CA (September 1956): 5-9; Demos Shakarian, *The Happiest People on Earth* (Old Tappan, NJ: Fleming H. Revell Company), 1975; "The Azusa Street Revival: Interesting and Unusual Facts," *Enrichment* journal (Spring 2006): 9; and Thomas R. Nickel, "The Shakarian Story," 2nd ed. (Los Angeles: Full Gospel Businessmen's Fellowship International), 3–14, also available at http://fgbmfi.org/who.htm (accessed July 11, 2008).

[56] Nickel, "The Shakarian Story," 3.

[57] *Full Gospel Men's Voice*, vol. IV, no. 8 (September 1956): 8.

[58] Charles E. Fuller (1887–1968), a prominent radio evangelist in the Los Angeles area who broadcast the "Old Fashioned Revival Hour," founded Fuller Theological Seminary in 1947. See http://fuller.edu/about-fuller/mission-and-history/history.aspx.

CHAPTER 2

Early Years in California

Grandpa Horton's Healing

After Harry Horton had been pastoring the Upper Room Mission for a few years, his parents came to California and lived for a time in an apartment before moving in with Harry's sister Bertha (Birdie) on Calzona Street.

While living at the Mission, Samuel ("Grandpa Horton"), now seventy-five years old, was hospitalized for surgery to remove prostate cancer. During the surgery, the doctor accidentally cut the urethra, which caused urine to flow through the wound. Since there were no antibiotics in those days, all that the doctors could do was send him home to die. Stanley was just five years old at the time but well remembers the black ambulance that brought his grandfather home and the medical personnel carrying his grandfather upstairs on a stretcher.

All the relatives came to be with Grandpa Horton, thinking he was going to die. However, Stanley's Uncle Joe Clark (who had married Harry's sister, Rachel) called the family together in another room to pray. How the Spirit of God came on that man! The next morning, Aunt Birdie went up to change Grandpa Horton's bandages and found that the wound was healed except for half an inch—and was perfectly clean!

Within a few days the wound healed the rest of the way, and Grandpa Horton went back to work. He lived to be eighty-seven and might not have died even then except that his wife had died, and he didn't take care of himself after that. All he wanted to do after his wife passed away was to be with Jesus and Margaret (his "Maggie"). He contracted tuberculosis and was sick for a while before he died on June 14, 1931. Young Stanley and the rest of the family all gathered around him and said their good-byes.

Grandma Horton and the Angels

Margaret Horton, Stanley's grandmother, was blind the last few years of her life, most likely from cataracts. Though she could not see the children as they would enter the room and approach her special chair where she always sat, she could recognize the sound of each child's footsteps, correctly greeting each one by name. In fact, she could recognize all members of the family by their steps. She was warm and loving to the children, calling each one over to administer a kiss and a hug.

Before she died, Grandma Horton was seriously ill for many months. However, her strong heart prolonged her life. Finally, she lay dying at Birdie's home on Calzona Street. There the whole family gathered around her bed. Suddenly, she rose up, and Stanley heard her say, "Don't you hear them? It's the angels! They are welcoming me home!" Immediately she fell back onto her pillow and was gone to be with Jesus. The children were overwhelmed and stood in stunned silence, unable to speak in that holy place. Having experienced such a godly moment at his grandmother's passing, Stanley often thought that if he could speak with any of his grandparents again, he wanted to ask them, "What is it like in heaven?"

A Family of Ten

One spring evening in Huntington Park, California, in 1916, a Pentecostal midwife was tending to Myrle Horton. There on

May 6, the eldest son of Harry and Myrle was born in a small house near the Upper Room Mission just next door to his Grandpa and Grandma Fisher. Named after his father's Welsh brother-in-law, Stanley Jones, and his father's great-grandfather George Monro,[1] Stanley Monroe Horton was the eldest of eight children, followed by Donald Kirk, Harold[2] Samuel, David Calvin (a "blue baby" who died about ten days after birth), Evelyn (Eva) May, Ruth Naomi, Clara Esther (who goes by "Esther"), and Gertrude ("Lois"). Stanley's father never called the girls by name. Rather, he called Eva "Sweetheart," Ruth "Lover," Esther "Honey," and Lois "Dolly." But he had no nicknames for the boys. Stanley was always just "Stanley," never "Stan."

Stanley M. Horton, 1916

Esther, Eva, and Ruth (Horton's three sisters)

Except for common childhood diseases, Stanley was rarely sick. He did have a bit of an adventure when he was three-and-a-half, though. One day, his parents realized he was breathing through only one nostril. He remembers being put on an operating table and instructed to "smell the oranges" (ether). The last thing he remembered was thinking he was rising toward the ceiling and about to hit the light overhead! Apparently when he was a baby, crawling around on the floor, he had picked up a shoe button and stuck it up his left nostril. By the time the problem was discovered, the surgeon could find only the rubber part of the shoe button; the iron hook had been absorbed! Stanley was always told that the shoe button experience had hindered his growth somewhat. Donald and Harold both did grow to be taller.

Stanley's father could not bear to see his children suffer pain, so when the children were all very young, in the 1920s, Harry arranged for Myrle to take a home-nursing course offered by the White Memorial Hospital in Los Angeles. With so many children, Harry thought that such training would help his wife deal with the many childhood illnesses or injuries that might occur. Stanley remembers his mother giving him fomentations when he had congestion. A year after Myrle's schooling, Stanley's sister, Eva, spent a year in a children's recovery home due to tuberculosis and fortunately came home with no problems.

With so many children and a Pentecostal ministry with people coming and going, life was never dull in the Horton household. One time when Stanley's brother Donald was just four years old, he came down with what the family at the time thought was the flu. Poor Donald could not even keep down a sip of water. Hearing about Donald's serious illness, a friend of Harry Horton's came over with a pillow and spent the night on his knees praying by Donald's bed. The next day Donald was better, though his eyes were crossed and he had to learn to

Harry S. Horton and his three sons, l to r: Harold, Stanley (in front), Donald

walk again. When he joined the Army, they told him there was evidence he had contracted polio. For a long time, Donald wore a patch over his good eye to make the lazy one work. In spite of that, he was a happy boy; everyone—especially his aunts—loved him very much.

In 1932, the Hortons lived in Palms, near Los Angeles. One night a significant earthquake hit. Stanley was sixteen at the time. He and Donald shared a bedroom across the hall from their sisters, Ruth and Esther. The quake struck in the middle of the night when everyone was sound asleep. When Esther awoke from the shaking, she heard the boys coughing and gagging. She ran into their room, and there they were on the bed—covered in plaster from head to toe! The house was an older house and did not withstand the quake well. When she looked up, there above their heads was a huge hole where the plaster had fallen. Thankfully, Donald and Stanley were not seriously injured.

Donald went on to get a bachelor's degree in physics and a master's degree in education. He'd only been in his undergraduate studies a couple of years when World War II began, and he was drafted into the Army. During the war, he served in a radio squad. On December 7, 1941, his squad was en route to Pearl Harbor on a Dollar Steamship liner that had been converted to a troop ship when they learned that Hawaii had been bombed. They decided to turn the ship around so as not to continue to Pearl Harbor, and on their return to the mainland, one of the ship's engines burned out. Somehow they made it back to San Francisco, and shortly thereafter Donald returned to Hawaii and Schofield Barracks to help rebuild the military installations there. Eventually, the Army sent him to the University of Hawaii in Honolulu where he studied math and also taught. He learned radar and was sent to the "Big Island" (i.e., Hawaii) to practice it. Later, he served as chief warrant officer in charge of all the radar in the invasion of Saipan and then worked with the Marines to set up radar systems there. When Donald returned from the war, he became a radio engineer for Aimee Semple McPherson[3] at Angelus Temple for KFSG (K Four Square Gospel). He later attended and served as a board member for Melodyland Christian Center,[4] a theater complex in Anaheim purchased from Disneyland in a bankruptcy sale and turned into a vibrant church. Stanley also enjoyed visits to Melodyland and was invited in later years to preach there. Eventually Hughes Aircraft chose Donald to be their chief human resources agent. In the 1960s, they sent him to Tehran to set up Iran Electronics Corporation. There five years, he also learned Farsi and worked with Christians in a couple of churches. Donald always served the Lord faithfully and taught a Sunday School class just about everywhere he went. He died in 1997.

Stanley's second-younger brother, Harold, took a job as a teenager in a photography lab in Palms. He also worked at MGM in Culver City. Even before Pearl Harbor, Harold got excited about the war and joined the Canadian Army. After the war, he married a Canadian Lutheran and went into real estate in Canada. Having developed an interest in politics, he became a campaign manager for a Pentecostal pastor in Kam Loops, British Columbia. The campaign was successful and the pastor was elected to one of the provincial offices.

At one point in his life, Harold was known as "Philip." After his Uncle Dwight died of appendicitis, his widow, Louise, had become involved in cultic matters, including certain letters of the alphabet being seen as lucky. Since *p* and *l* were considered good letters, Louise called Harold "Philip" to avoid "bad" letters. Eventually, Harold became entrenched in the same kinds of cultic practices as his aunt. For a time, the family had no knowledge of Harold's whereabouts and were very concerned about him. They found Harold only when his father was dying in 1949. At forty years of age, Harold finally rejected his cultic ideas and practices. By then, Stanley and his wife, Evelyn, were living in Springfield, Missouri. After reconnecting with his family, Harold lived fifty more years in Canada. His brother Donald and sisters Ruth and Esther would go to Canada to visit him. (His sister Eva had died already). Though Stanley kept in touch with Harold, he was never able to afford a visit there to see him. Harold died in 1999.

Stanley's youngest sister Lois died from cerebral meningitis at just three years old, when Stanley was fourteen. Lois ("Dolly") had been so sweet and so much fun as the youngest child in the family. Her death was very difficult, especially for Stanley's mother. Myrle wept bitterly and decided to take care that she wouldn't have any more children. Stanley's father hadn't believed in birth control. He had always told his wife that they wouldn't have any more children than God wanted them to have. He used to say God would let him have kids until He knew he couldn't take care of them any more. But following the birth of their eighth child, Lois, the doctor told Harry, "Enough kids. Your wife won't make it through any more." Not only did Myrle decide not to have any more children, but she also shocked Stanley's father by cutting her hair so she could take care of it more easily. The six children who were left needed all the time she could give. She had children to cook for and tend to, and dealing with her hair was just too cumbersome. Since Myrle was not from a Holiness background, cutting her hair short was a nonissue with the church; no one bothered her about it. She insisted she needed to do it because it was just too hot in Southern California.

Truly, Myrle's days were full. Her typical workday began at 4 AM with an hour of prayer. Harry would rise earlier than the children, to feed the chickens and the goats. By 6 AM, the children were washed and dressed for school—the older children tending to their own responsibilities—and the family sat down together for breakfast. Harry would offer a long prayer over the meal, and then following breakfast every morning, the family would have an altar time in the living room, including Scripture memorization. Stanley remembers that occasionally his parents would pray in tongues during this time. Harry and Myrle lovingly cared for the family's spiritual welfare. All the children were expected to contribute a prayer as soon as they were old enough. Committed to the memorization of Scripture, Harry and Myrle often quoted Bible verses to their children, especially from the Psalms. They had the children repeat Philippians 4:8[5] almost daily, to help them shape their basic attitudes and recognize the supporting hand of God. They made prayer time, family altars, Sunday School, and church enjoyable and never marred the family's enjoyment of their church experience by saying anything critical in the presence of their children against any preacher or any church member.[6] Instead, they told them of miracles they had experienced, such as the time the Lord told Stanley's father to leave San Francisco the day before the 1906 earthquake. At bedtime, Harry and Myrle would pray with the children as they knelt by the bed. They encouraged their children throughout their childhood to follow the Lord and saw to it that they were in church.

Myrle was a wonderful homemaker and a great cook. With very little to work with, she could make tasty meals. Stanley remembers that if he refused to eat soup, his mother would thicken it and called it stew! When she couldn't bribe him to eat spinach, she cooked Swiss chard. She was always very kind, gentle, and caring, often taking the children out individually for walks in the mountains behind Glendale and Pasadena to ask them questions, to allow them to express themselves, to try to remedy their problems, or just to discuss different things she felt were needed. On these hikes she would tell her children about her experiences with the Lord, often sharing with them many stories of Azusa Street. She read Bible storybooks, all the Mother Goose rhymes, and Hans Christian Andersen tales to the children and encouraged them to memorize Scripture. At night, she would often play the piano softly to help them go to sleep. Being a mother of so many children, especially during the Depression years, was no easy task. Stanley's youngest sister, Esther, remembers asking her mother on several occasions to say she loved *just her*. "Say, 'I love you,

Esther,'" she would plead. But in an attempt not to play favorites, "I love all my children the same" was Myrle's consistent reply.

As a pastor's wife, Myrle was also supportive of Harry's ministry. Besides carrying out other ministries, she often played the piano during worship services at the Upper Room Mission. The two always acted lovingly toward one another, often sitting on the couch together with Harry's arm around his wife. Harry was a "kind but strict" disciplinarian. The children had to get up on time, eat meals on time, and go to bed on time—and they did what he said. Stanley remembers that his father shaved with a straight razor and had a razor strop hanging behind the bathroom door. "I didn't love it when he had me hold out my hand because of some mischief and the strop stung," he recalls. "But I loved him for teaching me the difference between right and wrong."

One aspect of Harry's strictness was that he believed his sons should get the first and largest servings of food. Esther, the youngest, remembers that Stanley always got the first plate and she got the last. To this day she has kidded him about that, saying that since he was first in the family, he "got all the brains," and—since she was the last (and a girl, who subsequently would have had less to eat)—she "got none."

"I considered Stanley the smartest brother who ever lived," Esther reminisces. "I could ask him anything, and he would know it. I always told everybody that." Even in Esther's family now, her two grown children and one grown grandson say, "Well, if we want to know anything—especially about the Bible—we just call Uncle Stanley. He'll tell you all about it."

While Esther recalls with some humor these "injustices," Stanley remembers getting along fine within the family. His father took time with the children and helped them learn how to play well together and to share. When Stanley was about five years old, his Uncle Dwight brought the family their first radio. To find a station, they had to move a wire over a crystal until they found the station they were looking for, and then they could listen through a set of earphones. The radio had no speakers. Donald and Stanley would separate the earphones and each listen through one of them. They liked to listen to station KHJ that had children's programs, especially to an announcer called "Uncle John" who read stories for children.

Though life was serious and difficult at times and though Harry was quite strict in his child rearing, he still made life fun and interesting for his house full of children. During the time the family lived at the Mission, he would dress up at Christmastime with a Santa mask, dropping a trail of popcorn into the family's living room to signify snow. He also made mealtimes an occasion for stories, telling the children exciting tales of his boyhood in Canada and of his travels and ministry.

Those stories about the country so affected Stanley that one day, when a woman from their church who was visiting his mother asked him if he wanted to go to heaven, he said no. Myrle was shocked, until Stanley added, "I want to go to the country first!"

From 1916 to 1924, the Horton family lived in an apartment at the Upper Room Mission on Los Angeles Street. The apartment, with electricity and flush toilets but never a telephone,[7] was on the second floor of a large brick building that had two long, two-story wings filled with apartments where Chinese people lived. Between the wings was a large vacant lot where the children played ball with the neighbor kids. Two single men, "Brother Erickson" and "Brother Anderson,"

Stanley Horton on the top floor of the Upper Room Mission in Los Angeles, about 1918 or 1919. The mission was on the second floor, and the Horton family lived on the third floor.

also lived in the apartments. Both men would speak with the Horton children about the Lord, and Brother Erickson in particular would let them come in and cut up newspapers to try to make things. A spur[8] of the Southern Pacific Railroad (in what is now an Amtrak station) was at the end of the yard. The children liked to wave at the engineers as the trains went by. Across the way was a fire station. The front part of the building below the Mission housed a row of Chinese shops, each run by a family who lived in an apartment at the back of the shop.

The Horton children's best friends were their cousins, and they had plenty. They got to see each other often, for one of the Horton family's favorite pastimes was visiting the children's aunts and uncles on both sides of the family. They would also see the cousins when Myrle would go to the White Memorial Hospital to have another baby; they were farmed out to relatives for the two weeks she was there. The kids always had fun together. Sometimes, however, things would get a bit "interesting." Once when Stanley was staying with his Uncle Harold and Aunt Anna Fisher, he slept on the top bunk. After he had nodded off, his cousin Charles unwound a safety pin and stuck it up through the thin mattress, waking him up with a start! On another occasion when the kids were eating at Uncle Stanley and Aunt Amelia's in Fullerton, his aunt asked, "Stanley, may I cut your meat for you?" "No thank you," he said. "I can do it. We have tough meat at our house too." His mother never let him forget that one! Another time he was with his Uncle Joe and Aunt Rae Clark. The kids were acting up so much that Uncle Joe had to come out and draw a line in the backyard and say, "Howard, you stay on this side. Stanley, you stay on that side!"

Uncle Joe[9] pastored First Assembly in North Hollywood. Stanley enjoyed attending its Sunday School. It was there that he won his first whole Bible by memorizing Psalm 91. Before that time, Stanley had only read the family Bible, but now he had his own Bible for the first time.

Casitas Avenue

By 1923, Stanley's life was about to change. One day as his father was crossing Los Angeles Street near where the family lived, a bread truck whirled around the corner, hit him, and dragged him about ninety feet. His left leg was paralyzed, but God healed him from that so he could walk again. The bread company settled out of court for two thousand dollars, half of which went to lawyers. The other half served as a down payment for a five-thousand-dollar four-room house at 3252 Casitas Avenue in the Atwater Park district of Los Angeles, between Forest Lawn Memorial Park and Griffith Park near Glendale.

The four-room house on Casitas Avenue had a central hall with four doors: into the kitchen, the bathroom, the back bedroom, and the living room. The children would play "elevator," pretending that each door opened to a different floor. They ate their meals in a breakfast nook off the kitchen. A door from the living room went into the front bedroom where the parents slept, along with whatever baby was in the crib. The living room had a large window and a fake fireplace with a gas burner. One side of the room had bookcases that were well used.

The backyard was fenced, and the children were not allowed out without permission, nor did they go outside after dark. The single garage had a workbench along one side, but the children were never allowed to touch the tools out there. On the bench was a hand-turned coffee grinder. Stanley's father would buy a large bag of wheat and use the coffee grinder to grind wheat for Myrle to make her homemade whole grain bread and biscuits.

Next to the one-car garage, Harry built a playhouse the same size as the garage with sides constructed of crisscrossed boards like latticework, to make little open squares. He brought sand from the Los Angeles River for the children to play in since people were free to take it. The family could not afford pets; there were stray cats in the neighborhood, but the children would get upset when one would get into the playhouse (completely open at the front), because they would make their mess in the sand! Behind the garage and play place was a spot for the chickens that supplied the family with plenty of eggs.

At the end of the yard the Hortons had a pen with two white Toggenberg goats that provided them with milk. Each year when they would go dry for a period of time, Harry would take a large milk can and go to a local dairy where he could get it filled for free. (No one wanted skim milk in those days.) The rest of the yard was a vegetable garden with one white fig tree and one pomegranate tree. The soil was deep and had some clay in it, so the boys would dig down and make a tunnel to dig out a cave. Then they would use a posthole digger to dig a chimney. Each of them was allowed a small space to plant whatever they wanted. Stanley planted radishes (because they came up so quickly) and carnations (so the children would have some to wear on Mother's Day).

Behind the houses across the street from the Horton home on Casitas Avenue was the main line of the Southern Pacific Railroad. Though Stanley's father had a Model T Ford while living on Casitas, the family could take the Red Cars (Pacific Electric trains) into town for ten cents or into downtown Glendale for five cents—and they also did a lot of walking.

On the other side of the tracks was a large vegetable garden owned and worked by a Japanese family. On the San Fernando Road side of their property they had a stand to sell vegetables. The family's bathtub was out in the open, and they would take baths by turn, starting with the grandparents. Needless to say, this was quite a spectacle for the Horton children!

By the age of eight, Stanley loved to read and made regular trips to the local library. He also thoroughly enjoyed roller skating on the sidewalks. At one point he wanted to learn to play the piano, so he found a teacher who would give him lessons in exchange for watering her lawn every day in California's rainless summer. He loved the old hymns. He would try to pick out tunes on the piano such as "Jesus, Lover of My Soul." One time, his Sunday School superintendent had his friend Peter P. Bilhorn come and give a concert at the church. Peter had written "Sweet Peace, the Gift of God's Love" and other hymns. Of this man's music, Stanley reflects, "I have never heard a richer, more beautiful voice before or since." In his junior high years Stanley gave up trying to do better on the piano, bought a trumpet, and began to play in the church orchestra.[10]

During vacation time from school, the Horton boys would go swimming in the Griffith Park pool, visit the free zoo, or climb around on the hills and then walk home by way of the dry Los Angeles River, which was very sandy. One time when the boys were walking home in the sand, they took off their shoes and tied them to their belts with their shoelaces. Talking and running, they weren't paying attention to what was happening as they dragged their shoes along. Once home, they discovered to their chagrin that Donald was missing a shoe that must have dropped off along the way. The boys all retraced their steps but never did find that shoe. Shoes were almost too expensive to replace in those days, so this was a sad event indeed.

Closing the Mission

Harry Horton continued as pastor of the Upper Room Mission for several years; eventually that entire area of the city would be demolished to build Union Station for the region's principal railroads, but around 1925, Harry moved the services to a building in the Arroyo Seco[11] of South Pasadena, where he continued for about a year. Though he had no visible signs of physical trouble from being hit by the bread truck, his strength was never quite the same. Eventually, he could no longer preach full-time and with full strength, and the Upper Room Mission closed.

Since he had no stamina to labor full-time, he worked one day a week for a gardening firm and later, due to health concerns, as a night watchman for a supermarket. The supermarket job did help the family during these difficult times, as Harry was allowed to bring home bruised or outdated produce. The family's back porch was always full of these fruits and vegetables, and in between meals the children could go out and eat whatever was available.

The family also grew vegetables in their garden, but when none were available from that source, Harry would leave early in the morning and walk three or four miles to a farmers' market where he could get vegetables for one cent a bunch. In watermelon season, they would wait until the price went down to one cent a pound. They also enjoyed more meat when hamburger got down to ten cents a pound. The family was very poor, but they never went hungry.

Stanley's parents always made quite a celebration for the children's birthdays, complete with cake and candles. For Stanley's birthday, however, they made an exception—he insisted that his mother make him a rhubarb pie instead! Grandma Fisher and Grandma and Grandpa Horton were usually there to celebrate.

When Grandma Fisher came to visit the children, she sometimes would bring them a bag of toys and books, which Stanley vividly remembers because he loved to read so much. It was always only family over for parties, though—never neighborhood friends—because to attend other children's birthday parties in return would be too costly. One time when a neighbor girl did invite Stanley to a party, his mother took a handkerchief that had been given to her as a wedding gift and wrapped it up for Stanley and Donald to give the girl as a present so they could attend the party.

Such ingenuity and resourcefulness through difficult times blessed the Horton children even years later. Of her parents, Stanley's sister Ruth would say in her eighty-sixth year, "They were the best. I still wonder how they managed all us kids. Especially with my father not making much money, and it being Depression time. They always kept us going. They were special people."

Father's Questions

After his accident, Harry Horton went through some theological struggles. He befriended John Scheppe (pronounced "Shaypee"), a man born in Danzig as Hans Scheppe, who went to sea at fourteen, ended up in Oakland, and then married. When he got saved, his wife left him, so he moved to Los Angeles. In the 1913 worldwide camp meeting, he woke up everyone after having a vision of Jesus, shouting that the name of Jesus needed to be honored. Stanley remembers Scheppe sitting across from his father in the family's breakfast nook:

> Usually one of them was pounding the table as he vented his ideas. My father was influenced at one point by the Oneness, or Jesus Only, teaching, but eventually saw the error in their illustration. The Oneness folks called it a New Issue, but it wasn't new. It was just the old Sabellianism in a little different form. They compared God to a doctor who is called Dr. Jones in his office, Father or daddy at home, and Sam on the golf course. But Sam Jones on the golf course does not telephone Dr. Jones in the office and talk to him. Nor does Dr. Jones in the office telephone Father Jones at his home to ask how the children are.[12]

Another time Harry read Charles H. Pridgeon's book *Is Hell Eternal or Will God's Plan Fail?* He would never let Stanley read it, but he talked about the idea that God is so good that everyone will be saved, including the devil. The lake of fire will purify, and the sinners and fallen angels will come out saints. Later, he saw the fallacy in that idea. If the lake of fire can save people, why did Jesus have to die on the cross?

For a while, Harry also thought the family should please the Lord by keeping the Jewish biblical feast days and also observing Saturday as the Sabbath (by abstaining from work, having special times of Bible study and prayer, etc.). But after more closely examining Paul's epistles he changed his view on that; he was also turned off by the extremes some went to in observing the festivals.[13] Remembering Harry's struggles during this time helped Stanley later to search the Scriptures for the truth of God.

Since there were no Pentecostal churches nearby, Stanley's mother began taking her children to Atwater Park Baptist Church, the only church in the neighborhood. The Baptist Sunday School had excellent teachers. They emphasized Scripture memorization and taught God's Word in ways that children could understand—all of which had a strong impact on Stanley as a young boy. At the same time, the family kept in contact with area Pentecostal churches, occasionally visiting Bethel Temple Assembly of God and, not long after it was built in 1923, Angelus Temple.

On Saturday afternoons at Angelus Temple, Aimee Semple McPherson would hold children's meetings. Sometimes the family would take the streetcar to the services, and at other times a woman who had attended the Upper Room Mission would come to Stanley's home on Saturdays to take him and his brothers to the children's services. On one occasion—since Stanley's father was well known as the pastor of the Upper Room Mission—Stanley was brought up to the platform to lead in prayer. (He was so consumed with the need to pray that he didn't pay much attention to the lady who had brought him to Angelus Temple; he just marched right up to the platform!) When they brought him onto the platform, Sister Aimee, as she was called, dressed in her white apparel, beckoned to Stanley to sit on her lap until it was time for him to pray. "She was a first-rate sermonizer and a gracious lady," Stanley recalls of his visits there. "I will never forget her warm, friendly personality, nor . . . the marvelous musical cantatas she wrote. I used to love to sit in the audience after a service, too, and listen to Esther Fricke Green play an hour's organ concert."[14] Esther was a famous organist, and Stanley loved her concerts.

Harry and Myrle with Jesus

In 1949, Stanley's parents came to Springfield, Missouri, and stayed with Wesley and Ruth Steelberg, since at that time Stanley and Evelyn were living in a small duplex with their two children. Even though Harry Horton was then dying of throat cancer, God took the pain away. One day as Stanley knelt by his father's bed and began to pray for him, his father, sensing his own pending demise, stopped him and said, "Don't pray for me, Stanley; praise the Lord with me." Harry kept praising the Lord even though his voice was just a whisper—and that was how he slipped off to be with Jesus.

After her husband's death, Myrle passed a GED test, took sixteen hours of library science, and obtained employment as librarian at West Coast Bible School in Fresno, California, affiliated with the Church of God, Cleveland, Tennessee. Myrle's sister-in-law, Anna Fisher (mother of Dr. Robert Fisher of the Church of God, Cleveland), was the cook there. The two women had a great time there with the students. One term Myrle filled in teaching American history. A student once tried to stump her by asking about an Indian uprising in Canada. It just so happened that Harry had been in that area at the time and had told her all about it. So the students were surprised at her knowledge. She retired and lived alone in a trailer park in Fullerton, Orange County, California, until she passed away at age seventy-three, in 1968.

Aimee had many dedicated and gifted ministers working with her—especially in the "500 Room," where sinners sought the Lord for salvation, and in the "120 Room," where people came to receive the baptism in the Holy Spirit or came seeking healing. Stanley's father went to the 120 Room when Stanley was about twelve; Harry had developed a lump on his throat the size of a goose egg. A friend of Harry's, Brother Arthur, was in charge of that room. He prayed for Harry there, and the lump melted away. The whole family all praised the Lord when he came home, and the lump was totally gone!

During Stanley's high school years, he enjoyed continued interaction at times with the Foursquare. He loved to go to Angelus Temple whenever he could, as he'd done as a boy. Such events as the musical drama "Bells of Bethlehem" were always a favorite of his there. His uncle Harold Fisher was the official photographer for

Angelus Temple, and his brother Donald was engineer for their radio station, KFSG. Donald told Stanley that those closest to Sister Aimee never lost confidence in her through all her personal troubles.[15] He defended her honor, pointing out that the great love offerings went into the work and were handled by a board of twelve elders and that when she died, her total estate was only four thousand dollars. Years later, when Stanley was at UC Berkeley, his family attended a Foursquare church for a while.

Mostly as a result of his theological struggles at the time, but also due to his poor health, Stanley's father did not go with his wife and children to the Baptist church. Because he worked nights, he wasn't active there although he did attend with the family on occasion when they went to Angelus Temple or Bethel. Myrle stayed active, usually playing the piano for services, and she and Harry always made sure the kids went—Sunday morning, Sunday night, Wednesday night, and Friday night. In later years, after Stanley had left for college, his parents went to a Foursquare church on Hoover Boulevard pastored by Aubrey Lee. Also they were always happy about the ministry of Uncle Wesley and Aunt Ruth Steelberg in the Assemblies of God.

Uncle Wesley

Uncle Wesley's parents were Swedish immigrants. His father, a lay Methodist preacher in the Denver area who had worked as a machinist, became Pentecostal after Wesley's miraculous healing from a debilitating condition due to brain fever and spinal meningitis. The Steelbergs sacrificed greatly to help start Swedish churches in the Los Angeles area.

Horton's uncle,
Wesley Steelberg, 1952

69

Saved and filled with the Spirit at age eight and miraculously healed not long after, Wesley Steelberg was known in his youth as "The Boy Preacher."[16] Ordained with the Assemblies of God in 1919 at seventeen (only to have to return his credentials later when the Council voted that ministers had to be twenty-one for credentialing), Steelberg went on to serve the Lord as church planter; evangelist; pastor; radio minister; then district, general, and executive presbyter; district superintendent; assistant general superintendent (one of four at that time); national Christ's Ambassadors director (1945), and—upon the retirement of E. S. Williams—general superintendent of the Assemblies of God (1949). In 1945 Steelberg was one of the speakers at the General Council of the Assemblies of God in Springfield, Missouri. He exhorted those in attendance that the time had come for the Pentecostal movement to "make a choice between lapsing back into formalism . . . or consecrating to such an extent that the supernatural manifestation of God's Spirit would be perpetuated among us."[17]

Stanley Horton has very early memories not only of Wesley's father (who, as he remembers, used to break out in tongues at the table during grace) but also of his loving and entertaining Uncle Wesley, who encouraged him in the faith and had a tremendous impact on his life. One of his earliest memories,[18] at age four, is of attending his Aunt Ruth and Uncle Wesley's wedding in the Steelberg home. The daughter of Elmer and Clara Fisher, Horton's Aunt Ruth met this young, handsome preacher when he came to Los Angeles in 1919 to serve as assistant pastor of one of the first Pentecostal churches of the city, Victoria Hall.[19]

When seventeen-year-old Wesley and his equally young bride, Ruth, left for Arizona—shortly after their wedding in 1919—to do pioneer evangelistic work, Stanley's father gave them a car for the journey.

Those were still the days of the "wild west" and the young preacher's ministry was enriched by some exciting though trying experiences among gamblers, miners, and other rough men of this "frontier" area. Again and again attempts were made to destroy the meeting tent, but the Lord overshadowed Brother Steelberg and brought him through with a strengthened confidence in God's faithfulness.[20]

Later Steelberg visits throughout Stanley's adolescence continued to provide a source of great joy. Often Uncle Wesley would take the Horton kids to the beach to jump the waves or build sand castles. At Christmas when Wesley and Ruth would come for dinner, Stanley always had fun decorating the Christmas tree with strings of popcorn and other homemade things. He remembers too how his Uncle Wesley would play "Santa Claus to six little Horton boys and girls"[21] and that the Steelbergs would bring school clothes as gifts for all the kids.

Still later, while pastoring in Sacramento, Wesley and Ruth took the then fourteen-year-old Stanley and his brother Donald to be with them for the summer. They went to Yosemite National Park to show them Yosemite Falls, Vernal Falls, and the after-dark Firefall. Stanley remembers watching bears—as lights were turned on across a river—eating food put out for them. But most memorable was his trip with the Steelbergs to Sacramento for several weeks. The first Sunday in Uncle Wesley's church, Stanley sat a little behind a young man named Robert Carrington, who later became a pastor in the Northern California–Nevada district. During worship, Robert was raising his hands, and Stanley could see the glory of the Lord upon him. Stanley wanted that.

Stanley's hunger for more of God continued to increase during this Sacramento visit. One day Uncle Wesley took the Horton boys to a Pentecostal Ambassadors for Christ (PAC) convention in Turlock, California. Steelberg had envisioned and launched this youth organization, a precursor to what eventually became the national "Christ's Ambassadors" organization.[22] The service was wonderful, and Stanley went to the altar at the close. The Lord's presence was so real to him that he simply got lost in it and was unaware of anything around him. Then he felt a tap on his shoulder, and a man said, "Are you saved, brother?" Everyone else had gone, and this man wanted to put the lights out. Stanley was already saved, but that night he knew in a new way that Jesus was real.

Besides Steelberg influencing the young Horton boys during this visit, for several years his ministry in the Sacramento church resulted in many young people going into ministry.

Wesley Steelberg continued to be an influence throughout Horton's life. Not only had this wonderful and fun-loving man provided his nephew with cherished childhood memories, but he also served as a godly example, modeling the character of Christ and a zealous commitment to furthering the Kingdom. It is said of Steelberg that during his ministry in Sacramento, he

continued to demonstrate those qualities that gradually brought him to national recognition as one of the movement's outstanding leaders. He displayed a rare combination of faithfulness to the old paths of the Pentecostal movement and aggressiveness to meet the challenge of the days in which he lived. His daring faith to push ahead and risk all for God was tempered by sincere humility and dependence on God.[23]

"Rare combination" are words also often used to describe Stanley Horton's character. For those who have known Horton, it is clear that Wesley Steelberg indeed made his mark on his nephew. In the power of the Spirit and with a humble spirit of Christlike service for God's glory, both Steelberg and Horton accomplished much for the Kingdom.

Those years of service came to an end for Steelberg three years after becoming general superintendant of the Assemblies of God. After pouring himself out for God in the work of the ministry,

Wesley Steelberg preached his last message in Cardiff, Wales, at a minister's meeting in June and after suffering a heart attack went to be with the Lord at age fifty a month later.

In his testimony to CBI students just days prior to his Uncle's passing, Horton wrote, "My Aunt Ruth and Uncle Wesley['s] . . . never-failing love, faith, and interest have been a constant source of inspiration and encouragement to me. Uncle Wesley over Revival Time [sic] still stirs my heart and brings tears to my eyes, just as he always has."[24]

"Saved Indeed"

Stanley remembers giving his heart to the Lord in 1922 when he was just six years old. Right after that spiritual experience, he wanted to be baptized in water. But his father didn't want people to think he, as the pastor of the Mission, was pushing his son to be baptized too soon. Finally, he decided to turn Stanley over to a couple of his deacons to let them question him privately. Stanley doesn't remember their questions, but he never forgot the baptismal ceremony. "I can still picture it in my mind," he reminisces, "as well as the three women who were baptized right after me."

Six years later, after the Horton family had moved from the apartment at the Upper Room Mission, a French woman named Marie Carpentier began operating a rescue mission called "God's Mission" at that same property. Stanley's father served on its board of directors. Sometimes when Harry was there for a board meeting, Stanley would go down and eat with the men. One time when Stanley and his father were visiting the Mission, Marie gave Stanley a cake for his twelfth birthday. She sat down and spoke with the "birthday boy" about spiritual things. After listening to his story for a while, she told Stanley that she was not sure he really could have been saved when he was six years old. This bothered him a bit. So the next time he went downtown to the library, he slipped away and found another rescue mission where no one knew him. He went to the altar when they gave the invitation for salvation, and the Lord reassured him that he was indeed saved. "I remember presidents, beginning with Calvin Coolidge," Stanley remembers, "but I was not much impressed with them or other heroes as a child. Grandma Fisher told us stories about the Civil War and how her uncle marched through Georgia to the sea. That was interesting, but Jesus was my hero. I wanted to be just like Him."

When the family later moved to Palms, they began attending a nearby church that had once been Foursquare but had joined a Bible Standard group headquartered in Iowa. This group encouraged Stanley to seek for the baptism in the Holy Spirit. He had not sought earnestly before, probably because of a bad experience he'd had when he was about eight. Some friends Myrle Horton had known in the Azusa Street Mission persuaded Stanley's parents to visit a special meeting being held at Frank Ewart's church.[25] After the service Stanley went down to the altar and a woman started jiggling his chin, supposedly to help him speak in tongues. When Harry Horton saw what was happening to his son, he grabbed him and left, and the family never went back.

Smart from the Start

When it came time for Stanley to begin school, his mother found that the school near the Upper Room Mission was full of children who, as he put it, "used profanity and bad grammar and were badly behaved." So she went to the library and got material to homeschool her budding scholar. Stanley was an eager student, always wanting to do well. He also enjoyed talks with his mother during schooltime that had to do with spiritual things— especially when they would speak about the coming of the Lord.

Because she homeschooled him at the Mission, Stanley was already able to read when the family moved to Casitas Avenue in 1923. When he finally did go to public school at age seven, he skipped grade B1[26] at the Atwater Avenue Elementary School and went into A1 with Miss Slaughterhouse as his teacher. Then he skipped B2 and did well until the third grade, where he had Mrs. Bond as a teacher. His memories of this teacher and the experience of that particular segment of his schooling are less than pleasant. "I think she didn't believe in letting children skip grades. She so scared me that I wouldn't respond even though I knew the answer. By the end of the year I was almost a nervous wreck," he recalls. "Fortunately, my fourth grade teacher, Mrs. Merrick, was very affirming. She knew how to encourage me and brought me out of it." Altogether Stanley skipped five semesters, which allowed him to graduate from high school in January 1933 at the age of sixteen.

For school the Horton boys wore collared shirts with short pants and belts, and the girls wore dresses their mother made, sometimes from flour sacks. After school they changed to overalls and went barefoot. At graduation from the ninth grade, Stanley wore his first suit, with knickers (pants just below the knee), since boys didn't wear long pants until high school. When Stanley was twelve, a couple of boys in his class at school persuaded him to join the Glendale YMCA. Selling the *Saturday Evening Post* for five cents meant a two-cent profit for himself, so he was able to save enough to pay for his membership at the YMCA. He enjoyed the gym and swimming in the pool.

When Stanley reached the sixth grade, because his IQ was 160, they enrolled him in the gifted program, "Opportunity A" class, at Eagle Rock Elementary School, seven miles from his home. He took a streetcar to Eagle Rock Center then walked one-half mile. The school had extra activities for students—learning French, acting in plays, and much

Horton, ca. 1929 (age 13)

more. After that he attended Eagle Rock Junior High, where in the eighth grade he took typing as an elective for one semester. The best he could do at the time without errors was twenty-eight words a minute. Little did he know how persistence in this skill would pay off—helping him to be the most prolific writer in the Assemblies of God!

It was during this time that Stanley's love of writing began to emerge. Throughout his junior high years, he wanted to be a newspaper reporter, with the ultimate goal of becoming a foreign correspondent.

He had good friends as a teenager but became rather timid. "I never had a girlfriend or went on dates in this period," he recalls. "One embarrassing moment I remember was when a neighbor asked me to walk her daughter who was my age to the local library. Her name was Buena Sandal (she pronounced it "Byuna") from Texas. That really shook me up! I was just embarrassed to walk with a girl."

Stanley's most exciting events during his early teens were hikes in the mountains behind Glendale and Pasadena and roller coaster rides at the Venice pier. He loved to be up in the mountains where he could look down on Los Angeles (in a time of much less smog than now) and also enjoy the beautiful trees on the mountainside. He also enjoyed taking a five-cent bus from Palms to go by himself down to the water where he could watch and listen to the waves and go fishing. One time while fishing from a broken-down pier, he caught a small hammerhead shark, which he threw back, and a halibut, which his mother fixed for supper.

By the tenth grade, Stanley was at Eagle Rock High and began to realize he was having problems seeing. But no one realized he needed glasses[27] because his eyes could adjust to read the charts. On the ball field, though, his astigmatism prevented him from hitting the ball because his eyes weren't able to adjust fast enough. "I didn't realize you were supposed to see the ball," he remembers with a smile. "I thought you had to estimate the time, listen, and then swing! The coach told me he would give me a nickel if I would hit the ball. But I never could." So instead of allowing him to play ball, the coach took him out of the regular gym class and had him lie down and rest during that period. Stanley would bring his lunch and sit and visit with two of his buddies from the "Opportunity A" class, Humphrey Marshall and Haydn Lindsey, on a bench outside. Even though he missed out on gym class, Stanley still got exercise: to save money he often would bring his roller skates to school and skate home instead of taking the streetcar.

One tenth grade English class in particular greatly bored Stanley during these years. "I know I shouldn't have done it, but I would put my head down on my desk and close my eyes. When the teacher would ask me a question I could always pop up with the answer, so she ignored me most of the time." Finally, a new high school, John Marshall, named after the famous Supreme Court Chief Justice, was opened only two miles from Stanley's home, and he attended there for his junior and senior years. His graduating class was not large since some of the students in the district decided to go on and complete their last two years in the high school where they had started. Stanley got along well with fellow students and was elected to represent his class on the student council for his senior year.

The teachers at John Marshall were phenomenal. Stanley doesn't remember a boring class in the bunch. His history teacher had taught in China. His chemistry teacher had worked as a research chemist for an oil company. He got Stanley excited about chemistry, so much so that he decided to major in chemistry in college. His mother had wanted him to become an engineer, which she thought would be a dependable career. But he was too taken up with chemistry to do that. His physics teacher was also a good teacher; however, he was from upstate Vermont and didn't pronounce *r*'s in the middle or end of words—so he couldn't pronounce Stanley's name correctly. There was a Jewish girl in the class named Hotvedt. When the teacher called the roll, he would say, " . . . Hot'n, Hotvedt. "

French was also one of Stanley's early loves in high school. His sister Ruth remembers him sitting at the kitchen table speaking in French at mealtimes. "He would go on and on with his French, getting a big kick out of the fact that no one in the family was able to understand him!" Stanley would go to the foreign language department of the main library at 6th and Hope and look for interesting books in French. He read quite a number—a whole row—of Jules Verne's novels in French, some of which had never been translated into English. He also became interested in Indian literature at this time and wrote class papers about Hinduism and about Ghandi—in particular, why he did not become a Christian. In later years, Horton's interest in India would find great fulfillment, as he traveled there on numerous occasions to teach and preach.

When he first came to John Marshall High School, Stanley had noticed that the librarian, Miss Viola Estelle Stevens, was doing a lot of extra work after school. So he volunteered to help, collating and shelving books. In the process, he learned a great deal about library work and the Dewey decimal system of classifying books. That knowledge would later help him to get jobs in the libraries both at Los Angeles Junior College (1933–35) and Harvard Divinity School (1944–45), where he was a student.

Stanley kept good grades all through high school. At graduation, he was presented with a gold pin in the shape of a Greek lamp with a certificate of lifetime membership in the California Scholarship Federation. After Stanley graduated from high school in 1933, the Horton family moved to Culver City for a year and then to the Palms district of Los Angeles.

"God was so good to me during my high school years," Stanley recalls. "Grandpa Horton died during this period, but that was a blessed homegoing for him, and we did not grieve, as did those who have no hope. He called us in to say good-bye; my father grieved but told us kids that Grandpa was not suffering any more. I remember that even during those years, all I wanted to do was follow the Lord and do His will. I had wonderful parents and relatives who encouraged me. We didn't have much money, but we had everything we needed. This was an important time for me, as I was beginning to seek the Lord for the baptism in the Holy Spirit."

Endnotes

1 George Monro had no "e" on the end of his name. Stanley's parents didn't know that until later when it was too late and his middle name already had the "e."

2 Several *Pentecostal Evangel* articles exist authored by a Harold Horton. This man was not Stanley's brother, however, but an important British Assemblies of God theologian who was no relation. Stanley corresponded with him a few times.

3 "The early 20th century evangelist, Aimee Semple McPherson, was a pioneer of women in religion. Having experienced a profound religious conversion at age 17, Aimee began preaching across the United States and later, the world. In 1918, she established her base in Los Angeles, Calif., where in 1923, the 5,300 seat Angelus Temple was dedicated and became the center of her revival, healing, and benevolent ministries. She was the first woman to own and operate a Christian radio station. Her sermons were the first to incorporate the contemporary communications of that day into her preaching of the Gospel. From Angelus Temple she performed an extensive social ministry, providing hot meals for more than 1.5 million people during the Great Depression. She summarized her message into four major points known as 'The Foursquare Gospel,' and founded a denomination called The Foursquare Church." See "Aimee Semple McPherson: Our Founder," *The Foursquare Church*, http://www.foursquare.org/landing_pages/8,3.html (accessed September 4, 2008).

4 For more information, see "Melodyland Christian Center," in *The New International Dictionary of Pentecostal and Charismatic Movements*, 868.

5 "Finally, brethren, whatsoever things are true, whatsoever things are honest, whatsoever things are just, whatsoever things are pure, whatsoever things are lovely, whatsoever things are of good report; if there be any virtue, and if there be any praise, think on these things" (KJV).

6 Stanley Horton, "Word Study: Train a Child (*Chanokh*)," *Enrichment* journal, http://enrichmentjournal.ag.org/199902/090_train_a_child.cfm (accessed July 11, 2008), 1.

7 The family did not have a telephone until Stanley was in college.

8 "A spur is a railroad track on which cars are left for loading and unloading. Spurs are also used sometimes for railroad car storage. A spur can be single-ended or double-ended. A single-ended spur connects to the through track at only one end. A double-ended spur connects to the through track at both ends" (http://modeltrains. about.com/od/glossary/g/spur.htm).

9 Joseph Clark, married to Harry's sister Rachel, was pastor and founder of the Assembly of God in Los Angeles, in Lankershim (later North Hollywood). He was from England. His son Howard Clark graduated from L.I.F.E. (Lighthouse of International Foursquare Evangelism), pastored churches in Ohio, was superintendent of the Foursquare Eastern District, and president of a Bible school in Illinois before he retired. Uncle Joe's daughter's grandson is Kirk Noonan, an associate editor of *Today's Pentecostal Evangel*. Howard died in the late 1990s in New Hampshire. The rest of the Clark family went with the Assemblies of God.

10 Stanley played a trumpet in church throughout all his college days in California. Later when living in Boston as a student, he gave up the trumpet ("because it was too difficult to keep a stiff upper lip"), bought an accordion, and took lessons at the New England Conservatory. He played the accordion in street meetings and in churches he pastored in New Jersey and White Plains, New York. He played it some in Springfield, but one summer he left it upstairs at their Williams Street house while in New England for a summer vacation. When he returned, he realized the heat had melted the wax reeds and he had to discard it. "I was too busy to practice anymore by then anyway," he remembers.

11 Literally, "dry streambed" in Spanish. This area is a stream and watershed in Los Angeles County. "The Most Celebrated Canyon in Southern California. . . . The scenic Arroyo Seco begins high in the San Gabriel Mountains and flows through the communities of La Canada, Flintridge, Altadena, Pasadena, South Pasadena and Northeast Los Angeles to meet the Los Angeles River just north of downtown Los Angeles" (http://www.arroyoseco.org/watershed. htm).

12 Stanley M. Horton, original written response to "Life Chronicles" questions provided to him by author, 2006.

13 The leader of one little group in Los Angeles that kept the Sabbath and the Jewish feasts told his congregation that he had had a vision that they should not use salt or any condiments. When most of the husbands rebelled against this, the leader told them not to worry— they would have soul mates in heaven. Later he told them they could find their soul mates and get to know them now. One can guess what that led to.

14 Horton, *Reflections of an Early American Pentecostal*, 24, 58.

[15] See Edith L. Blumhofer's excellent biography *Aimee Semple McPherson: Everybody's Sister* (Grand Rapids: Eerdmans Publishing, 1993).

[16] "All for Jesus," *Pentecostal Evangel*, August 10, 1952, 3.

[17] Ibid., 10.

[18] Another early memory of Stanley's, from a time not too long after the wedding—when, as he put it, he was still short enough to walk under the table without bending over—he said to his Uncle Wesley during a family visit, "Uncle Wesley, when I see the stars they make me think of God."

[19] "All for Jesus," 4.

[20] Ibid.

[21] "My Testimony," *The Scroll*, May 19, 1950, 5.

[22] According to a letter (to "Sister Obera," December 18, 1975, FPHC) written by Ruth Steelberg Carter—the district PACs secretary and widow of Wesley Steelberg—the PACs first met for a convention at First Assembly [Ralph Harris' letter says Glad Tidings] in Oakland, California, on Memorial Day [in 1925] (p. 2). At a later convention, on November 11 of that year, the PACs name was adopted; Wesley Steelberg was chosen to be the chairman and a constitution for the group established.

While visiting family in Los Angeles in December 1925, the Steelbergs shared with Carl Hatch and others about God's blessings on the youth ministry in Northern California. Ruth Steelberg recounts how Hatch "had heard about the blessing on our conventions in the North and wanted to know all about them. [The Steelbergs] . . . were glad to share with them, the blessings that had come from the privilege of having such fellowship together" (Ruth Steelberg letter, p. 3). Not long after, Hatch headed a youth organization in Southern California named "Christ's Ambassadors" and sent a report of that convention to Springfield, which was published. (Two earlier reports sent to Springfield about the conventions in Northern California had not been published.)

According to Ralph Harris, the Christ's Ambassadors were recognized officially at the 1927 General Council held in Springfield, Missouri, although the organization was still understood to be organized state by state (*General Council Minutes*, 1931, 81). For ten years, Steelberg piloted PACs, known for its mass conventions with sometimes over three thousand youth in attendance ("All for Jesus," 4). Ruth Steelberg recounts that they continued "with much blessing . . . until we could hardly find auditoriums large enough" (p. 3).

In January 1936, when the Steelbergs felt called to go pastor Highway Tabernacle in Philadelphia, the decision was made to merge PACs with the Southern California group headed by Hatch, and the name "Christ's Ambassadors" was adopted for all the youth groups.

The first National Youth Conference was held in 1940 in Springfield at Central Bible Institute. Other conferences followed. A request was presented at the 1941 General Council to establish a national C.A. Department. Then in February 1943, Ralph Harris came to Springfield to work toward establishing a national C.A. Department, and the 1943 General Council approved this ("Report of the Young People's Committee," *General Council Minutes*, 1943, 24–27).

According to a June 1981 typed history by Ralph W. Harris on "The Development of the National Assemblies of God Youth Ministry" (FPHC), PACs began in 1926. His earlier "History of the National CA Department" (FPHC) written in the 1970s states 1925. In this history he states that "Both the Northern California and Southern California Districts are entitled to credit. Arkansas, too, had an elected young people's leader as early as 1925" (p. 1). As Ruth Steelberg said in her letter, however, "Surely no one can take any glory for what God does, as we are all just instruments in His hands that He can use for His glory, but the glory all belongs to Him" (p. 4).

23 "All for Jesus," 4.

24 "My Testimony," *The Scroll*, May 19, 1950, 5.

25 Ewart (1876–1947), a former Baptist minister, was baptized in the Spirit in 1908 and became assistant to Durham before pastoring in Belvedere, California. Ewart had told the Horton family that they would not be honoring Jesus properly unless they were baptized in the name of Jesus only. Some of his followers had even come to Myrle and told her that she would lose her salvation if she didn't get re-baptized. Myrle doubted the truth of this teaching, since she did not see how she could lose something so precious to her. She began to be angry, however, that something like not being baptized in Jesus' name only could rob her of this experience. Fearing that her anger over the issue itself might be the cause of her losing her salvation, this young eighteen-year-old Spirit-filled believer gave in and got re-baptized. Years later, upon rethinking her theology and doing a thorough study of the Bible, Myrle adopted a Trinitarian position and became a part of an AG church. (Horton, *Reflections of an Early American Pentecostal*, 19–20).

26 In Los Angeles at that time, "B" was the first semester of the year, and "A" the second. So they had started Stanley in the second semester of the first grade, and then he went to the second semester of the second grade.

27 Stanley did not get glasses until his last year at the University of California at Berkeley, in 1937 at age twenty-one. His doctor told him that he had never seen such eyes without glasses. Because of his bad eyesight (2400/2200 vision), the Army classified him as 1-B-O at the time of the draft in 1940.

CHAPTER 3

University

Early Adult Years

In thinking about where to go for college, Stanley considered trying to get a scholarship to Colgate University, where his great-great-grandfather had been the president. Though he would certainly have qualified academically, unfortunately there was no way he could get enough money even to travel to New York state had he received the scholarship!

So he took the English entrance exam at Los Angeles Junior College (LAJC, but later changed to Los Angeles City College) and of course passed with flying colors. The school had asked for an essay on how the Depression was affecting his family. Stanley wrote that it hadn't affected them at all! The family was already poor and had learned to get along on very little, so the current economic situation in the country altered nothing.

Only sixteen at the time, Stanley began classes at LAJC immediately after finishing high school in January of 1933. He arranged for rides to class with a neighbor boy who had a car and was also attending there. This young man was dating the daughter of the founder of Ralph's Groceries. One day when the boys stopped at her house on their way to class, Stanley saw for the first time a record player that could play twelve records. At the time, he was quite impressed with such progress!

His experience at LAJC was interesting on many counts—characterized by achievements as well as new challenges. He tested out of algebra and so was able to go immediately into calculus. In his second year, he took botany as an elective. "The professor tried to persuade us that there was no conflict between Christianity and Darwin's theory of evolution," he remembers. "I was not convinced."

He enjoyed the freshman chemistry lab, even though the lab instructor told them the class was too large and that after the first six-week test a third of the class would be out. The professor who taught the lecture sessions had a prejudice against freshmen: he didn't believe in giving them As, so Stanley had to be satisfied with a B, like it or not. He also took a piano class as an elective. When he went for his piano lesson, the teacher was surprised to learn that he was a chemistry major. "Didn't you notice the chemical stains on my fingers?" Stanley asked. Not only would this young man's stained fingers run over the piano keyboard, but in the words of the hymn writer Frances R. Havergal in 1874, the Lord would take those consecrated hands and let them move at the impulse of His love, using them in a multitude of ways for the furtherance of His kingdom.

When the Long Beach earthquake of 1933 took place at 5:55 PM on Friday, March 10, Stanley was working in the college library. "It sounded like a freight train coming," he recalls. "Then the lights, hanging on long cords, began to swing up to the ceiling." Though many schools in the area suffered serious damaged, the college did not. The quake measured 6.4 on the Richter scale and caused widespread damage to buildings throughout the area, estimated at forty million dollars, and 115 lives were lost.[1] Many of the people died when they ran outside and were hit by falling debris from tall buildings. Loss of life would have been much greater had the quake struck only a few hours earlier, when children were in school. As a result of this quake, new and improved building codes were implemented in hope of preventing such destruction and loss of life in the future.

When the time came in 1935 for Stanley to graduate from Los Angeles City College with his associate of arts degree, his entire family turned out for the event. They were all so proud of him. After graduation he worked at a restaurant for a while to save money for a suitcase and other items he would need to take with him to school. Then one day

Stanley M. Horton sitting in his dorm room at the University of California at Berkeley in 1937

someone passed his mother an unmarked envelope with fifty dollars in it for Stanley. That gave him enough to travel to Berkeley and pay his entrance fees at the University of California at Berkeley.[2]

Stanley had met a Pentecostal Christian who was a professor at Berkeley. This man had once told Stanley that he could stay with him if he came there to study. However, by the time Stanley arrived to register, the professor had gone on sabbatical, and Stanley had to stay elsewhere. He found a room in a YMCA where he stayed for a week, living on thirty-five cents worth of apples—which gave him hives! After that, he was able to make arrangements for an attic room in the home of the eighty-year-old Quaker mother-in-law of one of his mother's cousins, just two blocks from campus. He took care of her lawn and garden for his room. He arranged for his meals by working for a year serving tables at a Jewish fraternity house about a block off campus. Since the house was close by the school, he would return there to serve each meal. During his time there, he got to taste some Jewish food that was new to him, but he didn't get much opportunity to interact with the residents since he wasn't a member of the fraternity. He could only come in from the kitchen and serve the meals. He would listen in on their conversations, though, and it struck him that most of the young men there were quite liberal in their Jewish observance; he figured most were Reform Jews. Stanley didn't learn too much about Jews or Judaism there as the young men didn't want to discuss religion, but he did speak with one of the Jewish boys in one of his classes at Berkeley—a young man named Goldberg, who had changed his name to Gould to hide his Jewishness.

During Stanley's university years (1935–37), he could watch from the Berkeley campus as the Golden Gate Bridge was being built. "It was something to see the great cables spun in place," he remembers. "The day before the bridge was opened to traffic they had a pedestrian day [Thursday, May 27, 1937]. I still have the twenty-five-cent souvenir ticket needed to walk the mile each way. It was hot, sunny, and windy, and being prone to burn rather than tan, what a sunburn I got!"

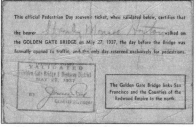

Front and back of the ticket given to Horton to cross
the Golden Gate Bridge on opening day, 1937

Stanley took swimming for the required gym course for his senior year and continued to swim for an hour each day at one of the college pools. He felt that swimming would exercise all of his body, and this was important to him because he believed the Lord wanted His children to be healthy.

He didn't have much time for any other activities, except an occasional trip on the ferry to Glad Tidings Tabernacle in San Francisco to hear the pastor preach or to go to the First

Pentecostal Church (AG) of Oakland for Sunday services, Tuesday evening prayer meetings, and Thursday evening testimony times. The pastor there, Rev. J. Narver Gortner,[3] was a solid biblical preacher. His preaching was always expository; he would begin his sermons reading the Scripture and saying, "I see seven points in this passage." Gortner played a significant role in mentoring the young Horton, instilling in him a love for the Bible.

Years later when reflecting on those who had mentored him and impacted his life, Stanley would recall, "How many others there are who have laid a good hand on my shoulder I could not begin to tell. There was J. Narver Gortner, who steadied a young man away from home in a great and godless University, and who later encouraged him as he sought a license to preach."[4] Gortner's contribution was practical as well. When days got colder Pastor Gortner took pity on Stanley—who wore no more than a heavy sweater in the Los Angeles winters—went to Goodwill, and bought for his young friend a gray overcoat that went half way to his ankles!

The people at the church were an encouragement to Stanley, too, in terms of praying for him as he sought the baptism in the Holy Spirit. The Sunday School superintendent at that church, a teacher at Oakland Junior High, also took an interest in Stanley, often taking time to talk with him about a wide variety of topics—his experiences with God, blessings in his life, teaching, and various practical things as well, just to help him along his way.

AG Executives, 1946. l to r: Fred Vogler, G. F. Lewis, J. Roswell Flower, W. I. Evans, Ralph Riggs, F. D. Davis, E. S. Williams, J. Narver Gortner, Wesley R. Steelberg

During Stanley's last year at Berkeley, Pastor

Gortner left his pastorate in Oakland to become president of Glad Tidings Bible Institute in San Francisco (now Bethany University in Santa Cruz). Rev. C. Stanley Cooke then became the pastor, and Stanley became good friends with his son, Leon. The two young men would go to street meetings and look for other ways to serve the Lord.

After his first year at the University of California, Stanley applied for the college summer program of President Roosevelt's National Youth Administration, open to any youth needing work. They sent him to a Civilian Conservation Corps (CCC) camp at Big Sur in central California, south of Monterey, where he followed a surveyor working on a road through the park. There he got his first case of poison oak, covering most of his body. In spite of this trial and other challenges that summer, Stanley did his best to be a good witness to the other young men in the camp, all of whom were poor farm boys from the backwoods of Arkansas.

Throughout that summer, Stanley was able to go on Sundays to the Assembly of God at Pacific Grove. One Sunday, he missed his ride back to the camp. As he walked on the road by the ocean, the famous Northern California fog rolled in, and the only way he could tell he was on the road was to feel the pavement under his feet! He came to a place where gravel had fallen across the road and then crept along until he found the pavement again. Finally, a man in a Ford pickup came by and took him the rest of the way.

During Stanley's last year at Berkeley he worked in one of the university laboratories doing chemical titrations for a graduate student's doctoral research project (dropping chemicals into a solution until the point that a reaction takes place). He decided to take some biochemical courses and found himself disheartened by some of the atheistic, hostile-to-faith professors who promoted the theory of evolution with no room for anything but chance. He was left uneasy by questions that would come up in class—offered by either the professor or students—or concerns that would come to his mind as a result of the material. One night while kneeling by his bed in that attic room, Stanley cried out to God. "I know I'm saved, but I just don't know the answers to some of the questions they are raising!" Stanley was young and didn't know about the many good books and other resources that could have helped him. Ironically, years later he would come to be seen as the "answer man" in the Assemblies of God, with his weekly Question and Answer column in the *Pentecostal Evangel*, by his role on the Commission for Doctrinal Purity, and in a multitude of other venues.

In this time of questioning and doubt, the Lord heard his cry and helped him, reminding him of all the testimonies of his family. Stanley recalled how as a five-year-old he used to have terrible earaches in the night; his father, to sooth him, would carry him outside at night to point out the stars, then bring him back in, and Stanley would fall asleep. One particular time, Stanley had an awful pain, like a knife sensation going ear to ear. His dad rebuked the devil, and the pain stopped. He had only one earache since that time, while studying for final exams at Berkeley. But he prayed, and the Lord healed him.

In the face of his doubts, Stanley also recalled how when he was five, he saw his grandfather healed and how at fourteen, his six-year-old cousin Charles was healed of polio. The doctors hadn't recognized the polio at first and just gave him some pills. But when the paralysis set in, they said, "Sorry, we cannot help you." But Charles' parents carried him into Angelus Temple, and Aimee Semple McPherson prayed for him. He walked out of there, went on to play football in high school, joined the Navy, and made it through World War II.

The way God had healed his father at Angelus Temple when the lump on his neck just melted away also came to Stanley's mind during this faith struggle at Berkeley, as well as how God had recently worked in his brother Donald's life. Stanley had just been home for Christmas vacation and saw how Donald had changed. Before Stanley had left for Berkeley, Donald—in spite of being healed of what may have been polio when he was four—had developed a bitter spirit toward their dad and the church. Donald still went to Sunday School and church—because that's what the family did. But his bitterness was coming through in ways then and began to grow. For example, to answer the roll in the Sunday School class each person was expected to quote a Scripture verse they had memorized that week; Donald would pick something out of the Psalms that pronounced judgment. He was not trying to be funny; he was just bitter. But while Stanley was at Berkeley, there was a real revival at the church. Donald repented, was baptized in the Holy Spirit, and his whole attitude changed. He served the Lord faithfully all his life after that.

As Stanley recalled these stories, his heart was encouraged and his faith convictions were strengthened. Often while at Berkeley, these stories from his past sustained him and saw him through. Shortly after this crisis of faith, Stanley received the baptism in the Holy Spirit on New Year's Day of 1936. As he recalls:

Jesus was so real to me. I could feel His touch like never before. I was so overwhelmed with the presence of Jesus that I was hardly conscious of speaking in tongues; I did speak in tongues, but not for very long. That night I remembered an evangelist saying something derogatory about young people who spoke only a few words in tongues, while he spoke for hours. The next night I went to the altar; no one gathered around to pray for me, but I simply said, "Lord, if there is a freedom in this, I want it." Suddenly it was like a dam broke, and my praises and prayers to God in a heavenly language poured out of my mouth. For a couple of weeks I could hardly pray in English.

Then Sister Lehmann, mother of missionary Harold Lehmann, came to me and said, "Stanley, God has done something wonderful for you. Do not let a day go by without coming before the Lord and letting Him recreate it in you." I still thank God for that advice in a day when some received the baptism, and once they had received it, never spoke in tongues again.[5]

In addition to following this godly sister's advice, Stanley also learned from 1 Corinthians that speaking in tongues edifies believers spiritually. Not only did the baptism edify Stanley; this experience also brought a desire in him to quit the university and go to Bible school. In addition to his own questions, there were those who encouraged him to "quit the godless University of California."[6] He prayed and struggled and prayed some more. Finally he told the Lord that if He wanted him to stay at Berkeley and get a degree in science, he would stay. As he later recounted, "God gave me no peace until I was willing to stick it out there in Berkeley."[7] As soon as he gave in to the Lord's desire for him to stay at Berkeley, Stanley felt a "warm feeling" go all through him. Only later when Central Bible Institute (CBI) in Springfield, Missouri, needed a science teacher did Stanley understand why God wanted him to have an undergraduate degree in science. Finally in his last year at Berkeley, he took a graduate course in advanced biochemistry that was open to seniors. The professor there believed in intelligent design, rather than in Darwinian evolution, and that encouraged him.

Being filled with the Spirit continued to make a profound impact on Stanley's life. One time while at a downtown Assembly of God in Oakland in 1937, he had a "glorious experience" dancing in the Spirit. After it happened, however, he felt such a sense of shame, believing that he had done this "in the flesh" and had brought dishonor to the Lord. Sometime later, though, an elderly woman came to him and told him how blessed she had been observing him dancing in the Spirit. Then he knew in his heart that this experience had truly been of the Spirit, not of his own flesh, and he was able to own the experience as a godly visitation.

Peas, Preachers, and Providence

Stanley graduated with a bachelor of science degree in December of 1937 from the University of California at Berkeley. At that time, jobs were scarce. These were still the years of the Great Depression, and Stanley nearly wore out his shoes looking for work. Finally, he went to see the director of the land research department for the California Packing Corporation in Rio Vista that put out Del Monte foods. Stanley heard the director tell the young man ahead of him that he had nothing open in his department, but if he really wanted a job he could work on one of their five-thousand-acre ranches in Rio Vista, where the Sacramento and San Joaquin rivers came together. The man ahead of him said no and left. But since Stanley's shoes were wearing thin, he accepted and went to the ranch. When he arrived, the man in charge of field research said he'd come "just at the right time" and that he could use him in their research of the best fertilizer combination for asparagus. Stanley enjoyed working out in the sunshine. He was fascinated by the mechanical pea harvester in an adjoining field that went through and separated the peas from the vines according to size, processing them into the Del Monte cans before noon.

Spiritually, life in Rio Vista was difficult for the young Berkeley grad. There was only a Baptist church in town, with a rather liberal pastor and a less-than-inspiring youth group. Stanley recalls that at one young people's meeting he attended, they spent their whole time arguing about whom they should invite to come to a special picnic and whom they should not. Hungry for God and good fellowship, Stanley was relieved when he was able to buy a 1929 Hudson so he could drive the forty miles to Sacramento's Bethel Temple. W. T. Gaston, a former general superintendent of the Assemblies of God,[8] pastored the eight-hundred-member congregation. Stanley flourished in this church's Christ's Ambassadors (C.A.s) young people's group. Every Sunday many of the people gathered in a large prayer room behind the pulpit, and they would often pray until the wee hours of the morning. On one occasion, pastor Gaston gave the young Horton just the right word as he was answering God's call to prepare for a full-time ministry. He told Stanley to obey the Lord and trust Him to guide him and provide the way.

After working eight months at the packing company in Rio Vista in 1938, Stanley took a civil service exam for work in the California Department of Agriculture chemistry laboratory in Sacramento. He was interviewed and hired. He boarded in Sacramento with a deacon and his wife, the Haysteads, both from England.[9] Soon Stanley found himself feeling a bit jealous of the Haystead's son Clarence. Besides having a terrific singing voice, he was big, handsome, and popular with the girls. Everything seemed to come easy for Clarence. In his jealousy, Stanley began to see all kinds of things wrong with Clarence. But then, as he recalls, "The Lord rebuked me, and I had to repent."

Over his initial spiritual hurdle at the Haysteads, Stanley began to go to street meetings with the youth from Sacramento's Bethel Temple on Saturday evenings and Sunday afternoons. Many young men had left the Dust Bowl[10] to work on ranches in California. They would come into town on Saturdays, and so the street meetings always drew a crowd. Still timid when it came to public speaking, every time Stanley would get up his courage to speak, someone would step out and give such a great testimony that he would think he couldn't say anything worth people's attention after that. So he quit going to the street meetings and tried to convince himself he just wasn't called to that type of ministry. Soon the Lord spoke to his heart, though, and told him to go to a street meeting and look at the people's faces. When he did, he saw the marks of sin in some of them. The Lord spoke to his heart again, and said, "Haven't I done anything for you?" Stanley forgot his pride and fears and had no trouble testifying after that.

Even at this young age, Stanley was able to offer clarity and biblical wisdom to the youth group. During one convention, the youth leaders were working on modifying a "do not" kind of statement that members would need to sign relative to going to theaters and so forth. Some of the young people wanted to add that members shouldn't go to roller skating rinks. Stanley got up and said, "I think we need to put a more positive emphasis on what we believe and what God wants us to do rather than putting all the emphasis on the negative." He told them straightforwardly that things like theaters and roller skating weren't his problem, that there were other things that were larger temptations for him, like reading fiction! As he recalled years later, "I could spend all my time reading fiction rather than studying!" He asked the group, "Shall we add 'Not reading fiction' to our list? No, we need to let the Holy Spirit guide us about what we should and shouldn't do instead of making a list." And so the group voted not to keep adding these types of things to their list.

Stanley spent three years in Sacramento busily working for the Lord. In addition to serving as vice president of the youth group, he taught a junior high Sunday School class, visited rest homes, passed out tracts on the street, and even sang in the choir. (As Stanley recalls, "The choir director said he didn't mind if a person was a little flat now and then!") He thought he was doing what the Lord wanted him to do. During this time, he began thinking of going to graduate school to get a higher degree in some scientific area. However, God had other plans.

One Sunday, Stanley's pastor, Rev. Gaston, announced a special prayer meeting to take place that afternoon. Stanley attended and by about four o'clock, realized that everyone else was gone. Praying there alone in the church, he felt an unusual presence of the Lord and heard an audible voice speak to him: "I want you to go back to school and prepare to teach in Bible school." As he would recount years later, "That was the furthest thing from my mind, and no one else would have thought of it either!" In fact, when he did decide to go, some of the people in the church told him he was foolish to leave his career in science. Regardless,

Stanley would not be swayed by their doubts. He was sure he had heard the very words of God that day. "Though I have had many great moments throughout my life, far beyond anything I have deserved, I believe that this was the most important day of my life, when in 1940 the Lord spoke to me to go back to school and prepare to teach in Bible school." Many among the thousands of those who have been his students over the decades or read his prolific writings would agree.

Uncle Sam

While living and working in Sacramento, Stanley received notification to register for the draft. On October 16, 1940, he registered with the Selective Service System as a conscientious objector.[11] He was classified as 1-B-O, meaning he would not have to fulfill his military service unless the country actually went to war, and that if he did have to serve, he could fulfill his obligation in civilian service. The "B" part of the classification indicated his poor eyesight. By the time the United States entered World War II in 1941, Stanley had a 4-D classification, granted to ministers of religion or divinity students, and was not required to serve in the military.

Stanley's difficult decision to become a conscientious objector was influenced by the early Assemblies of God position on pacifism, the literature of the time,[12] and the position of his pastor, W. T. Gaston.[13] This decision placed Stanley in a small minority in the AG (less than twenty young men[14]), as most Assemblies of God pacifists at the time "chose the route of non-combatant service."[15] Martin Mittelstadt and Matthew Paugh note, however:

> In the years following WWII, Horton began to notice a slight shift in his pacifist position. As a young college professor, he noted adjustments based upon encounters with students returning from active duty. He recalled numerous testimonies of conversion while overseas and one student

who received the baptism in the Holy Spirit while in a submarine. Horton tells of the migration of former soldiers to American Bible colleges: "In my first teaching job at the Metropolitan Bible Institute in New Jersey, I think half of the students there were on the GI Bill. . . . Some of them were saved while they were in the army or one of the services, and there wasn't too much I could say about that, because I had to accept that the Lord had called them. They showed that they really loved the Lord, and they have gone out to do great things. A number of those students I had [in classes] went out, and some of them became district superintendents, evangelists, pastors."[16]

Stanley's brother Donald did go in the Army and was with the Marines in the invasion of Saipan as the chief warrant officer in charge of radar. Throughout the war, Stanley kept in touch with his brother. Donald had several narrow escapes as well as contracting dengue fever but through everything kept a good witness for the Lord.

Gordon Divinity

In the providence of God, Harold Needham, principal of the Southern California Bible Institute (SCBI)[17] came through Sacramento. Horton asked him about going to SCBI. He was told, "You already have an undergraduate degree. We are going to need teachers with graduate degrees for the sake of our accreditation. So I think you should find a seminary to go to." Stanley wrote to seminaries all over the country and finally decided that Dallas Theological Seminary sounded good. He filled out the application and was about to sign it when he felt a strong check in his spirit. He prayed and again felt that check, so he put the unsigned application back in his desk drawer. Much later, he found out that at the time Dallas Theological Seminary would have let him come but would not have given him a degree without his signing their statement of faith—which he couldn't have done because its view of dispensationalism[18] ruled out Pentecostalism. His experience in the Holy Spirit was an integral part of who he was, and he would never deny that reality.

Content that God had something else in mind, Stanley worked another year in the chemistry lab, until 1941, returning there again in the summer of 1942 after his first year at Gordon. During that time, a Baptist evangelist named Harry Anderson held a campaign in Sacramento. He came to Stanley's young people's meeting and invited them to visit his campaign. He told them that the very presence of Pentecostal young people in his meetings seemed to make a difference! The young Horton talked to him about his calling to go to seminary. Anderson told Stanley about Gordon Divinity School (now Gordon-Conwell Theological Seminary) in Boston's Back Bay district. Sensitive to the Spirit's leading, he felt this was of the Lord, so he wrote and was accepted. That fall of 1941 he took the bus to Boston.

Gordon Divinity School began as the Boston Missionary Training School, founded by Rev. A. J. Gordon in 1889; the school was named Gordon Divinity upon its founder's death. Five years earlier in Philadelphia, Dr. Russell Conwell had begun the Conwell School of Theology as a night school in the basement of the Baptist Temple. In 1969, the two schools merged and became known as Gordon-Conwell Theological Seminary.[19] Appropriately, the closing words of Dr. Conwell's book, *Acres of Diamonds* (quoting the English poet, Phillip James Bailey), can be applied to the life of Stanley Horton, the young man who came to Gordon in 1941 and who would become one of the school's most prominent graduates: "He most lives who thinks most, who feels the noblest, and who acts the best."[20]

Stanley blossomed at Gordon. He enjoyed New Testament subjects and Greek under Dr. Merrill Tenney (who later went to Wheaton College), Old Testament subjects and Hebrew under Dr. Burton Goddard, and theology under Dr. Nathan R. Wood.

His book, *The Secret of the Universe* (reprinted under a different title), had a view of the Trinity and how God related to the universe that resonated with Stanley. Dr. Ernest Palmer was another Old Testament theology teacher who instilled in Stanley a love for the Scriptures. These professors were earnest Christians who encouraged Stanley and showed a personal interest in him, encouraging him to continue his studies.

During Christmas break of Stanley's first year at Gordon, he went to Philadelphia where his Uncle Wesley Steelberg was then pastoring Highway Mission Tabernacle. As he walked into the church, he knew something was happening. He felt the power of God and fell on his knees. In regular services, revival was taking place—people were getting saved and many were being baptized in the Holy Spirit. On Christmas Day, Uncle Wesley gave Stanley a book of Spurgeon's sermons, and one of his young cousins said, "Now, Stanley, you can *really* preach!"

Evelyn

Shortly after Stanley arrived in Boston in the fall of 1941 to study at Gordon, he went to a fellowship meeting in a suburb north of Boston where a California evangelist was speaking. He met the pastor that first Sunday and in their conversation mentioned that he was a student at Gordon. The church was only a five-cent bus ride from the school, so Stanley decided to go there again the next week. That second Sunday, the pastor—who had seen Stanley come in the building—spent his entire

Stanley and Evelyn as newlyweds in Boston, 1945

sermon speaking against higher education! A bit frustrated and discouraged on his bus ride back to Gordon, Stanley told himself he would *never* go to *that* church again. But the Lord spoke strongly to his heart saying, "That's where I want you to go." Apparently, God had other things in mind.

Sensitive to the Spirit's leading, Stanley obeyed and soon was asked to teach a Sunday School class. To get to his class, he had to walk through a classroom where a lovely young woman, Evelyn Gertrude Parsons, was teaching. Evelyn also played the piano and organ for a Christian radio program, as well as for the church, and a pump organ for street meetings in downtown Boston. Her parents invited Stanley for dinner several times.[21] At the time, she was dating a young pastor in another Boston suburb, but Stanley felt a "strong feeling from the Lord" that she was the one for him!

Somehow Evelyn's young pastor friend faded into the distance, and she began spending time with the handsome Gordon student whose company her parents seemed to enjoy. On their first date, Stanley took Evelyn to a basketball game where the Gordon team was playing. Not long after, he took her to a symphony concert. On Sunday afternoons when Evelyn would play the piano for a downtown mission church, Stanley would go there to be with her. He would take her flowers or a box of Whitman's Samplers. Clearly, as this young scholar was finding out, there were

Stanley Horton, MBI yearbook, 1947
(used by permission of VFCC)

"many" reasons God wanted him at that church! That winter a baseball diamond near Gordon flooded and froze over, and became a perfect place for Stanley and Evelyn to go ice-skating. The two enjoyed one another's company immensely, and soon their relationship blossomed.

The summer of 1942, after his first year at Gordon, Stanley hitchhiked back to California (something still safe to do in those days) and worked in the chemistry laboratory again. At the Northern California–Nevada district camp meeting, the credentials committee approved Stanley for a license to preach, and in the fall the young Reverend Horton returned to Gordon and to Evelyn.

For her birthday on November 9, 1943, Stanley gave his sweetheart a locket with a small picture of him in it. Then he asked her to close her eyes and slipped a diamond engagement ring on her finger. He had saved enough money from his work that summer in Maine. At age ninety-two, having spent over sixty years of his life with Evelyn, Stanley would say of the engagement ring: "This was the best purchase I ever made!"

One of Stanley's fellow students worked at a jewelry store in Boston. He had bought a diamond for his girlfriend at the wholesale company where the jewelry store bought their diamonds.

Horton visiting the Steelbergs in Philadelphia on his way home to Los Angeles for the summer after his first year at Gordon, 1943. Stanley would often hitchhike across the country during his school years to get back and forth between school on the East Coast and his family's home in California.

Through that connection, Stanley purchased Evelyn's diamond and a matching wedding ring. The diamond was between a third- and a half-carat with smaller side diamonds. The wedding ring had an insert of six small diamonds. As Stanley recalls: "Evelyn was ecstatic to show off her ring at work the next day."

Seminary Pastor

Even as a busy seminary student, Stanley was presented with ample opportunity for pastoral and preaching opportunities. During the spring semester of his second year at Gordon, he filled in for several weeks at Faith Assembly of God in Hyannis on Cape Cod. Then later that summer he asked Roy Smuland, district superintendent of what was then the New England District Council, if there was a town in New England where he might get a job and also help a local pastor. Smuland didn't seem to like that idea, but he told Stanley that the district had bought a former Methodist church building in Monson, Maine. The pastor there had separated from his wife, she left the town, and the church was closed. "See if you can do anything with it," Smuland offered. Stanley borrowed money for the bus fare and stopped at Dover-Foxcroft, Maine, where Rev. Joseph R. Flower—later New York district superintendent and then general secretary of the Assemblies of God—was pastor. During the course of Stanley's short visit, Flower encouraged him to go ahead.

In Monson, Stanley found a job in a slate mill. The machine workers there made the slate pieces into backings for electrical installations. Not only was this job carrying slate a source of much needed income, but it was also an opportunity to get to know the men—who taught the young Horton how to bear the weight of his load with his legs instead of with his back.

The two other churches in Monson—one Baptist, the other Presbyterian—had also been closed, so the newly minted Rev. Horton was free to visit in all the homes. Most of the people in the town were Swedish. When he would visit them, they would always offer him coffee. He refused at first because he had never learned to like coffee. But some of them made such a fuss that he gave in and has been a coffee drinker ever since!

Soon Pastor Horton had a congregation of thirty or thirty-five. He also held his first funeral service. His sister Ruth remembers that during this time Stanley wrote home to their mom saying he was going to do his first funeral and that he was concerned about it. His mother encouraged him, as always, and the funeral went "just fine."

In the Monson Assembly was a backslidden Pentecostal who used to come regularly to the services. One time, Stanley had a sermon he felt would be "just right" for this man. He prepared and prayed, prayed and prepared. When Sunday came, the man was away, visiting relatives—the only time he was not in church all summer! Stanley didn't have anything else prepared, so he had to preach that sermon. After the service, a woman came to him and said, "That sermon was just what I needed!" After that, he learned to let the Holy Spirit guide him for what he should preach.

The end of the summer arrived, and since Stanley was committed to go back to Boston for his last year at Gordon (1943–44), Brother Smuland sent a recent graduate of CBI to take his place.

During the fall semester of 1943, Stanley would take the train from Boston to Providence every weekend where a deacon of the First Baptist Church of North Kingston, Rhode Island, would meet him and bring him to the church. Stanley served as interim pastor there during that semester, since it was the time of World War II, and the pastor who was there had gone into the Army as a chaplain. The church had sent notice to Gordon Divinity School requesting that someone fill in on Sunday mornings—and Stanley served as pastor since he was "the only one available."

Encouragement from the Lord

Even with these pastoring opportunities, however, God chose Stanley Horton's teaching career for him. God had called him to teach in 1940 and was continuing to see him through difficult and discouraging times in his years of preparation. At Gordon, a Baptist minister lived for a time across from Stanley in the dorm. This man had pastored for ten years and had come back to finish his degree. The two would often talk and pray together. One day the man said, "Stanley, you need to go back to your chemistry. You will never be enough of a politician to get anywhere in the ministry." That bothered Stanley a little, but he knew he was in God's will and that God had called him to teach, so he shrugged off the comment.

Other discouraging times would come, and Stanley would have to learn how to deal with those challenges as they arose. While at Gordon, he needed to work part-time in order to pay his expenses; for a while, the only job he could get was the evening shift at a gas station about two miles away. Having given up his car in order to be able to come to Gordon, Stanley was forced to walk back and forth to work. One night, he was at the station all alone. It was cold and dark, and

Youth Program

◆ TED KLINE, Converted Sonqwriter and Jewish Christian
◆ STAN HORTON & his Accordion
◆ ARCH MARTIN, Athlete and Track Friend of Gil Dodds

Delinquency Film, Special Dodds Film Accordion Music, Youth Messages

Christian Youth Association

2115 E. 6th St.   Los Angeles, 33 Calif.

Ministry promotional piece, 1944: Stanley Horton (with accordion), Ted Kline, and Arch Martin, Gordon students, drove back to CA for the summer in 1944 with Stanley and ministered there with him. During that summer, Stanley worked for his uncle in a photo lab and held other odd jobs while living with his parents.

he was beginning to feel deeply discouraged—even ready to give it all up. On the way walking back to campus that night, Stanley met Gil Dodds. Gil was in one of Stanley's classes at Gordon and had just recently set the world record for the indoor mile (4:06.4).[22] The two men talked, and Gil began encouraging Stanley. Being an athlete, Gil pointed out to Stanley that walking back and forth was good for his health! He encouraged him in other ways, and their time together was a real turning point for Stanley at Gordon.

Gordon Commencement

Because of the excellence of Stanley's grades, Gordon's president, Dr. Nathan Wood, called him in to ask him to serve as one of the 1944 commencement speakers. Stanley was so honored. That June, when he graduated from the divinity school with his M.Div.,[23] the ceremony included Gordon College and was held at the Park Street Church with 1600 in attendance. The first young man who spoke represented the college and spoke on the loss of the absolute. "He sounded as if he had swallowed a philosophy book," recalls Stanley, for he was over the heads of many.

When Stanley stood to represent the seminary, he could see people settling back in their seats as if to say, "One more, and this will be over!" To this day, Stanley is surprised that the faculty approved his message. His text was Mark 12:24 (KJV), where Jesus said to the Sadducees, "Ye know not the scriptures, neither the power of God," and his theme was that one cannot truly know the Scriptures unless one knows the power of God! As he got up to speak, Stanley felt a strong anointing of the Holy Spirit. He could see people suddenly sit up straight in their seats. They hadn't heard anything like this before. Emphasizing a theme that would later be a hallmark of his many writings and teachings, the young Stanley Horton proclaimed that "the difference between liberals and conservatives is at the point of the supernatural. . . .There is no fence to sit on. Either you believe in the supernatural, the miracles, the virgin birth, the resurrection, or you do not."[24] He recounted some of the miracles of healing that had taken place in his own family and how those miracles had made the Bible more real to him.

Afterward, Stanley's Baptist friend who had told him to go back to his chemistry came to him with tears in his eyes and told him, "Forget what I said before."

He already had.

A Pentecostal at Harvard

Stanley's Hebrew professor at Gordon, Dr. Burton Goddard, was a very kind man who encouraged him to go to Harvard to do the S.T.M. degree (Scientiae Theologicae Magistri, master of the knowledge of theology) and also helped him get a scholarship that covered tuition and his room, which happened to be in the same building where he went to class. A couple who lived in an apartment in the basement would come in after Stanley went to class to make his bed and clean his room. "I never had it so good!" he recalled. But when he told Brother Smuland, the New England district superintendent of the Assemblies of God, that he felt the Lord had made this possible for him, Smuland asked, "Was that the Lord or the devil?" Shocked, Stanley couldn't believe his ears. But he didn't let that discourage him. Often over the years, he had come up against those who were against higher education. But just as with the Baptist preacher who told him he should go back to chemistry, the fact that God had spoken to him in a way that was so real helped him to stay the course. Reflecting on this part of his life years later, Dr. Horton would recount:

> I just couldn't let anything else get in the way. I just had to follow the Lord. I felt as though higher education was a calling, and that if I did not fulfill that calling, I would have been disobedient to the Lord. Even when I had two master's [degrees], I felt like I should do a doctorate. I didn't know

Horton on steps of his
Harvard dorm in 1944

how it would all play out in the future. I just knew He wanted me to do it. He just led me a step at a time.

Pressing onward, Stanley began at Harvard in the fall of 1944. He enjoyed good classes in Greek, Hebrew, and Aramaic, as well as homiletics. At that time, all Harvard Divinity students had to take a yearlong course in some other religion, so he chose Islam. The professor was much more conservative than others Stanley had taken there. This man had written many books and articles and communicated to his students a quality understanding of Islam, its theology, as well as its cults. One unusual thing he told his students was that Mohammed was loyal to his first wife Kadija, but when she died, he married a number of women. When his wives would be in an argument and he could not settle it, he would go into a trance and come out with another chapter of the Koran, and that would settle it!

Horton considered the other professors he had at Harvard as all being "old-line liberals."[25] Dr. Robert Pfeiffer was Stanley's adviser and taught him Old Testament and Hebrew. Pfeiffer told his students, "You can believe that Sunday School stuff. I don't." Once Stanley and a fellow student, Samuel Shultz (later a professor of Old Testament at Wheaton College), were in a class of twenty-five, reading the Book of Isaiah. All the other students in the class were rabbis working on their doctorates in Semitics. Stanley and

Samuel had to work to keep up with their Jewish colleagues. When it came time for the class to study the fifty-third chapter of Isaiah, the rabbis wanted to skip it, but Sam and Stanley insisted. When they finished, one of the Jewish men said, "Our rabbis teach that the Suffering Servant here is the Jewish people, and since we do not have a temple or sacrifices, we are made acceptable to God by our own sufferings." Then Dr. Pfeiffer said (perhaps with tongue in cheek), "Look at this passage. It is vicarious suffering, vicarious suffering all through it. Can you Jews say you have never sinned and never brought any of your sufferings on yourselves?" They said, "Let's go to the next chapter."

On another occasion, the class was reading Amos in Hebrew. Dr. Pfeiffer said of one verse, "I don't believe Amos wrote this verse." A student asked him why, and he said, "It says the same thing a few verses before, and in my opinion Amos was too good a preacher to repeat himself." But Stanley remembers thinking to himself at the time, repetition is one of the chief ways of emphasis in the Old Testament!

Toward the end of his time at Harvard, Stanley had to pass a final written exam and an oral exam before the whole faculty, each asking questions that related to their discipline. For example, the New Testament professor asked him questions about how the Old Testament was used in the New Testament. The only question he didn't know the answer to was asked by Dr. LaPiana, the church history professor: "Augustine used both the Hebrew and the Greek Septuagint and knew they had some differences. How did he reconcile the differences?" When Stanley said he didn't know, LaPiana laughed and said, "He didn't reconcile them. He thought they were both inspired."

At his May 1945 commencement ceremony, Stanley wore the Harvard doctoral cap and gown, since the S.T.M. degree was considered a step higher than the M.Div.

After Stanley proposed to Evelyn in November of 1943, the young couple had decided to wait to get married until he finished his degree at Harvard. During that year (1944–45), the Hill Memorial Baptist Church across the river from Harvard had called the divinity school for a student to fill in on Sunday morning services while their pulpit committee took three months to search for a new pastor. The only one available at the time, Stanley was their man. Again, God was leading and providing.

One of Evelyn's relatives was a member of that church, and they welcomed her young beau to be their interim pastor. He gave them a series of sermons on basic Bible doctrines. One Sunday after a message on what the Bible teaches about hell, a woman said to him, "You are different. Our last pastor believed in purgatory, and the one before him believed God was too good to send anyone to hell." Another time, an elderly woman said to Stanley, "I wish you could stay and be our pastor. It has been so long since we have had anyone who could really preach!" When he told the congregation he was getting married and was going to go teach at Metropolitan Bible Institute (MBI), they invited the young couple to have their wedding at that church and even offered to provide the reception.

In later years when he was a young instructor at Central Bible Institute, Stanley wrote out his testimony for the school's publication, then called *The Scroll*, including a note about his Evelyn: "It was in Boston . . . that God gave me a sweetheart who became my wife, and whose unfeigned faith is one of the great joys of my life."[26]

Metropolitan Bible Institute

In 1945, Rev. Thomas Brubaker, superintendent of what was then the New York-New Jersey district of the Assemblies of God, came to Horton and asked him to become a full-time teacher at the Metropolitan Bible Institute in North Bergen, New Jersey.[27]

In 1941, with district assistance, Rev. Nicholas Nikoloff,[28] then pastoring a church in North Bergen, had reorganized Beulah

Nicholas Nikoloff

Born in Bulgaria in 1900, Nicholas Nikoloff came to the U.S. in 1920 after his aunt, who was one of several missionaries to Russia, introduced him to the Pentecostal experience. After she heard that he had given his life to Christ, her first words to him were, "Have ye received the Holy Ghost since ye believed?" Nikoloff was challenged by this question and began to search the Scriptures. In November of 1921 he was filled with the Holy Spirit at Glad Tidings Tabernacle in New York City.

One of the few ministers with graduate degrees in his day, Nikoloff went beyond his theological training at Bethel Bible Institute in Newark to receive a Master in Religious Education from Biblical Seminary in New York. He received his Ph.D. from New York University in 1955, writing his thesis on the Bogomils, a religious and social reform movement in Bulgaria. His great grandfather was a Greek Orthodox priest who "advocated freedom for Bulgaria from Greek and Turkish religious and political bondage. He was betrayed to Turkish authorities and committed suicide on the way to his execution. . . . Nikoloff's father was a government doctor who died while on duty as a result of exposure to freezing weather" (Norma Jean Black, "Instructor Nikoloff Reviews Past," *The Scroll*, September 27, 1952, 2).

Heights Training School,[29] established in 1912 in North Bergen, and served as its first president. A number of early Assemblies of God missionaries had graduated from Beulah Heights, but the school had fallen on hard times. MBI used the Beulah Heights facilities in North Bergen from 1945 to 1947, moved to Patterson, New Jersey, for its third year (1947–48), then finally to Suffern, New York, for the 1948–49 year.

In 1950, MBI merged with the two-year-old New England Bible Institute (NEBI) at Framingham, Massachusetts. Nikoloff served at NEBI for a year as president before coming to Springfield to be on the CBI faculty, where he and Horton taught together for several years. In 1952, Northwood Bible School, which was founded in 1930 in Northwood, New Hampshire, also merged with NEBI. But soon the most significant merger in the history of these schools would take place when in 1957 NEBI merged with Eastern Bible Institute (EBI) in Green Lane, Pennsylvania. EBI was a three-year Bible school that had emerged out of a summer Bible school started by Rev. J. Roswell Flower and Alice Reynolds Flower in 1932 on the campgrounds of Maranatha Park in Green Lane. EBI was formed in 1938, merged with Pine Crest Bible Institute in 1962 (a school begun by the Italian district of the Assemblies of God in Salisbury Center, New York), and that same year became Northeast Bible Institute. NBI was renamed Northeast Bible College (NBC) in 1975, finally becoming Valley Forge Christian College (VFCC) in 1976–77.[30]

When Stanley Horton was asked to come to MBI in 1945, the district's offer was fifty dollars a month and room and board for him and Evelyn for the eight months of the school year. When he told his Harvard professor Dr. Pfieffer about this, Pfieffer told him he didn't have to suffer that way, that Harvard could get him a job teaching for a good salary. But Horton prayed about it, considered the counsel of his Uncle Wesley Steelberg, who had encouraged him to go to MBI, and ultimately knew that was where the Lord wanted him.

Endnotes

[1] "Historic Earthquakes: Long Beach, California," *U. S. Geological Survey*, http://earthquake.usgs.gov/regional/states/events/1933_03_11.php (accessed July 22, 2008).

[2] While he was at the university at Berkeley, his family moved again, attended a Foursquare church, and eventually joined an Assemblies of God church.

[3] J. Narver Gortner served as a pastor, writer, teacher, district superintendent, executive presbyter (for twenty-six years), and president of Glad Tidings Bible Institute (now Bethany University). See Wayne Warner, "The Pentecostal Methodist: J. Narver Gortner," *AG Heritage*, vol. 8 no. 2 (Summer 1988): 12–14, for the account of how this Methodist preacher was filled with the Spirit and healed when Smith Wigglesworth prayed for him. In 1927, Gortner accepted invitations from two feuding Oakland, California, churches to serve as their pastor on the condition

that they merge—which they did, as First Pentecostal Church. "Under Gortner's ten-year ministry, First Pentecostal Church became one of the strongest Assemblies of God congregations in the country. By 1943, on the fifteenth anniversary of the merger, more than twenty-five people in the church had entered the ministry" (13). One of those was Stanley Horton.

4   "My Testimony," *The Scroll*, May 19, 1950, 5.

5   Horton, interview by author, May 26, 2008; *Reflections of an Early American Pentecostal*, 28.

6   Horton, *Reflections*, 28.

7   "My Testimony," *The Scroll*, May 19, 1950, 5.

8   W. T. Gaston (1886–1956) was elected "general chairman" of the Assemblies of God in 1925 and served to 1929. The title was changed to general superintendent in 1927 (http://www.flickr.com/photos/ifphc/255039878/). Gaston was one of five future Assemblies of God general superintendents who attended the first General Council of the Assemblies of God in 1914 (http://ag.org/enrichmentjournal/199904/021_ag_supts.cfm). During Gaston's administration, the General Council moved from a loosely operated Fellowship to the formal adoption of a constitution. He later served as superintendent of the Northern California–Nevada district (See "Assemblies of God Superintendents," *Enrichment* journal, http://ag.org/enrichmentjournal/199904/gs_04_gaston.cfm).

9   The Haysteads also had a son named Ken who was Stanley's age; Ken had already left home by the time Stanley stayed there. He graduated from Southern California Bible School and pastored for a number of years.

10 "Dust Bowl" was the name given to the American and Canadian prairie lands from 1930 to 1936, and in some places to 1939, due to drought and improper farming techniques that killed the natural grasses, resulting in major damage to the land, culture, and economy of the Midwest after severe dust storms. See "Timeline of the Dust Bowl," PBS, http://www.pbs.org/wgbh/amex/dustbowl/timeline/ (accessed July 5, 2008).

11 A Conscientious Objector classification of 1-O meant that one was opposed to both combatant and noncombatant service (http://www.sss.gov/classif.htm). A classification of 1-A-O meant one was opposed to training and military service with arms and could fulfill one's obligation through noncombatant service. At the time of the World War II draft, however, because of the additional issue of Horton's poor eyesight, his Conscientious Objector status was 1-B-O. The 4-F status during World War II referred to those with physical deterrents to serving; Horton would have had that status due to his eyesight but was already in the 4-D category as a divinity student.

12 Martin William Mittelstadt and Matthew Paugh, "The Social Conscience of Stanley Horton," *Heritage,* 2009, 16. Mittelstadt and Paugh note that "Pacifism remained the official position of the AG until 1967" (19) and

offer Jay Beaman's *Pentecostal Pacifism: The Origin, Development, and Rejection of Pacific Belief Among the Pentecostals* (Hillsboro, KS: Center for Mennonite Brethren Studies, 1989) as a "helpful historical trajectory of Pentecostal responses to non-violence." They also note "other early and important pacifist publications," such as Arthur Sydney Booth-Clibborn's *Blood Against Blood* (New York: Charles C. Cook, n.d.); Frank Bartleman's *War and the Christian* (n.p.; n.d.); Donald Gee's articles "War, the Bible, and the Christian" (two parts), *Pentecostal Evangel*, November 8, 15, 1930, 6, 2, and "Conscientious Objection," *Pentecostal Evangel*, May 4, 1940, 4; E. S. Williams' "In Case of War," *Pentecostal Evangel*, March 19, 1938, 4; and J. Roswell Flower's "The Plight of the Conscientious Objector in the Present World Conflict," *Pentecostal Evangel*, July 3, 1943, 2–3.

[13] Gaston served as general superintendent of the Assemblies of God from 1925–29 and later served as superintendent of the Northern California-Nevada district. See his "Looking for the Blessed Hope," *Enrichment* journal, http://www.ag.org/enrichmentjournal/199904/gs_04_gaston.cfm (accessed August 9, 2008).

[14] Mittelstadt and Paugh, 15, summarizing J. Roswell Flower, "The Plight of the Conscientious Objector in the Present World Conflict," 2–3, note the "vast majority of young men who sought and gained status as non-combatants" and E. S. Williams' article "In Case of War," 4, in which Williams advocated non-combatant service.

[15] Ibid., 16.

[16] Ibid.

[17] Harold K. Needham, D. W. Kerr (who wrote the first draft of the Assemblies of God Statement of Fundamental Truths), and W. C. Pierce began SCBI in the summer of 1920. The school moved from Los Angeles to South Pasadena in 1927. It was the first four-year institution of the Assemblies of God. It moved to Costa Mesa, California, in 1950. The name was changed to Southern California College in 1959 and has since become Vanguard University. (See http://www.vanguard.edu/index.aspx?id=1422 for more on the school's history.)

[18] See chapter 8 on Horton's influence in diminishing the importance of dispensationalism in the Assemblies of God.

[19] Conwell became Temple College in 1888 and Temple University in 1907. For more on Gordon-Conwell's history, see http://www.gcts.edu/about/history.php.

[20] Russell H. Conwell, *Acres of Diamonds*, Temple University, http://www.temple.edu/about/Acres_of_Diamonds.htm (accessed July 5, 2008).

[21] Evelyn's father, Edward G. Parsons, was born in Freshwater, Newfoundland, to Methodist parents. Her mother, Katie Parsons, formerly known as Katie Babcock, was born in Bay Roberts, Newfoundland, also to Methodist parents. They met in the Boston area and married. After the wedding, they returned to Bay Roberts, where their son Ralph was born. After a while, they came back to Boston where Hannah was born, then

Edward III (Ted), Marian, Edith, Dorothy, and finally Evelyn. Evelyn's father was a painting contractor.

Katie's brother and sister-in-law, Richard and Beatrice Babcock, were in the first graduating class of CBI in Springfield, Missouri. After graduating, they began an Assemblies of God church in Cambridge, Massachusetts. Katie's parents got saved and filled with the Holy Spirit at that church, as did Evelyn and two of her sisters, Edith and Dorothy. Edith went to Zion Bible Institute in East Providence, Rhode Island, and married Aaron Kelley, who became a pastor. Dorothy married Frank Musker (ninety-seven years old in 2008) who taught gymnastics at Boston University.

22 See *Gil Dodds: The Flying Parson*, by Mel Larson (Chicago: Evangelical Beacon, 1945). See also "Preacher's Comeback," *Time*, February 3, 1947; http://www.time.com/time/magazine/article/0,9171,886330,00.html.

23 This degree was originally the bachelor of divinity degree—the standard seminary degree at that time. It was renamed the master of divinity (M.Div.) degree in October 1973.

24 Horton, *Reflections*, 33.

25 When asked about his view of the higher criticism approach to the study of Scriptures, about the relationship between "fundamentalists" and "liberals," and about how he thinks he was influenced by his study at Gordon and then at Harvard, Horton replied: "The more I study the Bible, the more I have confidence in its inspiration and reliability. I feel that the liberals are influenced more by their philosophies than they are by the Bible. And their philosophies are mostly humanistic. The liberals reject the Holy Spirit's inspiration of the Bible as well as the work of the Holy Spirit in our own lives. And I found that the arguments of the liberals are very shallow. And as far as the evangelicals are concerned [i.e., Gordon and the people who were at Biblical Seminary in New York, too], their influence on me was to emphasize that the Bible can interpret itself. But they fail to realize that the Holy Spirit can also help us to understand what the Bible is talking about. When we experience the power of the Holy Spirit, it helps the Bible to come alive to us." (Horton, interview by author, April 26, 2008). For more on Dr. Horton's views about liberals, see *Reflections of an Early American Pentecostal* (Baguio City, Philippines: APTS Press, 2001), 1–11.

26 "My Testimony," *The Scroll*, May 19, 1950, 5.

27 Brubaker later became president of MBI after Horton left and after Wesley Steelberg served as president there for a short time.

28 Norma Jean Black, "Instructor Nikoloff Reviews Past," *The Scroll*, September 27, 1952, 2. See also *The Centralite*, November 22, 1955, 1, 3.

29 The founder of Beulah Heights Assembly and Training School was Mrs. Virginia E. Moss (1875–1919). To read her remarkable testimony and the story of the founding of the school, see her autobiographical piece, *Following the Shepherd: Testimony of Mrs. Virginia E. Moss*,

North Bergen, N.J., 1923, n.p. When the Lord directed Mrs. Moss to open a school, she told the Lord that "people would not stand with me, for this was the day of receiving the Holy Spirit and going right to the field, and they would not believe in schools" (32), but the Lord confirmed His message to her through Scripture, and she obeyed—opening the school in 1912. She died within a month of the school's seventh-year graduation in 1919. See also a newspaper article commemorating the fiftieth anniversary of the church Moss founded in 1911, North Bergen Church, which became Gospel Tabernacle: "To Hold Golden Anniversary Celebration at Gospel Tabernacle in North Bergen," *Hudson Dispatch*, September 15, 1961, 8.

[30] See Reuben Hartwick's "Pentecost Comes to the Northeast: A Survey of the Early Events and Influential Leaders," *Heritage* (Spring 1990): 3–5. (Note: Hartwick gives 1942 as the Beulah Heights reorganization date, 1977 as the date for the school being renamed NBC, and 1978 for the name change to VFCC. These dates do not correspond to the "VFCC Family Tree" put out by the college in their 1998 and 2007 alumni directories or to a FPHC analysis of *Pentecostal Evangel* articles, school correspondence, and handbooks.)

CHAPTER 4

Beginning a
Teaching Ministry

The Wedding

On September 11, 1945, Evelyn's uncle and brother-in-law conducted the wedding ceremony together. "I was so thrilled as I saw Evelyn coming down the aisle," remembers the young groom. "She looked so beautiful."

Stanley had rented an apartment in Cambridge that summer, so he and Evelyn stayed there the night they were married.[1] The next morning they took a Greyhound bus through Vermont to Montreal for their honeymoon. Stanley had made a reservation for the Mount Royal Hotel, but the bus was late, and so the hotel sold the newlyweds' room to someone else. Eventually, Stanley and Evelyn found an old-fashioned rooming house where they could stay for the night. The next day they took a horse-drawn bus tour of the city and returned to the Mount Royal where there was now a room available. In the morning they boarded a

Stanley and Evelyn on their honeymoon, 1945

train to Quebec City, where they found an Irish driver of a horse-drawn cab who showed them around the city.

A friend of Stanley's from California, Kenneth Haystead, who had been an evangelist, was then pastoring a Pentecostal assembly in Ottawa, Canada's capital city. He and his wife invited the newlyweds to spend a few days with them. So the young couple took the train to Ottawa, where Ken showed them around the Parliament buildings and other sites. Back in Montreal, Stanley and Evelyn missed the train they were to take back to Boston, so they decided to make the most of their time and see if anything interesting was going on in the city. Upon asking their taxi driver for ideas, he took them to a rodeo—the only one Stanley has ever gone to in his life!

Immediately after the honeymoon, Stanley went down to North Bergen, New Jersey, to begin teaching at Metropolitan Bible Institute. Evelyn decided to continue her clerical job at Brockway-Smith-Haigh-Lovell in Boston until after New Year's, when she was due to get a good bonus. Throughout the fall of 1945, she lived with her parents and would come down to New Jersey on the weekends to be with Stanley, which greatly improved the countenance of the young instructor!

Life at Metropolitan Bible Institute

Finally, after many long weeks and months apart, Evelyn came down after New Year's to stay with Stanley permanently in North Bergen. For the next two years, they shared a second-floor, two-bedroom apartment with John and Evelyn Lewis, who had been missionaries to India.[2] Stanley carried a heavy load in his years teaching at Metropolitan Bible Institute (MBI). At the beginning of each semester, pastors would come to a faculty meeting, and each one would pick a subject to teach for two hours one day a week. Nicholas Nikoloff[3] would teach a couple of courses, a woman came up from Eastern Bible Institute (EBI) to teach the Christian education courses, and Horton would teach the rest,

Stanley at MBI in North Bergen, 1945

Stanley's 1948 MBI yearbook picture (used by permission from VFCC)

MBI faculty, North Bergen, NJ
Front row, l to r: Robert McGlasson, Russell Goodwin, Milton Wells, R. D. E. Smith, Thomas Brubaker, Sr., Nicholas Nikoloff, unknown, Stanley Horton
Back row, l to r: unknown, Agnes (Mrs. Russell) Goodwin, unknown, Eva Teresa Sisco, unknown, unknown, Mrs. Nicholas Nikoloff; unknown, Evelyn Horton

MBI faculty and students, North Bergen, NJ
Stanley and Evelyn Horton are located on the second row, fifth and fourth from the right

usually twenty-one or twenty-two hours a week. During his time there, he taught nearly every subject in the catalog—including even English composition and literature—and encouraged his students to write, as a part of whatever ministry God would have for them. Though the load was heavy, the classes were not large, and Horton just accepted this responsibility as an open door to do what God wanted him to do.

Not long after Stanley arrived at MBI, a local pastor in Morristown, New Jersey, left his storefront church, Morristown Gospel Tabernacle.[4] To fill the void, Superintendent Tom Brubaker asked Horton to take a group of students with him and see what he could do with the church. Stanley had no car, but one of the students, Alice Gothard, had one and offered to drive the ministry team down each week. They visited homes and left *Pentecostal Evangel* magazines. Almost every Sunday they had new people come. However, they would come only once. When Stanley inquired into this situ-

Horton with Wesley R. Steelberg outside the Morristown Gospel Tabernacle, Morristown, NJ, 1945

ation, he found that a couple who attended the church regularly would visit newcomers and tell them that Stanley was making a lot of money teaching, that he was just there for the money, and that they shouldn't come back! This couple had been a part of a Church of God congregation that had collapsed. They didn't want to see the little Assemblies of God church succeed, so every time new people came, they'd get a visit from this couple with a tall tale to tell.

Stanley pastored the Morristown church for about ten months, struggling along faithfully, never finding out about this couple's sabotage until near the end of his time there. When he did discover it, he told the district officers that for him to continue there was not a good idea at the time. He took a pastorate at the Assembly of God in White Plains, New York,[5] where he ended up staying for the next two years—all while carrying a full teaching load at Metropolitan.

As if pastoring and teaching at MBI were not enough to fill his days, Horton took additional courses in Bible and psychology at Biblical Seminary of New York (now New York Theological Seminary). From time to time during 1946–47, he would cross the river to New York City for the seminary's Saturday program. "I just wanted to keep up with my studies after finishing at Harvard," he explained.

In 1946, Superintendent Brubaker brought Horton to their credentials committee, and they quickly approved him for his ordination at the district council on May 9.[6] A "Brother McDowell" was the speaker at the ceremony, and Stanley recalls that it was a powerful service.

Stan, Jr.

Almost exactly nine months later, in the midst of a February snowstorm, Stanley, Jr., was born in Christ Hospital, Jersey City, on February 7, 1947. Encouraged through the early months of parenthood by the wise counsel of the Lewises (with whom they were still living), Stanley and Evelyn entered into the new adventure of raising a child. The Lewises proved to be helpful friends. John encouraged the new father to be involved in taking care of the baby, even changing diapers. Hanging diapers out the window was not a good idea because of smoke and pollutants in the air in New Jersey, so the Hortons found a diaper service that picked them up twice a week. They also got a lot of help from Evelyn's family in Boston after Stan was born, enjoying visits back and forth with them. While Stanley taught and carried on pastoral duties, Evelyn stayed busy with the care of Stan, Jr., and helped out at the church teaching Sunday School, playing the piano, and helping in visitation.

The Move to Suffern

After Stanley's second year teaching at MBI, the district officers proposed moving the school to a better location. The faculty had a prayer meeting and felt the school should stay where it was—so convenient to New York City. Students could be in Times Square in twenty minutes by bus through the Lincoln Tunnel. There were opportunities for work and ministry for the students all around that area. The school even had extension classes in New York City. However, the district sold the property and bought an estate with a big house and a lake at Suffern, New York, an hour's bus ride from New York City. Stanley believed that this move was not God's will and felt led of the Spirit to write to CBI to inquire about employment. They had already filled all their positions for the year, so he asked them to consider him for the next year and stayed on through 1947–48 at MBI.

The town of Suffern where the school planned to move was small. The citizens there didn't want a lot of students in their town, so they obtained an injunction against using the property as a school. This held up the school's move from North Bergen. Faced with that obstacle, classes for the 1947–48 academic year were held in Patterson, New Jersey, where the Assemblies of God had a large Sunday School building that MBI could use during the week.

Meanwhile, Stanley and Evelyn moved to the new property at Suffern; this allowed them to keep an eye on the property for the school and also provided them with more room for their growing family. With his salary of one hundred dollars a month, Stanley purchased a small car from one of the members of the White Plains Assembly to drive back and forth to Patterson. In addition to teaching, the school asked him to serve as librarian, providing him with one student as a helper. The library was meager, composed solely of donated books. Stanley decided that the Dewey decimal system didn't have enough classifications for religion and theology, so sending for cards from the Library of Congress, he adopted their system of classification. That same system was later adopted by some of the other Assemblies of God Bible colleges.

Central Bible Institute

On October 2, 1922, Central Bible Institute (CBI) began as a "co-educational institute for the training of men and women to become ministers and missionaries on the home and foreign fields."[7] The first school quarters were in the basement of a small white church—Central Assembly on Calhoun and Campbell—that had a seating capacity of four hundred. By October 8, 1924, the students were settled in their new building. J. Roswell Flower[8] and others helped choose the site for the school. The Commercial Club of Springfield donated fifteen acres to the General Council for CBI on a "quiet, oak-timbered spot, just the place for worship and rest and study."[9] The front page of the *Pentecostal Evangel* in the summer of 1924 displayed a large picture of the new facility, describing the campus as "beautiful for situation." The oaks around the campus were seen as "significant of the strength of Pentecostal truth in the plan of God. . . . These trees seem to be fitting symbols of the strength that is to be found in well-trained students that we all pray will throng its halls until Jesus comes."[10]

Five years after this article was written, Bethel Bible Training School in Newark, New Jersey, merged with CBI;[11] its principal, W. I. Evans, became CBI's third principal. Bethel had grown out of a Pentecostal mission begun by Minnie Draper and a missionary rest home with Eleanor Smith (Bowie) as matron. Evans, Frank M. Boyd, and Ralph M. Riggs, who all later served at CBI and played significant leadership roles within the AG, were originally teachers at Bethel.

It was to this school that Stanley Horton would end up devoting years of his life—thirty in full-time teaching and six more in part-time, after leaving CBC in 1978 to teach at the new AG Graduate School.

In the spring of 1948, Ralph Riggs[12] contacted Stanley Horton to come to Springfield for an interview to teach at what was then Central Bible Institute and Seminary (CBIS).[13] Again, Uncle Wesley Steelberg's counsel to make the move played a significant role. Steelberg was living in Springfield by that time, serving as an assistant general superintendent. Stanley and Evelyn stayed at the Steelbergs' home for a few weeks while construction on their duplex at 533 Williams Street was completed. CBI owned land on the street just one block south of campus, and for a few years after World War II had been building rental houses for CBI faculty and staff. After a few weeks with the Steelbergs, Stanley, Evelyn, and their son, Stan, Jr., moved into the duplex next door to Hardy Steinberg,[14] who taught theology at CBI. Thus, they entered into a community of leaders who would impact the future of the Assemblies of God for decades to come. Stanley Horton would live on Williams Street until 2003.

Endnotes

[1] Evelyn's uncle was Richard Babcock (who graduated from CBI's very first graduating class and went on to pioneer a Pentecostal church in Newfoundland). Her brother-in-law was Aaron Kelley (who graduated from Zion Bible Institute).

[2] During the three years Stanley taught at MBI, John Lewis was dean of men and taught English; his wife Evelyn served as dean of women, or matron. The Lewises had many fascinating stories to tell about India. However, sometimes John's stories would take precedence over instruction. "John was a good English teacher, but if a student mentioned India, we wouldn't have English; we'd have India!" one student remembers. [Comment by Priscilla Edwards, my mother, who had John Lewis for English at MBI. The Lewises' son Clifford became an official in the Eastern District Council of the AG.] After their years at MBI, the Lewises returned to India, where John eventually went to be with the Lord.

[3] While at Metropolitan, Nikoloff encouraged the young instructor Horton to be sure to clarify his theological terms so people would understand

them. Perhaps the AG and Pentecostal world in general has Nikoloff to thank to some extent for Horton's commitment to clarity in his writings.

Upon Horton taking his leave from MBI in 1948, Nikoloff, serving both as president of the school as well as secretary of the New York–New Jersey district, transferred Stanley's ministerial credentials to the Southern Missouri district without Stanley's knowledge or approval—not entirely happy that this promising young instructor was leaving MBI for CBI. Horton has been a member of the Southern Missouri District Council of the Assemblies of God since that time.

4 The storefront church was next to a furniture store. In the winter, the furniture store would turn off their heat on the weekends, and so the parishioners were forced to wear their overcoats during the service.

5 A "Brother Walegir" became pastor of the White Plains church after that, and the church has since grown into a wonderful church.

6 Ernest S. Williams was general superintendent at this time, and J. Roswell Flower was general secretary.

7 CBC Golden Anniversary Book, *Year of Jubilee: A Pictorial History of CBI-CBC* (Springfield, MO: CBC, 1972), 18.

8 J. R. and Alice Reynolds Flower experienced the early Pentecostal revival, began the *Christian Evangel* (later *Today's Pentecostal Evangel*) in 1913, and joined the AG at its organizational General Council in 1914, where J. R. became founding secretary-treasurer. Flower assisted in the selection of Springfield, Missouri, as the AG national headquarters in 1918 and served as the AG's first missionary secretary-treasurer in 1919. The Flowers devoted the rest of their lives to service within the AG in pastoral, district, and national capacities, and J. R. played a key role in the entry of the AG into the National Association of Evangelicals. The couple also founded Maranatha Summer Bible School, which ultimately became Valley Forge Christian College. (See McGee, *People of the Spirit*, 116, 201–04, 221, 230–31 (sidebar), 291, and *The New International Dictionary of Pentecostal and Charismatic Movements*, s.v. "Flower, Joseph James Roswell (1888–1970), and Alice Reynolds (1890–1991)," 642–644.

9 CBC Golden Anniversary Book, 18.

10 "The New Nearly-Completed Bible School," *Pentecostal Evangel*, August 9, 1924, 1.

11 Two other schools later merged with CBI—South Central Bible Institute in Hot Springs, Arkansas, (1953) and Great Lakes Bible Institute in Zion, Illinois (Fall, 1954). The school's name change from CBI to CBC was announced in the September 29, 1965, issue of *The Centralite* after becoming official at the general presbyters' meeting of the 1965 General Council.

CBI's principals and presidents have included D. W. Kerr (1922–23), Frank Boyd (1923–29), W. I. Evans (1929–31, who later served as dean 1948–54), J. W. Welch (1931–39), E. S. Williams (1939–48), Bartlett Peterson (1948–58), J. Robert Ashcroft (1958–63), Philip Crouch (1963–80), H. Maurice Lednicky (1980–2001), Wayne Benson (2001–04), and Gary Denbow (2005–). CBC received accreditation with the North Central Association of Colleges and Secondary Schools in 2005.

[12] Riggs was one of four Assemblies of God assistant general superintendents at the time. Education was part of his responsibility, and CBIS was a General Council school, so he interviewed prospective teachers.

[13] See chapter 7 for a description of the evolution of Assemblies of God graduate and seminary education.

[14] Hardy Steinberg was president of Great Lakes Bible Institute in 1949 until its merger with CBI in the fall of 1954, when he came to CBI to serve as dean of men and to teach systematic theology and homiletics. He became a valued friend and colleague of Horton's for many years. Later, he worked with Berean School of the Bible, an AG correspondence institute. After he passed away, his wife, Francis, became the second wife of Robert C. Cunningham, longtime editor of the *Pentecostal Evangel*. See Steinberg's article "Christ Prays for You," in *The Scroll*, September 30, 1954, 2.

CHAPTER 5

Family Life

Not long after the Hortons arrived in Springfield, Evelyn became pregnant with their second child. During this pregnancy in 1949, she suffered quite a loss of blood. The doctor had her stay in bed for over a month before the baby was born. Stanley had to do everything for her, even carry her to the bathroom. When their son Edward was born, the doctor told Evelyn that she had two fibroid tumors that had been causing the problem. Not believing the tumors should be removed due to medical reasons related to the way they were positioned, he advised the Hortons not to have any more children. After three years, however, Evelyn felt the Lord had touched her, so she went for an examination and the doctor could not find the tumors! She waited six months and went to another doctor. He couldn't find them either. Then time went by, and the Hortons kept praying for another child; finally, seven-and-one-half years after Edward was born, his little sister, Faith,[1] was born in December of 1956. When the nurse brought the news that Evelyn had given birth to a girl, Evelyn's mother, overcome with joy, danced down the hall at the new St. John's Hospital in Springfield, Missouri!

Burning the Midnight Oil

The Hortons lived in the duplex on Williams Street from 1948 to 1952, when they moved five houses down to 615 Williams, at that time with their two young sons, Stan, Jr., and Ed. A year before moving into the new house, the Assemblies of God Church School Literature Department of Gospel Publishing House, desirous of having the lessons for the *Adult Teacher's* Sunday School periodical published earlier, asked several people to write some lessons to move the issues ahead a quarter. Horton wrote two lessons. Then one of the writers—also serving as a pastor—became too busy to continue, so Horton "fell into that job," one he continued to do faithfully for twenty-five years.[2] At first, he would spend many afternoons and evenings at a desk in the old Gospel Publishing House[3] on Pacific Street in Springfield. Later, he worked at home. But since the boys' beds were in the same room upstairs where his office was, he'd wait until they went to sleep before working. With his teaching load at CBI and his responsibilities for the *Adult Teacher*, Horton soon became known for long work hours and little sleep. His neighbors sometimes reminded him that they noticed his light on late. Dr. William Menzies, who lived five doors down from the Hortons, at 527 Williams, for many years, noted, "For twenty-five years of his writing the adult quarterly, I dare say that a good bit of what he wrote was written after midnight—long hours, and for very little pay."[4]

For many years, this young CBI instructor, who would become the Assemblies of God's premier theologian, received one dollar an hour for writing the *Adult Teacher*. Later, when he wrote the lessons at home, he was paid on a flat rate basis for each quarterly. Though this income was paltry, it did help augment his salary from CBI, which in the early years was particularly low. Horton's "magnificent salary" as he later would put it—when he was hired to teach at CBIS for the fall of 1948[5]—was twenty-four hundred dollars a year, paid at sixty dollars a week for forty weeks. The twelve weeks of summer he had to look for other work. For a while, he served as pastor of a country schoolhouse church called Potter Assembly[6], about a mile north of Strafford, Missouri (1949–51), and later pastored Sparta Assembly of God[7] (1951–52). After three years teaching at CBI and with two boys needing many things, Horton needed a raise. Two other teachers who had come at the same time he did were paid more, apparently because they asked for it. So he finally asked the president, E. Bartlett Peterson,[8] for a raise. Peterson gave him ten dollars a week more, but that was the last time Horton ever asked for more money.

In retrospect, however, none of these financial issues ever appears to have discouraged Horton or derailed his focus from what he felt the Spirit was leading him to do and be. "God always supplied our needs," he says. "We were never able to save enough for a down payment for our own home, but we enjoyed the house we rented at a special rate from CBC. All I ever wanted to do was do the Lord's will and take the doors He opened for me. Teaching at Central Bible College for thirty years was my most enjoyable job." This eternal optimist viewed his modest income as a good situation, as it propelled him into writing.

Horton authored all the volumes of the *Adult Teacher* from 1952–1971. He also contributed the biblical exposition to issues of the *Adult Teacher* from 1971–1978 and except for 1982, wrote or contributed to several volumes until 1992. Over the years, he would receive letters or comments from individuals throughout the Movement regarding how much the *Adult Teacher* materials had meant to them and helped them in their

Horton at desk at Gospel Publishing House working on the *Adult Teacher*, 1955

Church School Literature department at 11th National Sunday School Convention, St. Louis, Missouri, March 30–April 2, 1954.
l to r: Stanley Horton, Zella Lindsey, Juanita Brown, Genevieve Howard, Ellis Martin (Stevens), Ralph Harris

Church School Literature Editorial Staff, l to r: Donald Johns, Stanley M. Horton, Ellis Martin, Dorothy Morris, Ralph W. Harris (editor-in-chief), Nicholas Nikoloff, Mary Virginia Bryant

understanding of Scripture. *Revivaltime* preacher C. M. Ward told Horton once that he found much material in the *Adult Teacher* to use in his radio sermons. Many pastors and congregants kept the *Adult Teacher* quarterlies to use as commentaries. Russell Wisehart, current Sunday School Bible and doctrine editor, was a student of Horton's at CBC and later worked with him on the methodology for Horton's *1 & 2 Corinthians* Adult and Student curriculum (1982). "I have all Horton's quarterlies from '51 on," he reported, "except for just a couple. I depend a lot on Dr. Horton's ideas when I'm editing the current material. His work is one of the first sources I go to. If I have a question, I always look at the older lessons from the '50s for clarification on theological issues." [9]

Without a doubt, through his writing of the adult Sunday school curriculum for twenty-five years in a time when the term "adult elective" was unheard of, Horton helped shape the theological values and beliefs of a Movement. Robert Cooley, Horton's student at CBI in 1949 and later his colleague on the faculty there—would later comment about his writing:

> He modeled a biblical scholarship that was practically applied. So if you read the adult quarterly for twenty-five years, you can see that the lesson material grew out of an academic understanding of Scripture but was very practical. It was the same with his articles and other books—a technical understanding of the biblical text but a remarkable way of translating that into a body of applied theology. This is the meaning of his life, that he had a wonderful way to do that. His scholarship was never esoteric; it was for everyone. To be able to go from an exegetical theology to an applied theology was a real gift. [10]

When asked to reflect on the impact of that influence, Horton humbly noted, "I don't know. From what people tell me, it helped their understanding of the Bible, so that would certainly have helped shape their theological thinking." Horton felt that producing this Christian education curriculum was one of his greatest privileges, because during the years he was writing, the majority of Assemblies of God churches used the *Adult Teacher* for what was often their "auditorium class," where most or all the adults would gather to study the Scriptures for Sunday School. He spent many seasons in prayer in connection with writing these materials, seeking God for wisdom to write the lessons and researching the original Greek and Hebrew of the biblical passages. Even though he wrote over a year ahead of the time the lessons were used, he often received letters telling how a particular lesson had met a real need in a particular adult Sunday School class. His writing also helped him in his teaching and later in his doctoral studies.

"Dad Was Always Busy"

With such a heavy teaching and writing workload, it is not surprising that one of Stan, Jr., and Ed's earliest memories is the sound of a typewriter. They remember him working until 4 or 5 in the morning doing the quarterly, getting two or three hours' sleep, and then rushing off to a 7:30 AM class. Their mother would stay up with their father to keep him company while he was writing, but she was also concerned that he'd be late for his classes. She was afraid that his having had so little rest would cause him to sleep through his alarm. (Apparently it must have happened once or twice for her to be that concerned!) William Menzies, Horton's neighbor and colleague for many years, recalls Horton running to cross Norton Road to get to classes early in the morning, and how sometimes fellow CBC personnel would affectionately refer to Stanley and Evelyn as "The Late Hortons" because they were always rushing to get places.

"Dad was always on the run. Dad running out the door so he wouldn't be late. Dad coming home for lunch. Dad after supper going up to the office grading papers," his son Ed recalls. "You're going to bed and you hear the typewriter going *tap, tap, tap*, and you're going to sleep to the typewriter sound."

Holy Spirit Empowered Th.D.

The sound of the typewriter in the upstairs office increased even more after 1953, when Horton was accepted for the doctor of theology program at Central Baptist Theological Seminary in Kansas City, Kansas. He arranged his courses at CBC to be on Mondays, Wednesdays, and Fridays in order to accommodate the fact that the seminary had doctoral seminars only on Tuesdays. This arrangement required him to take the 2 AM Tuesday morning train to Kansas City, Missouri, then take a bus across the river to the seminary for classes all day. After that, he would spend time in the library, take a bus home—arriving at midnight—and still get up for a 7:30 class the next morning.

Following this two-year period of course work, Horton spent three years visiting libraries in Chicago, New York, and Boston doing research for his dissertation, "A Defense on Historical Grounds of the Isaian Authorship of the Passages in Isaiah Referring to Babylon."[11] German scholars had done most of the archaeological work on Babylon. So Horton spent two weeks in the basement of the Harvard Divinity School library going through German periodicals that had never been translated into English. He remembers how the Lord helped him through the final stage of his doctoral work:

> Finally I had a great deal of material, but I was having a terrible time organizing it into a logical order for my dissertation. One day I left my desk remembering that the Bible says that the one who speaks in a tongue edifies himself. As I continued to pray in tongues I did feel that edification. I went back to my desk and everything fell into place! My dissertation was accepted, and I was happy

Stanley and Evelyn at graduation

that my wife and my mother were able to be at the commencement on May 28, 1959, to see me get my Th.D. degree.[12]

The CBI faculty gathered on May 12, 1959, to honor Horton's achievement, and the students from Horton's Hebrew classes honored him by presenting him with a copy of *Brown-Driver-Briggs Hebrew and English Lexicon* in appreciation for his outstanding work in Hebrew.

In light of such a schedule, it is remarkable that Horton recalls: "I never felt a conflict or pressure between work and family." What concerned him more than his absence was what his boys might be doing in their absence. "The most difficult thing about being a parent was when we didn't have a TV and our boys would be at friends' homes watching we didn't know what. We finally bought a small TV and set standards for watching. There were other times when they wondered why some children were allowed to do things we didn't let them do. We would tell them what we felt was right."

Not only did Stanley try to do what was right with his children according to standards of behavior, but he also—as his father had done with him through difficult times—tried to make life fun and enjoyable for the family. He played ball with the boys and helped them to learn how to ride their bikes. And he was an excellent storyteller. When the boys were little, he'd try to find time to tell them stories before bed. When Faith was growing up, however, life was less hectic, so without fail Stanley would—after his nightly routine of watching the 5:30 news, reading his paper, and doing the daily crossword puzzle in it—tell a bedtime story to his daughter.

Saturday mornings were special because the children got to see their dad a little more. In the early years, CBC had a baker who would make fresh pecan rolls and other pastries on Saturday mornings for the students. Stan, Jr., and Ed would take turns running over to the campus to buy these delicacies for the family breakfast. After a while the school quit providing the pastries, so Stanley made Saturday mornings special by preparing banana pancakes, waffles, or omelets for the family. This little routine, this break from rushing to and fro the rest of the week, was a delight to his children. Faith remembers how he used to make the pancakes in the shape of an *F* for her, *S* for Stan, and *E* for Ed. On Sundays, they would buy pastries for breakfast so they didn't have to take the time to cook and could just concentrate on getting ready for church.

Boston and Cape Cod

Stanley and Evelyn would also take the children to various places and go for rides in the country, where they would enjoy good times together. Every summer the family would drive back to Boston, Massachusetts, to see Evelyn's relatives. They would go to different beaches close by and occasionally take in a Red Sox baseball game. Every Christmas until Evelyn's mother passed away, the family visited their "Nana." In later years, many summer vacations were spent staying with Evelyn's sister in a rented house on Cape Cod and swimming in the warm waters of the south shore.[13] One sister in particular would send them money to help with the trip.

"We had a used '55 Buick Roadmaster, and Dad would drive all night and all day, pull into a little coffee shop or rest area, snooze, then drive some more," Ed reminisces. "Stan would lay on the seat, and I'd lay on the floorboards. There were no seatbelts of course. Sometimes I'd get behind Dad and whisper in his ear, 'Faster, Dad! Go faster!' So he'd go faster, and then Mom would say, 'Stanley! You're going too fast!' So he'd go back down."

One summer he stopped the car in New York City in the middle of the night, had the kids all roll their windows down, look up, and then said to them, "This is the Empire State Building!" Since it was night, though, they didn't venture out of the car but just continued on to Boston.

On another trip, this time at Christmas, the family was making their way to Boston in a blizzard. Stanley drove into a snow-drift and the family had to be rescued. While Evelyn and the kids were taken somewhere to be safe and warm, Stanley waited alone in the car for the tow truck—much to the anxiety of his young daughter who was afraid another car might come along and run into him.

Even after the boys were grown and married with children, the Cape was a special place for family gatherings and time together.

Making Ends Meet

Aside from weekends and vacation breaks, though, the boys were on their own a lot during their growing up years. Life was busy, finances tight, and Dad was often busy or away. So the boys were one another's best company. "Stan and I were always together," Ed remembers. "I was his shadow. Our parents would have been shocked if they had known where we were! It was a different world in the '50s than even when Faith was growing up ten years later. We were everywhere. We went caving and biking. We roller-skated all over CBC and made a nuisance of ourselves in the summer. We ice-skated on the lakes in the winter, we played in the creeks, we went exploring in the parks. All that was our entertainment. When Doling Park would have 'Dr. Pepper Free Ride Day' we'd ride to all the filling stations and stores to see if we could have their bottle caps out of the machine so we could ride for free, because we had no money to go on those rides the rest of the year."

In the early years at CBC, everyone was struggling financially, not just the Hortons. Eventually, though, other families were able to move away to nicer houses, but the Hortons stayed at Williams. Stanley and Evelyn looked at a lot of houses, but never moved. At one time, they tried to buy the house they rented on Williams Street, but CBC wouldn't sell it to them. Ed remembers that when he was about fourteen or fifteen, his father got an offer to teach in California. "At that position, he would have made more money. And we

Stanley and Evelyn in 1949

would have loved to go to California. But Dad just didn't feel it was right, that it was what the Lord wanted. He felt the Lord wanted him to stay at CBC." With Stanley Horton, it never was about the money. His focus was on ministry and on doing what God had asked him to do—whether he was well paid or not. Many times on the weekends, he would minister even hundreds of miles away at some little country church, often at great personal cost to himself. "It didn't matter how far it was," his son Ed recalls. "He just did it because he wanted to serve the Lord."

In order to have money for the things they wanted to do as kids, Stan and Ed would often ride their bikes up and down Kansas and Glenstone streets looking for pop bottles so they could trade them in to get a pop. "We could get a small bottle for seven cents and a big bottle for twelve cents. And it was two cents a bottle if you brought a bottle back." The boys had other entrepreneurial means as well: "We picked walnuts. We mowed lawns. We sold things door to door—needles, seeds, pens, light bulbs."

Finances weren't quite as tight when Faith was growing up, but still the budget was limiting. "I don't remember Dad ever worrying about it though," Faith recounts. "In fact, I remember him talking about how God always came through. One time, money was very tight and they couldn't pay some bills. Then the doorbell rang, and my parents went to the door; there on the steps was some money in an envelope."

Protecting the Family

In their early years at CBI, Evelyn would accompany Stanley to Christmas parties, get involved in campus activities such as the women's auxiliary, and have people over, but as the years went by, the school became larger, many faculty were younger, and Evelyn's lack of formal education became a personal concern in public settings. Though early on this did not bother her at all, later she felt a bit hurt when at times her response to the question, "And where did you go to school?" was coldly received. This made her take a step back and be protective of herself and her family, erecting a barrier between the worlds of home and work.

Perhaps some of Evelyn's desire to stay out of the spotlight and to be protective of the Horton home and family matters was also because of their financial struggles. She sought to have a haven for the family from the world of ministry where people would not know their business. This translated into her not wanting her children to have friends in the house. As son Ed recalls, "The folks were funny about giving us keys. I can remember when we were kids, the house would be locked up all the time if they'd gone out. So if we got home from a football game or somewhere, and they were gone, we'd have to climb up over the roof to get in an upstairs window. I think they didn't want us to have a key to the front door because Mom was so private. We had to go up to other people's houses in order to play Monopoly or anything." By the time Faith was grown, this had changed.

Her parents ceremoniously gave her a back door key in the seventh grade and a front door key in the ninth grade—with a long talk about the responsibility of having it!

Evelyn was also concerned for the family image and what people thought of them. In addition to her apprehension that—even on a family vacation in Cape Cod—someone would see Stanley Horton without a tie on,[14] she was also concerned (on the other end of the spectrum) that people would ever think they were putting on airs. "I can remember when they got a Chrysler New Yorker, in the late '80s. And it had the little sidelights on the back of the roof. She was so concerned even then with what people would think—that we were getting too wealthy, too fancy, or something. But that was just Mom." Evelyn was also concerned about how the house looked, since she had heard comments about how much nicer other people's homes and belongings were than theirs. When Faith was allowed to have a friend over, she had to first spend half a day helping her mother clean the house before the friend could enter the house. Of course, the friends didn't care—they just wanted to play. But Evelyn was very conscientious about things being just right.

Generosity Overflowing

Ironically, though the Hortons did not have much in the way of finances or worldly goods themselves, they were very generous over the years to others. When they saw or heard about a need, they often gave, whether it was to help pay a bill, buy food, help with medical care, or cover school expenses. And they usually gave anonymously if they could get away with it, because they didn't want any glory from it. Stanley told his daughter years later that their generosity was usually due to her mother's inspiration from the Lord. "She had a loving, giving heart," he said, "and was always an encouragement to others."

Only years later did one of Horton's closest associates discover just how much he and Evelyn had given away. William

139

Menzies recalls riding together with Horton to a district func-tion in Nebraska in the 1980s where both men (now at AGTS) were participants. "I discovered on that trip just how generous he and his wife had been, giving to every appeal that came and ultimately giving away so much of their resources. Because they had given so much away, they had no resources to buy a house of their own. But there was no bitterness in his quiet report to me. They really had always just trusted the Lord to meet all their needs. Surely they invested in eternal values!"[15]

As their father became increasingly well known, the unreal-istic expectations and outside pressures related to being "Stan-ley Horton's son" or "Stanley Horton's daughter" did become a bit of an issue. The children never felt this pressure from their father, but Evelyn did remind her children at times, "You've got to be careful what you do, because what you do reflects on your dad." When Faith asked her father about that in high school, he wasn't troubled about that. He understood his wife's concern but told his daughter she didn't need to worry about being so careful because of being *his* daughter, but just should always do what she knew *God* wanted her to do.

As uncomfortable as that concern may have been at times, in the close-knit church culture of Springfield, it was often a reality—especially when the boys were younger. Son Ed remem-bers that when he was about six, the family went to a *Revivaltime* broadcast at CBC. "For some reason I was asked to pray, and I was extremely shy as a kid. Terrified. For a long time I didn't want people to know I was Dr. Horton's son. When we'd go to churches for him to minister, I'd hide in the back of the church. Because they'd ask, 'You're *Dr. Horton's* son?' and for some rea-son they'd act as though because of that I'm automatically a Bible scholar and a world prayer leader and a theologian! But it doesn't work that way. Dad's special, and Dad's unique. I'm not Dad. Stan's not Dad. Faith's not Dad. But people somehow wanted to translate whatever Dad was to us."

When Faith went to CBC, she would sometimes get that kind of comment—not from the people who worked there, but from other students. "They'd expect me to get lots of As or to know things that I didn't know. Or, if I *did* know something, it was *because* I was his daughter, and it was just something genetically passed on."

The kids learned to deal with the expectations, however, accepting it as a part of their lives. "It was just something we grew up with; that's simply the way it always was." But this reality did not stop them from doing what they felt led to do. As Faith noted, "I went to CBC because I wanted to study the Bible, and I knew the best person to study the Bible under was Dad!"

Worshipping Together

When they first arrived in Springfield in 1948, the Hortons joined Central Assembly of God. Not long after, Stanley served as a pastor in Strafford, Missouri, and then Sparta, Missouri, from 1949 to 1952, eventually resigning to have more time to work on the *Adult Teacher*. They returned to Central, but at that time, all the Sunday School classes there were being taught by others who'd been at the church longer. So in 1954, when Stanley was offered the opportunity to teach the adult class at Bethel, a Central Assembly church plant in the north part of Springfield,[16] he left. Evelyn was playing piano[17] at that time for one of the large adult Sunday School classes at Central, so she stayed there for six more months until finally being persuaded by the pastor of Bethel, Pauline Mastries, to come play piano for services. When she did come to Bethel, she ended up playing piano and organ for about forty years. She was faithful to her ministry there and had a key role in the service—so much so that one day when someone from children's church asked a child to deliver a note to Dr. Horton, the child's response was, "I know Mrs. Horton who plays the organ, but who is Dr. Horton?" Surprised, the person had to explain, "Well, you know, that's Sister Horton's husband!"

An intelligent woman, Evelyn often enjoyed conversations with Stanley about various subjects, but mostly the two enjoyed mutually shared spiritual experiences. With such a rich Pentecostal heritage, they appreciated sweet times of prayer, praise, and the moving of the Holy Spirit in the services. Evelyn also often ministered to and counseled many people in her own quiet way, encouraging them in the Lord and praying with them.

The family was at church "every time the doors were open." All three children were saved when quite young. Their father had the privilege of baptizing them in water and was delighted when each was bap-

Horton family, ca. 1954; l to r: Evelyn, Stan, Jr., Stanley, Ed

tized in the Holy Spirit. The Horton boys had started out in the Boy Scout troop at Central Assembly, but later became part of the first Royal Rangers[18] outpost—established at Bethel as a trial group. The boys even had the great distinction of having their pictures in the first published Royal Rangers handbook!

Sunday afternoons, however, were extremely quiet at the Horton home. Due to a tradition their mother had grown up with and passed on to her own family, the children were not allowed to play outside on Sundays but had to be confined inside. Though Stanley—as his children only learned in their later adults years—would have been fine with letting his children play outside on Sunday afternoons, he deferred to his wife on this issue. "I hated it," remembers their daughter. "It was hard watching all the other kids out the backdoor playing and running back and forth in the yard. And we weren't allowed to go out there."

The Hortons stayed at Bethel for decades, in spite of the fact that this little church did not have all the amenities of a larger congregation. There was no youth group, and the Horton boys remember looking longingly at the activities and trips going on in other youth groups (although Faith did make some good friends and enjoyed various activities).[19] "We were like the little stepchild church. And I always thought we were there because of Mom. But come to find out after she died, Dad said, 'No, it was because I was offered the opportunity to teach the adult class.'" Though they were primarily there because of his desire to teach, Stanley was also supportive and appreciative of Evelyn's ministry there at the church. Charles Harris, who came to Springfield in 1958 to pastor Bethel and attend CBC, remembers that when he arrived, the Hortons' daughter, Faith, was quite young. "Indicative of the kind, gentle man he is, if Faith was restless in the service, Dr. Horton would go outside with her, walk around with her, and carry her on his hip, so her mother could minister at the keyboard."

Stanley Horton, though a world-famous theologian and author, continued to teach the adult class at Bethel Assembly for over forty years, cutting back some only when his wife took ill and needed his care. Sometimes, he would have as many as seventy-five students, many other times as few as ten. And these were simple, average folk, not well educated. But they loved the Lord and wanted to learn, so it didn't matter to him if he was teaching one person or fifty or a thousand. Besides, the people at Bethel were always very caring of Horton, and he had a deep love for them as well. A statement his pastor has heard him say on many occasions, "Central may have the brass, but I have the gold," is indicative of his commitment to and appreciation of the people at Bethel. Staying at his post exemplifies his devotion and humility as well. Though especially in later years he could have taught anywhere, for him to put himself forward would have been to deny who he was. He wasn't *trying* to be humble. That's just who he was—a man with a gracious, meek spirit.

When Charles Harris arrived in Springfield, he already knew the name *Stanley Horton* because by then Horton was serving as sole author of the adult Sunday School teachers' quarterly. "Coming here from my pastorate in Arkansas and looking down and seeing the noted Stanley Horton sitting in my congregation was a bit intimidating," he recalls. "Although he didn't have his doctorate yet, he was a noted man of God. But for all his accomplishments, I never had anyone treat me with greater respect or give me more encouragement than he did. He was always supportive in every way of his pastor." Harris also had Horton as his professor during his years at CBC, 1958–63. He recalls:

> In the classroom, he didn't need any notes. It just rolled out of him. He could make Scripture come alive. And I've always appreciated his scholarship. He's a great scholar, but he has remained a man of God, and genuinely Pentecostal. He's a defender of the faith, a man of the church, and totally loyal to the Assemblies of God.
>
> I had several courses with Dr. Horton. I was always grateful that I had him for science. His bachelor's was in science. So he gave me a very understandable and genuinely biblical view of evolution and the major planks in this platform, every one of which he could answer from his own knowledge of scientific theory and biblical teaching. I had him for Old Testament History and Literature. I studied Hebrew with him two years. And in all of my dealings with him, I can say he is a genuine Christian gentleman and a scholar, a man of God, and a man of the church.[20]

Harris continued to pastor Bethel while working on his master's degree in counseling at Southwest Missouri State Univeristy (now Missouri State University). In 1967 he went to teach at CBC and eventually did a doctorate at the University of Tulsa. Thus, he had the rare distinction of having been Horton's pastor, student, and—during Harris' thirty-eight years at CBC—his colleague.

In 1967, Derreld Wartenbee came to Bethel as pastor. He too had been Horton's student while at CBC from 1951–54. "When I came to CBC, I had such a insatiable desire for God's Word," he recalls.

> My first semester and a half I read the Bible through. There were so many questions I had about what a particular Scripture meant. And inevitably I'd come into Dr. Horton's class, and that subject would come up, and I'd have my answer. God certainly has had His anointing on Dr. Horton. The way I put it is, he takes the cookies from way up on the shelf and puts them down where common, ordinary people can reach them.[21]

Now at age ninety-two, Dr. Horton attends Central Assembly on Sunday mornings with his family but continues to attend Bethel Assembly on Sunday evenings. The pastor or a deacon picks him up for services. This congregation has been home to him. He loves, trusts, and confides in his pastor and has a great affection for the people there—some of whom even provided financial support for him to travel to Alaska for ministry several years ago. When Horton was writing his book, *What the Bible Says about the Holy Spirit*, one church member at Bethel, a retired minister, offered to edit it for him. Not averse to getting help from anyone, even those not nearly as educated as he, Horton gave this elderly preacher something to do.

Stanley told his pastor one time, "You know, I really don't have a friend. When you have a lot of education, people sometimes are nervous about being around you." But people at Bethel have befriended and cared for him—especially in his older age. When he was younger, he was so busy, and time for friends was just a luxury. But now he appreciates even more the times of fellowship and people's care for him—especially in the years since Evelyn passed away.

A Loving Father

The Horton children did well in school. Both Stan and Ed played instruments in their high school marching band. Stan, Jr., later played the bassoon in the Springfield Symphony orchestra, and Faith sang in many school choir ensembles. Ed remembers that if he ever had a problem in algebra or chemistry or physics, he had ready assistance right there in his father. "My joke about Dad is that if he ever gets senile and loses half his intelligence," Ed says, "he'll still be twice as smart as me. He's just unique. I mean he's got all these blends. And he could have been a rocket scientist if he'd wanted, if that had been his mission."

By the time Faith came along, her growing up experience was quite different from her brothers, because they were so much older. Since the boys were gone when Faith was around ten, she went through her adolescent and teen years essentially as an only

The Hortons
Ed, Faith, Evelyn, Stanley, Stan, Jr.

child, doing everything with her parents and feeling very close to them. "Any time I had a problem or would come home from school upset about something, I could go up the stairs to my Dad's little office and tell him what had happened. I remember he would smile or look concerned and say something like, 'You know, I felt just like that when I was your age.' That always made me feel so much better, because it wasn't just *me*.

And he always had some word of wisdom of how to handle it."

Faith's bond with her father was strong. He always did a lot of things with her. On visits out East when her mom was spending time with her sisters, Stanley would take Faith to different tourist sites or out to

Faith with her Dad on his ninetieth birthday

eat. "It was just the two of us. We spent a lot of time together. I didn't have a sibling who was my age to spend time with. So in a lot of ways Dad was that for me." When she was in high school, she often stopped at his CBC office when walking home. She'd knock on his window and he'd move the curtain, smile at her, and wave her in. She'd come in and spend some time talking about the day. "I loved those moments alone with Dad to talk," she recalls.

Though the boys rode their bikes everywhere and walked to school during their childhood, times had changed by the time Faith was older. "I couldn't ride my bike a block away from the house without getting in trouble!" Instead, she remembers her parents—especially her father—driving her everywhere: to school each morning (if he did not have an early class), to various Christian events she wanted to take part in, and to high school activities. "A lot of parents complain about having to take their kids places," Faith comments, "but he never once complained—even if it was really late. I was involved in a

Christian coffeehouse downtown in my sophomore and junior years in high school. And it was open 7:30 to midnight on Friday and Saturday nights. Dad would drop me off and pick me up. And he was never late picking me up. He never complained how late it was, even though we always had to be at church the next morning." In Faith's growing up years, her father was not rushing to and fro so much, but was always there, making the family's life a joy and going places with his wife and daughter. "I remember he was always available to answer any question I ever had on any subject," Faith recalls. "Sure, he had interruptions with the phone to answer a pastor's question from somewhere across the country, but it was our normal life, and we all knew he loved us."

Empty Nest

Each time one of the children left home, Stanley and Evelyn were prepared. "Evelyn would cry a little," Stanley recalls,

Stan, Jr., and Stanley

"but both of us knew we had to let them go." As a result the children always had a good, close relationship with their parents. Reminiscing about his role as a father, Stanley states: "I suppose there are some things that should have been changed, but I do not have any regrets. I'm glad we took good care of our children and disciplined them when necessary. Sometimes parents don't always know what to do, but somehow the Lord helps us through. I think the worst decision I ever made was to let a surgeon sew up a cut on Stan, Jr.'s, forehead . . . without anesthetic—while we held his feet and arms and he screamed. He probably doesn't remember that, since he was only three, but I do!

"The whole 'life in a fishbowl' thing may have bothered them a little, but on the whole I think they made their own way without problems. I never tried to tell them what they should do as far as their work was concerned and so on. We encouraged them in whatever path they were going to take. It is important to encourage your children to follow the Lord and then set a good example for them. My greatest hope for my children and grandchildren is that they will keep looking to Jesus, as their mother and I did these many years, and be faithful to serve the Lord and love each other."

The example that his grandparents and parents set for him certainly did have a profound impact on Stanley. His parents made times of family and communal worship enjoyable for everyone—including the children. In later years, when writing a word study on "training" a child, Dr. Horton would note that the idea of this word (Hebrew, *chanokh*) not only involves discipline but also entails "dedicating a child to the Lord and raising that child in such a way that the child will enjoy the house of God and the things of God."[22] The role his own parents played in providing spiritual guidance certainly instilled in him a love for times in God's presence and with the people of God.

Because CBC did not have a teaching degree at the time, both Stan and Ed went to Evangel College—Stan because he wanted to major in music and teaching[23] and Ed because he wanted to major in science and teaching. Both young men married after their third year of school and finished at Southwest Missouri State University (now MSU). Ed went on to get a master's degree in science education and taught high school and middle school science for twenty-five years before retiring. When Ed was a senior at SMSU, his draft number came up to go to Vietnam. The government said if he joined the Army Reserves, they'd let him finish school. By the time he completed his college work, the war was over. When he had just six months left before his retirement, he was called up during Desert Storm to serve a medical detachment, and spent eight months testing water at camps in Saudi Arabia, near Kuwait.

Stanley Horton
with his younger son Ed, 2008

Neither Ed nor his siblings ever knew[24] until the writing of this book that their father was a conscientious objector in World War II. He had never spoken with them about that detail of his life nor ever said a contradictory word about Ed's military service. Stanley had told them only of his 4-D status; he felt no need to further discuss his conscientious objector position since after the war he had modified his views about the value of the military experience. However, pacifism is still of concern to Horton. As Mittelstadt and Paugh note:

> Today, Horton continues to deliberate on the Christian response to war. In the current climate of war and a predominant culture of violence, he retains his earliest sympathies and returns to the Scriptures. Horton encourages Christian responsibility concerning the place of earthly kingdoms: "Of course, you can't forget what Jesus said to Pilate, 'If My kingdom were of this world, my soldiers would fight. But my kingdom is not of this world.' So our primary concern needs to be for the kingdom of God and

not primarily for the kingdoms of this earth" [Paraphrase of John 18:36]. While Horton recognizes the value of citizenship and its ensuing responsibilities, he maintains Christians must not lose sight of their higher citizenship, namely, the kingdom of God. With the same passionate conviction found in his teaching and writing, Horton calls for young people to engage the mission field: "We should encourage young people . . . to spread the gospel, and establish the church, and not be so quick to think that they can solve the world's problems with war and conflict, which I still don't believe that we can."[25]

Thus, Stanley was supportive of his children doing whatever they chose to do. "I knew I wasn't going to be a minister or Bible teacher like Dad. I can remember graduating from high school and there was the Vietnam War. The choice was, go to college or go to war. I definitely wasn't mature enough for college, but I didn't want to go to war either," remembers Ed. But his father didn't push him in any way. He left all three of his children free to choose on their own. Faith graduated from CBC, went to a seminary in Ohio for a year, and then returned to Springfield to work as a med tech at Maranatha Lodge. She married and is a stay-at-home mom, homeschooling her son.

"Papa" and "Papa the Great"

Having survived life under a microscope, the Horton children emerged triumphant. All remain close to the Lord, one another, and their parents. Stan met and married Linda Self.[26] Ed married Diana Dykes, and they had two children—Matthew and Monica. Matt married Darci Stonebreaker and they had Cale and Aven. Monica married Matthew Bryant and they had Asher, Noah, and are expecting a baby girl in March 2009. Faith married Brent Stilts, and they had a son, Zachary Andrew Horton Stilts (so part of his name is after his Papa). To his grandchildren, Stanley

Horton is "Papa," and to his great-grandchildren, "Papa the Great."

Some of Ed's most favorite memories of his Dad are with his own children, Matt and Monica when they were growing up. From the time they were little, they loved being at Nana and

Family portrait, Horton's 90th birthday, 2006. l to r: Darci Horton, Cale Horton in Matt Horton's arms, Linda Horton, Stan Horton, Jr., Ed Horton, Diana Horton, Monica Bryant holding Asher Bryant, Faith Stilts, Brent Stilts, Faith Lueth (niece from Boston). Stanley Horton in chair with Zachary Stilts on his left side.

Papa's house. When the children were about four and two, Ed and Diana moved to a house a couple of miles from his parents. One day after they'd been at the new house a couple of weeks, Ed was in the front yard working on the bushes. After a few minutes, he looked up, and to his horror—the kids were gone! His wife was at work, and he was panicking, with no idea where the kids had disappeared. He looked around frantically, got in his car and drove through the neighborhood but didn't find them. Finally he swung over to his folks' house, but they weren't home. As he was backing out of the driveway, there came the sheriff up Williams Street with the kids. They had walked along Valley Water Mill Road where it curves and becomes National Avenue. A lady saw them walking and called the sheriff. The kids couldn't tell them how to go the two blocks back to their own house, but they could tell them how to go two miles to Nana and Papa's house!

Stanley and Evelyn would also take the grandkids on trips, play with them in the backyard, and sometimes Papa would be on the floor and the kids would ride on his back. He was the horse and they were the riders. "He was totally into being Papa," remembers Diana. Even in his eighties after Faith's son Zachary was born, Papa would get down on the floor and play with him. "Even though he's an older grandpa now and physically can't do what he did with Matt and Monia, he's really tried hard to give Zachary a good grandfather experience and good memories," says Faith. The two of them have spent a lot of time together and go out to eat or do different things. And as always, Stanley remains an excellent storyteller. Not surprisingly, his Papa has also been a great source of encouragement and wisdom for Zachary, who has already learned to go to his Papa for answers to his biggest Bible questions.

At Stanley and Evelyn's fiftieth anniversary in September of 1995, the family gathered to celebrate, and each one shared a special thought in the Hortons' honor. Ed and Diana's son Matt was at the time a freshman in college. When it was his turn, he said, "If I have a question on whether something is the right thing to do, I just ask myself, is it something Papa would do? And that answers the question."

Endnotes

[1] So named because of the faith required over the many long years of wanting a girl. They never gave up believing that God would answer that prayer. They also named her Faith after Evelyn's niece Faith who spent quite a bit of time with the Hortons.

[2] The back flap of the *Adult Teacher* volumes through 1959 reads, "Author for the *Adult Teacher* is Stanley Horton, B.S., B.D., S.T.M. (Harvard), Professor at Central Bible Institute. He brings to this work the mind of a Bible craftsman, the humility of a true scholar, a devoted love for the Word of God, and the anointing of the Holy Spirit." After 1960, his Th.D. was added, and in later years, "he offers inspiring, Bible-centered lessons from an evangelical and Pentecostal viewpoint."

[3] Once the Assemblies of God General Council offices moved from 434 W. Pacific Street to 1445 Boonville Avenue in 1962, Horton had an office in the old Safeway store on Boonville. See "Assemblies Plan 2½ Million Building," *The Centralite*, May 18, 1960, p. 3: "The four-floor structure will be the largest and most costly office building constructed in the Ozarks in more than 25 years." Also: "Assemblies Accomplishes Move to New Building," *The Centralite*, January 31, 1962, p. 3: "The Assemblies of God occupied the old building [on Pacific], an abandoned meat market and grocery store, in the spring of 1918 after moving from St. Louis, Mo. At that time, less than a dozen employees were associated with the denomination's offices which today has approximately 550." The new headquarters building was considered "one of the most modern in the nation." It was only years later, after his retirement from AGTS, that he had an office in the headquarters building, in Gospel Publishing House's Book Editing section, headed by Glen Ellard, to work with the Assemblies of God Higher Education Commission on the Logion Pentecostal Textbook series.

[4] William Menzies, interview by author, April 10, 2008.

[5] The new CBC campus publication *The Scroll* recorded the 1948 enrollment of 669 students as the "largest in the history of CBI . . . [with students] enrolled from forty-three states . . . and twenty-two foreign" countries ("Peterson Becomes School President," *The Scroll*, October 22, 1948, 1).

[6] This church later moved to Strafford and became First Assembly of God in Strafford.

[7] In Sparta, Missouri. This church later moved to a new building but kept the same name. Horton resigned this church to have more time to write the *Adult Teacher.*

[8] Succeeding E. S. Williams as president, Peterson arrived at CBIS in 1948 from Minneapolis, where he had served as superintendent of the North Central District Council for three years. Before leading the North Central district, Peterson had served as field secretary for six years and was associated with North Central Bible Institute and Seminary for nine years as an instructor and as a member of the board of directors. "Peterson Becomes School President," *The Scroll*, October 22, 1948, 1.

[9] Russell Wisehart, telephone interview by author, May 19, 2008.

[10] Robert Cooley, telephone interview by author, August 28, 2008.

[11] "Research on Isaiah Marks Work on Doctoral Degree: CBI Faculty Member Receives Honor May 28," May 3, 1959, Sunday *News Leader*, C7: "During his doctoral research the Rev. Horton correlated important, previously overlooked evidence supporting Isaiah's authorship of passages referring to Babylon in the 13th, 14th, 21st, and 47th chapters of the Old Testament book bearing his name.

"Most modern Old Testament scholars, including S. R. Driver, and George Adams Smith in The Expositor's Bible, have contended that these sections of the book [of] Isaiah were written by a 'second Isaiah' approximately 540 B.C., the Rev. Horton explains. The prophet Isaiah ministered from around 740 B.C. to 685 B.C.

"To establish his thesis that the parts of the book [of] Isaiah in question were written before 689 B.C., the Rev. Horton referred to the records of Sennacherib, Assyrian monarch who destroyed Babylon in 689 B.C. According to these records, Sennacherib captured and destroyed Babylon in exactly the manner predicted in the given passages of Isaiah, the Springfield scholar found.

"Sennacherib boasts in his inscription that he diverted water from the Euphrates River and its canals to make Babylon a swamp. In Isaiah 14:23 the prophet predicted that Babylon would be made 'a possession for the bittern (a species of heron), and pools of water.'

"Driver and Smith have asserted that the disputed passages of Isaiah were written 150 years after Sennacherib, and refer to the occupation of Babylon by the Persian conqueror Cyrus in 539 B.C. However, modern archaeological discoveries cited by Horton prove that the Babylonians welcomed Cyrus as a deliverer, and he did not destroy the city."

[12] Horton also received an honorary doctorate (L.H.D. [Litterarum Humanorum Doctor], i.e., Doctor of Humane Letters) from Faraston Theological Seminary in 1991. The president of the school, Dr. Rick Walston, had been one of Horton's students at CBC and wanted to honor him in this way. Walston also wrote a book that Horton edited for him.

[13] The December 15, 1953, issue of *The Scroll*, p. 6, CBI's campus publication, featured pictures of several faculty families with captions about their Christmas vacation plans. Along with the Donald Johns family and the J. Robert Ashcroft family and others is a picture of Stanley, Evelyn, and their two boys (ages 6 and 4); their caption reads: "The Stanley Horton family. They will be taking one of the longest trips of all the faculty families. They are going to Boston." The Ashcroft caption reads: "J. Robert Ashcroft, a family man, will be busy at the G.P.H. during vacation. A man who usually does not have more time than money." The following year, in a December 11, 1954, issue of *The Scroll*, Stan and Ed are pictured in a column called "Faculty Children." The caption reads: "Rev. and Mrs. S. M. Horton have two young gentlemen to supervise their home and its surroundings. Stanley Jr. is seven and has begun piano this year. Stan is planning to join the Cub Scouts to help round out his activities, which also include a stamp collection. Five-year-old Edward is enjoying kindergarten very much. . . . The boys pray for CBI students every day. Stanley insists that God has definitely spoken to him and that he is to be a missionary. Others may change their childish ambitions but not Stan; he is determined that he shall follow through. Stanley also has exceptional ability in arithmetic."

[14] Ed remembers, "I don't care where we were—even when we'd go back east to visit mom's family and we'd be on a beach on Cape Cod—and he'd go to leave for the grocery store, she'd say, 'Stan, put a tie on. Someone might see you.'" But it was true that Horton never knew when

someone might recognize him. Even on vacations or other trips, former students or just someone who had read one of his books would stop him and talk with him. Faith recalls, "I remember at a CBC picnic one time all the other professors were kidding dad because he showed up in a tie." The "tie thing" was such an issue that his son Ed says now, "I tell my Dad now if we're going on a trip together, 'Now, Dad, no ties!' I have a tie phobia now!"

[15] William Menzies, interview by author, April 10, 2008. (Also from his letter to Horton on his ninetieth birthday.) "In a way," Menzies continued, "Stan needed to be protected from the world. He was such a genuine, sensitive, spiritually minded fellow that in some ways he just needed to be protected. I would use that term. One time at the seminary on a Monday morning he was late for a meeting, and I discovered that he was at home with his daughter, Faith, who was terribly ill. They didn't know at the time, but she was in a diabetic coma. So at the seminary we raised the money to get Faith the care she needed. He was just so intent on the work God had called him to that sometimes he just needed assistance to deal with the normal activities, the normal responsibilities, of life."

[16] Bethel started as Northeast Assembly of God under the sponsorship of Ralph Riggs and Central Assembly in 1935 with an evangelistic crusade featuring K. H. Lawson. Gene Hogan was the first pastor. It changed its name to Bethel in 1952. When Horton came to Bethel and began teaching the Auditorium Adult Sunday School Class in 1954, Emil Balliet was pastor of Central, since Riggs had been elected as general superintendent. The Bethel Assembly congregation met in several places before building at 1005 East Dale Street. They eventually sold that building to a Ukrainian Pentecostal group that wanted to identify with the Assemblies of God and then built their new building in 2008 on land they'd owned on Grant Street for twenty years. The Hortons did not transfer their membership from Central to Bethel until after Charles Harris became pastor of Bethel in 1958.

[17] Beginning at age twelve, Evelyn was playing piano and later pump organ for street meetings. She also played for a Sunday afternoon radio show. Many people over the years commented on how beautifully she played the piano and organ—her music just flowed. "The way I heard it described was that she 'caressed' the keys," her daughter remembers. One time when the family was at a service at Central, Evelyn listened to the organist play a piece she'd never heard before. She took her pencil out and wrote the music out as the musician played it, then took it home and played it herself!

[18] Johnny Barnes became the first leader of the Royal Rangers program in 1962 to provide a means of motivating boys spiritually, mentally, and physically and to enhance their church and community life. For more on the history of Royal Rangers, see http://royalrangers.ag.org/about/history.cfm.

[19] Faith eventually got involved in revival meetings at another church in her junior year of high school. When she asked, they gave her permission to

attend that church, giving her a ride there for every service, then going on to Bethel themselves.

[20] Charles Harris, interview by author, May 6, 2008.

[21] Derreld Wartenbee, personal interview by author, May 6, 2008.

[22] Stanley Horton, "Word Study: Train a Child (*Chanokh*)," *Enrichment* journal, http://enrichmentjournal.ag.org/199902/090_train_a_child.cfm (accessed July 11, 2008), 1.

[23] Stan taught music at Bakersfield, Missouri, for one year. He had all the music from the 4th grade through high school. To have a school band he would go around those hills giving free lessons to kids. But because it was a small school, it wouldn't give him the equipment he needed. Stan told the school that if they didn't give him the equipment he needed, he was going to resign. In the meantime, the head chef at the Hickory Hills Country Club—with whom Stan had worked for several summers in college—heard Stan was having a hard time and offered him a job. He trained there and eventually became head chef at the Kansas City Club and later at the Advertising Executives Club. After two years he felt God wanted him to come to Springfield, so he did—without any promise of a job. He worked construction for a while, then soon got a job as banquet chef of what was then the Hilton and eventually became head chef. Later, he became the chef at the Assemblies of God General Council national office, but when they turned over the food service to an outside company in 2006, he began working in the warehouse at Gospel Publishing House, as he only had a few more years before retiring.

[24] In addition to not knowing their father was a conscientious objector or that he hitchhiked back and forth across the country during his college years, another story that wasn't told the children as they were growing up was the tale of their strong roots to the Azusa Street Revival and Upper Room Mission. At the time, the children never realized how strongly their own story connected to Pentecostal history. It wasn't until after he was married that Ed knew the whole story. "I wouldn't have known to even ask. It just wasn't something that came out."

[25] Mittelstadt and Paugh, 16–17. "Finally, Horton reiterates (as anyone with nonviolent sympathies) Jesus' paradigmatic role: 'I think that Jesus was certainly the model . . . that Jesus was here to give His life in order to save others, rather than to take life. And that there was a complete change here in the way that God was dealing with people, now that Jesus had come.' In this manner, Horton reminds Pentecostals of the radical nature of the kingdom. Jesus provides a model for a holistic approach to the value of human life as the embodiment of the 'good news of peace' (Acts 10:36).

"When questioned about the current attention given to pacifism in the Assemblies of God, Horton provides a poignant response: 'I stopped by the table there at SPS [Society for Pentecostal Studies] because they had information materials about pacifism. And I was surprised because that is the first time I have seen anything like that for all these years. And so I was surprised to see that there were still some who were encouraged about that. And I think there should be room for people who, by their own conscience, feel that they should be conscientious objectors.' [Horton refers to the growing influence of the Pentecostal Charismatic Peace Fellowship. See www.pcpf.org for further information.] In reflecting upon the current global crises, Horton recalls the difficulty of his own decision at the outbreak of World War II and calls for ongoing rigorous engagement of the Scriptures and our rich heritage on the question of the Christian's responsibility during a time of war" (Ibid., 17).

26 While working as an Evangel student at a nearby gas station on Glenstone Avenue, Stan, Jr., met a young lady who lived with her parents in the neighborhood and gassed up her car at the station regularly. Eventually after speaking with her week after week, he asked her out, and she said yes.

CHAPTER 6

Central Bible College Years

At the request of Ralph Riggs, then one of four assistant general superintendents of the Assemblies of God, Stanley Horton had arrived in Springfield in 1948. For the next thirty years, Horton taught Bible (specializing in Old Testament), Hebrew, Science, Theology, Apologetics, Archaeology, and other courses such as Religions of Mission Fields (1949) and Pentecostal Truths (1950) at CBI.[1] He also served as chair of the Bible Department, later called the Division for Biblical Education, for thirty years. For about three years, CBI did not have anyone able to teach the year of science the accrediting association required. So, having done his undergraduate degree in science, Horton prepared a semester of physical science and another of biological science. He enjoyed refreshing his knowledge of science and teaching the students. After Evangel College was established, CBI procured a couple of Evangel's teachers to come teach the required science courses, and Horton was able to focus solely on Bible and Hebrew.

Into All Truth

Within a year or two of arriving in Springfield, Horton had joined the Society of Biblical Literature and Exegesis[2] and was also writing study guides used in Sunday School workers' training courses. A few years after beginning to write for the *Adult Teacher*, he wrote *Into All Truth* and its Instructor's Guide

(1955). This book was chosen as the 1956 Workers' Training Month selection.[3] Each year the Assemblies of God published a different book for training Sunday School teachers across the country. Some years Horton would write the book; other years a different author would write the book, but Stanley would go do the training. For several years throughout the 1950s and 1960s—sometimes in the summer, sometimes during the school year while carrying a full load at CBI and needing to get up the next morning for 7:30 classes—Horton would go throughout Missouri and surrounding states for a week or so at a time to train teachers. These sessions would be held either at single churches or at a location where several churches had joined together. At one session in Tulsa, Oklahoma, thirty ministers from forty churches joined together to make the course a great success, and over one thousand people were enrolled for the course.[4]

Ray and Joyce Peters were members of Ferndale Assembly of God in Michigan in the late 1950s when Horton came through to conduct training sessions. Ray, who taught Sunday School faithfully for sixty-two years, still remembers the impact of this training upon their local church ministry. During Horton's one-week training session (or "Sunday School Convention" as Ray called it),[5] Horton told the teachers that to get the gospel out and reach people means more than just telling them they have to be saved. Believers should embrace families, get involved with them, go into their homes, see if the families have any needs, and if they do, meet them as best as possible. This might mean going over to someone's home and cutting the grass, playing with the kids, helping out single moms whose husbands may have left them, providing guidance for parenting or counseling for improving a parent-child relationship—whatever one had to do to help. After sixty years, Ray still remembers Dr. Horton's words: "You have to meet people where they are, relate to them on their level, and let them know you love them." In this teaching, Horton was showing his commitment to "friendship evangelism"—decades before it was a buzz word and in an era when many were still leery of anything that smacked of the "social gospel." In this, he was a man ahead of his time.

Horton authored additional materials for these training sessions, including *Panorama of the Bible* (1961), *Great Psalms* (1962), *Bible Prophecy* (1963), *Gospel of John* (1965), *The Promise of His Coming: A New Testament Study of the Second Coming of Christ* (later reissued as *Welcome Back, Jesus*), and *Desire Spiritual Gifts—Earnestly: A Consideration of First Corinthians 12–14* (1972). Regarding the impact of his writing, Gary B. McGee and E. J. Gitre point out that Horton became "an influential writer in the Assemblies of God at a time when only a few Pentecostals were professionally trained at the graduate level in theology and biblical languages. Theologically, he has had a profound influence on the course of Assemblies of God theology in the last five decades."[6]

Though a multitude of others have noted Horton's profound influence on Assemblies of God theology, true to his personality and his sense that it has been God's Spirit that has called and empowered him, Horton has characteristically downplayed his own importance. For example, one time after a discussion regarding what it took to be identified as a theologian, someone asked Horton, "Do you consider yourself to be a theologian?" In his humble, quiet way, one of the few who actually could have answered yes responded, "No, I consider myself to be a student of the Bible."[7]

Identifying Horton with the party line, some viewed his approach to theology as confessional, his writings tasting a bit like the last word on correct doctrine in the Assemblies of God. At times, however, Horton's theology did go against the flow, serving to keep the Assemblies of God out of the dispensationalist camp.[8] Those same colleagues who identified him with the party line, however, greatly valued that he got his doctorate in the field—considering him an anchor in the Movement, and one with the academic goods to teach. To them, the spirituality of this very charismatic and genuinely Pentecostal man was a breath of fresh air.

Horton's spirituality was also evident in the stability and continuity he provided to a young movement in the midst of change. As his colleague William Menzies notes:

> Over the years there have been many fads and ripples in the currents of this revival movement. But he has attempted to capture the heartbeat of the revival theologically and to put it in a biblical perspective. He has been able to highlight the things that are worthwhile and important in the midst of rapid changes. Stanley Horton represents solid evangelical theology and a strong commitment to the authority of Scripture and to the value of objective hermeneutics. And he has used that as a basis for providing an underpinning for developing a coherent Pentecostal theology. And over the years he has not wavered. His contribution as the premier Pentecostal theologian is recognized far beyond the contours of the Assemblies of God. People outside of our circles—in major Baptist denominations and elsewhere—immediately think of Stanley Horton when they think of Pentecostal theology, because he has articulated what is generally recognized as the heartbeat of that theology.[9]

Horton wrote a great deal on premillennial eschatology, including *Bible Prophecy* (1963); *The Promise of His Coming* and its reissue: *Welcome Back, Jesus* (1967); *It's Getting Late: A Practical Commentary on the Epistles to the Thessalonians* (1975); *The Ultimate Victory: An Exposition of the Book of Revelation* (1991); "The Last Things" and "Eschatology" in *Systematic Theology: A Pentecostal Perspective* (1994, 1995, 2007); *Bible Prophecy: Understanding Future Events* (1995); and *Our*

Destiny: Biblical Teachings on the Last Things (1996). However, in all this, he was "courageous enough to avoid dispensational terminology."[10] He wrote on this topic in such a way that "rather than being disruptive, he has been able to write books that have been well received and that have not caused controversy—when many others who might have tried such a thing," as Menzies notes with a chuckle, "would have run into a buzz saw!"[11]

Not surprisingly, Horton's interest in and contribution to the fields of prophecy and eschatology has generated "interesting" (and at times bizarre) comments and questions over the years. Several people have taken great pains to explain to him who they thought was the Antichrist. While in Israel in 1962, Horton met a messianic Jew who said he thought Richard Nixon was the Antichrist because, "If you put Richard Nixon into Hebrew letters, Rikard Nigson, that adds up to 666!" An Italian Pentecostal (also in Israel) told Horton that if one looks at what is written in Latin around the top wall of St. Peter's Cathedral in Rome, takes the letters Latin uses for numbers, and adds them up, "You get 666—so it has to be that the Pope's the Antichrist!"

But the most popular candidate for Antichrist for quite some time in Horton's younger years was Mussolini. Horton reminisces about how people thought Mussolini—even more so than Hitler—was going to be the Antichrist, because he was in Rome and had made a conquest of Ethiopia. The day after Mussolini died, however, Horton walked into the Biola College (then Bible Institute of Los Angeles) bookstore. And there, just inside the door, was a pile of books about four feet high with a sign that said, "Five cents each." Even now, over sixty years later, Horton gets a chuckle when he tells the punch line of this story, that the title of this book on sale for five cents was, *Is Mussolini the Anti-Christ?*

Beloved Professor

Horton's CBC years were full—day and night. In addition to the effort involved in his massive output of published works,

163

the time and care committed to raising his young family, and the spiritual expenditure of ministering on weekends, Horton carried a full teaching load. In spite of the heavy schedule, however, he loved his students and always made time for them. From his very early years at CBI, Horton communicated to his students his love for God, his hunger for the Spirit's work, and his appreciation for his Pentecostal heritage. His 1950 testimony in CBI's campus publication, *The Scroll*, highlighted the story of his parents and grandparents' salvation and infilling with the Holy Spirit in connection with the Azusa Street Revival. "I thank God for a home that was always 100 percent

Stanley Horton teaching Hebrew at CBI, *The Cup,* 1969 (used by permission from CBC)

Pentecostal," he wrote, "a home where hallelujahs were genuine and faith was real; where prayer and the word of God were loved, and where special family praise services in the middle of the living room floor followed frequent and wonderful answers to prayer."[12]

Stanley Horton, CBC, 1965 (used by permission from CBC)

Desiring not only that his students love God and hunger for the Spirit's work, he hoped also that they would "fall in love with the Word of God."[13] He would encourage them to go beyond a superficial study of the Scripture, to try to see what the Bible as a whole teaches, rather than taking a verse here and there to fit their own ideas. He especially enjoyed teaching Old Testament Survey to the freshmen. Most were not too familiar with the Old Testament, and it was a joy to "see the light come on" when they'd begin to realize there was something good and important in it. Even some students who had a Bible background were fortunate to have the "light" go on in Horton's classes. One such student was Dan Betzer. As Dan recalls:

> It was the fall of 1954. I had just graduated from high school and had enrolled at Central Bible Institute. . . . My first class, Mondays, Wednesdays and Fridays . . . was Old Testament Survey. The teacher was Dr. Stanley Horton. I had grown up in a full-gospel church that featured a top-flight Sunday School. I do not recall ever missing a Sunday in my grade school or junior high school days, so I thought I had a pretty good working knowledge of the Old Testament. Well, was I ever in for a shock!

Horton at his desk at CBC, *The Cup,* 1972 (used by permission from CBC)

Dr. Horton brought a wealth of information and insight into the Hebrew Scriptures that still serve me well this half-century later. Dr. Horton is a statesman in the world of academia. It was my good fortune to be influenced by his ministry early in life.[14]

Horton's influence served Betzer well. Dan went on to have one of the most well-known names in the Assemblies of God: as a pastor (First Assembly of God in Fort Myers, Florida, since 1987), author, television and radio host, recording artist, children's minister with his famous "Dan and Louie" ministry, district and national executive, and *Revivaltime* preacher for seventeen years.

Horton's classes also instilled a love for the Old Testament in the heart of a young man named Don Meyer, now president of Valley Forge Christian College:

I will never forget Dr. Stanley Horton. His influence on my life was profound. My love for the Old Testament was birthed in all of the classes I took from him at Central Bible College from 1964–1968. I think I took just about every course he taught. My first class was Pentateuch. I marveled at his knowledge of the scriptures. His gentle, godly manner with a deeply sensitive spirituality let me know one could be well educated and also a man of God. And as we asked him questions, he always shared a wise answer grounded in scripture. Much of my ministry has involved teaching and preaching from the Old Testament and I will always be grateful for what I received from him. These words don't begin to convey my love and admiration for Dr. Horton. He really has been one of my "heroes of the faith."[15]

Another student who had Horton for Old Testament Survey was Robert Cooley. Having taken this class in 1949, Cooley recalls:

I was impressed with Dr. Horton's understanding of the Old Testament text and appreciated his analysis of the biblical books and the biblical message. It was more than exposition of the text; it was the development of a theology and how the meaning of the Old Testament applied to life. This was long before OT theology courses. He was expressing his own academic experience (his experience in biblical theology from Harvard). His passion for a technical study of Scripture and a Pentecostal theology attached to it struck me. His was a passionate message. Most important was the impression [he] made [regarding] the value of . . . higher education.[16]

Horton's impact on this young scholar was profound. Cooley graduated from CBI in 1952 and went on to do a B.A. in biblical studies and archaeology (1955) and an M.A. in religious education (1957) at Wheaton before returning to teach and serve as dean of men at CBI in 1957. In 1957–58, he served on the graduate school committee with Horton and taught in the master's ("fifth year") program at CBI. The following year he did independent study with Horton to prepare for Hebrew study at Concordia. In the spring of 1959, Cooley went to Jordan to excavate—the first of a multitude of trips to the Middle East for archaeological research.[17] Cooley completed a Ph.D. in Hebrew studies and Near Eastern archaeology at New York University in 1963 and went on to teach and serve as academic dean at Evangel College. He began the Center for Archaeological Research at what was then Southwest Missouri State University (now MSU) in the fall of 1973, serving also as professor of anthropology, archaeology, and religious studies there until 1981, when he became the second president of Gordon-Conwell Theological Seminary.

Cooley's story is one among many from students whose lives Horton touched with his teaching and who went on to serve the

Lord in vital ministry posts around the world—teaching, preaching, pastoring, evangelizing, building churches and Bible colleges, being missionaries. One of the greatest desires of this son of the Azusa Street Revival was to instill vision in his students—particularly missionary vision. Horton would encourage these young people to believe that God had a place for them and would tell some, "I expect you to be my district superintendent or general superintendent one day!"

Many of Horton's students—appreciative of his humility, love for Jesus, commitment to the authority of God's Word, and blessed by various other things he did or taught that changed their lives—have kept in touch with him over the years, expressing that appreciation or even continuing to ask him theological questions relevant to their various ministries.[18] One of Horton's supreme blessings as he's gone around the world has been to find former students doing great things for God.

One of those students, Spencer Jones, was the first black student at CBC. He experienced Horton's gracious and persistent encouragement, and it changed his life.[19] Spencer had committed himself to God at the age of nine in his hometown of Poplar Bluff, Missouri, but had drifted from God. While serving in Vietnam in 1966, he met a Pentecostal believer who overflowed with the vibrant love of Jesus. Spencer wanted the kind of power that believer had! After this friend prayed with him, Spencer was filled with the Holy Spirit on July 13, 1967. This friend saw the call of God on his life and repeatedly urged him to go to Bible school. Finally, "to get the guy off my back," Spencer came to CBC in the fall of 1968.

By the following spring, however, he found himself in a cloud of discouragement. Just as Spencer was about to leave college, Dr. Horton happened to meet him one day outside his classroom. "I was just about to quit," Spencer recalls. "I would have, but he encouraged me day in and day out."[20] Not long afterward, Spencer felt God calling him to pastor in Chicago. The following year while still in school, he became the pastor of Tampa Street Assembly, a predominantly black church in Springfield where he had attended since his freshman year. After graduation in the spring of 1972, Spencer went to Chicago to serve as pastor of Southside Tabernacle Assembly of God, which has served as the training center for planting over thirty churches across America.[21] As Mittelstadt and Paugh point out in their *Heritage* article examining "The Social Conscience of Stanley Horton," Jones went on to impact

Spencer Jones, first African-American student at CBC, 1970 (*The Centralite*, January 23, 1970. Used with permission.)

the national Assemblies of God through his involvement in U.S. Missions, National Inner City Workers Conference, National Black Fellowship, Evangel University, and the Assemblies of God Executive Presbytery.

Throughout his years of ministry, Rev. Jones has not forgotten the role that Horton played during his college years: "I've always alluded to the fact that I am doing what I'm doing now because of his impact on my life. If he had not done that, I wouldn't be doing what I'm doing for God in the cities of America." As Horton mentored him, Jones now reflects that same "mentoring spirit" in his interactions with young ministers. He gives back by discerning "when people are going through some tough times whether it's in a racial way, whether it's in a financial way, whether it's whatever." As Horton was a resource for him, Jones makes himself available for encouragement, prayer, and attentive listening.[22]

Horton also provided similar guidance and godly mentoring to another young African-American student at CBC, now a Church of God in Christ bishop, Lemuel Thuston. Horton was a remarkable example of academic excellence, spiritual depth, and Christlike graciousness to Thuston. He also showed a personal interest in Thuston—encouraging him in his undergraduate work when the way was difficult, spurring him on to graduate work

Spencer Jones (far right) in a meeting with the AG Executive Presbytery and Evangel and CBC presidents along with black church leaders and black students from both schools. This meeting was the culmination of talks between Robert Harrison, Thurmon Faison, and the AG executives on ways the AG could "assist in a meaningful way in meeting the spiritual needs of the black community in America. The occasion gave the executives an opportunity to become better acquainted with the students and to learn their needs and any problems they might have in their educational program" (*The Centralite*, March 20, 1970, 3).

Seated (l to r): John January, Robert (Bob) Harrison, C. W. H. Scott, Martin B. Netzel, Kermit Reneau, T. E. Gannon, Gloria Grayson, G. Raymond Carlson, Veronica Tate, Philip Crouch (CBC president) Standing (l to r): J. Robert Ashcroft (Evangel College president), Frank Davis, Thomas F. Zimmerman, Jerry Lee, J. Philip Hogan, Bartlett Peterson, Bernadine Brown, Thurman Faison, Spencer Jones (Used with permission from CBC.)

at the new Assemblies of God Graduate School, guiding him in his Ancient Near Eastern History specialty at SMSU, connecting him with Spencer Jones to do an internship in Chicago's inner city, and providing Thuston with the "first and only" scholarship he ever received. "Horton was the inspiration for much of what I was able to accomplish and pursue academically and in other areas," he acknowledged gratefully. "I probably would not have finished if it was not for him."[23]

The scholarship Thuston received was due to Horton's concern about Assemblies of God churches moving out of the inner city to the suburbs and his hope that churches staying in the inner city could be multicultural. Toward this concern, Horton established the "Dr. Stanley Horton Scholarship," designated for a CBC student who planned to be involved in inner-city ministry. "I don't know of anyone in the Fellowship who had been that visionary at that time," the bishop recalls.

Horton first became keenly aware of social justice issues, such as poverty and race relations, as a result of his time in the New York City area in 1946–47 while studying at Biblical Seminary. "There wasn't a whole lot I could do besides give something, because I was teaching. I didn't write anything, but I

> "I always have been impressed by Stan Horton's concern for social justice. At moments he stood alone on this issue."
> —Stanley M. Burgess, editor of *The New International Dictionary of Pentecostal and Charismatic Movements*

would talk to people and just try to get them involved. Most white preachers weren't concerned with this too much at the time," Horton recalls. "Most of the California churches I had grown up in or attended were not multicultural. When my father had to leave the old Upper Room Mission and they tore down Chinatown to build the new railway station, we moved out to a building in Arroyo Seco in South Pasadena, and that church was multicultural. Even though the old Upper Room Mission was in Chinatown, that church wasn't multicultural."

Horton's support of multicultural churches found concrete fulfillment right in Springfield, Missouri. The year was 1972. Frank Davis, who had come to CBC in the fall of 1969 and his fiancé, Nancy, had recently graduated. Soon after, Nancy left for Ohio to work while Frank finished up some summer courses. Though the young couple had already decided to get married, Frank went in during that summer session to counsel with his professor Dr. Stanley Horton about interracial marriage.[24] When Frank asked Horton for his opinion on this issue, Horton told him that there was no biblical injunction against blacks and whites marrying; it was in society where the problem lay. "Just make sure you love one another," he said.

Frank's dad was a Missionary Baptist pastor who lived in North Carolina. When Frank called his dad and asked him to marry them, his father was reticent. On the heels of the 1960s, racial tension was high, and Frank's dad was concerned. "Frank, I really don't think I can marry you," he said. "It's going to cause racial tensions and could even cause riots." As Frank reflected later, "Maybe he thought I would give up; I'm not sure."

As Frank hung up, he was sad. "Who can I get to marry us?" he thought. Immediately Dr. Horton came to mind. Frank already had a good relationship with him. He had taken Horton for Old Testament and had enjoyed discussing a paper he wrote for that class, on intermarriage in the Old Testament. Another time, when Frank took Horton for Hebrew, they organized a "Hebrew choir." Since he'd been a music major in the secular college he'd attended previously, Frank directed the choir, and Horton played the piano while the group sang songs in Hebrew. "We'd do presentations at model Seders, for events and so on. We really enjoyed having Dr. Horton as a part of that Hebrew choir for the school," Frank remembers. He also appreciated Horton's teaching, his perspective on things, and the fact that he didn't hide his views on controversial issues. One example of this was Horton serving as faculty sponsor for a campus organization that

African-American student Spencer Jones began at CBC for black and minority students. "He was pretty sharp with the Scripture, and yet was a humble man," Frank remembers. "I trusted him, and I knew whatever he'd counsel me would be helpful."

Since Frank had already counseled with Dr. Horton in the past, as he pondered what to do, he decided to call him to request that he marry them. "I just felt Dr. Horton was the kind of man who would have married us," he recalls. Frank was getting ready to phone Horton when his dad called back and said, "I'll do the wedding."

Frank's father made the trip to Warren, Ohio, and married the couple. The Assemblies of God church there at that time would not allow Frank and Nancy to use their building for an interracial wedding. Nancy had even gone before the board at that church, and they "raked her over the coals." They just didn't feel the couple should get married. Nancy examined the possibility of one of the Presbyterian or Methodist churches allowing the use of their building for the wedding, but ultimately the couple decided to get married in the home of her oldest sister, Barbara, instead.

After they were married, Frank and Nancy moved back to Springfield, Missouri, where Frank had already been pastoring Tampa Assembly of God.[25] The years that followed the couple's time at CBC saw an increase in African-American students on campus. Frank attributes that increase to the work Spencer Jones was doing, and to the efforts of General Superintendent Thomas F. Zimmerman on racial issues during those years.

The Davises have been at Tampa Assembly close to thirty-eight years now. The church is a beautiful representation of a multicultural congregation—something still too unique and rare in American Pentecostal circles. Over the years, Frank has invited Dr. Horton to come and speak for the congregation. In addition, Horton's son Stan and daughter-in-law Linda are members there. Stan has served on the church board and as the church's missions coordinator. Every year the church has its Christmas banquet at the Elfindale Mansion in Springfield. Dr. Horton has been the speaker for that Christmas event—and on Father's Day—for the last three years. "He's really gotten better with age," says Frank. "He knows how to identify the practical side of the Word of God so anyone can understand what he's saying. He has always been the same man. I've appreciated his influence on students and yet his humbleness, his being up-front about things, and his lack of fear about what was going on in the culture. He's been such a wonderful blessing to us."

When reading through the book of well-wishings to Stanley Horton set down for him on his ninetieth birthday,[26] one cannot help but stand in awe at the touch of God's Spirit on his life and the blessing he has been to countless students through his teaching, preaching, and writing, but also through his encouragement, compassion, generosity, and graciousness.[27] In the same way that Stanley experienced a word of encouragement at just the right moment when he was a young teenager, he showered that same godly kindness onto the lives of those who would come after him.

One of those students was a young woman named Wanda Grace. She was a bright student, only eleven years old when she began high school. Not long after her sixteenth birthday and high school graduation, Wanda's father had a stroke. For the next year, she—along with her three younger siblings—ran the family farm. But the next summer, her mother was eager for Wanda to attend college. Though accepted and enrolled at Columbia University for engineering, that summer Wanda felt led by the Spirit to go to CBI. Toward the end of her freshman semester in November of 1954, Wanda's father, having suffered numerous other strokes from a brain tumor, passed away.

When Wanda returned to CBI at the end of November to turn in makeup tests to professors, quietly bearing the weight of her unbelievable grief, her visit to the Horton office in the boys' dorm provided great comfort. "Where does the soul really go?" she managed to ask him. She was encouraged by Horton's words from Scripture, that to be "absent from the body" is to "be present with the Lord." The following spring semester, when Evelyn wanted to sit in on a night class Stanley was teaching, the Hortons asked Wanda Grace to babysit their two young sons a couple of evenings each week. The Hortons showed great sensitivity to how difficult things were for Wanda and what pressure she was under. Their ongoing understanding and compassion for her circumstances touched this young teenager, and they became like family to her. Wanda later recounted how being allowed to be in a family situation like that even for a little while made a big difference.

The Hortons' friendship with Wanda has continued to this day. Wanda (who affectionately refers to Dr. Horton as "Papa") was privileged that spring of 1955 to have him come preach an Easter service at the church she attended in Fristoe, Missouri, and later preach a Sunday night service in Chicago where she was working. In recent years, Wanda and her husband, Hoyt Bostick, a physicist with a Ph.D. from Berkeley (who has greatly enjoyed his visits with his fellow scientist and Berkeley-ite) have opened their California home to "Papa" for extended visits in conjunction with various meetings or in preparation for one of Horton's many trips to teach overseas.

Another student of Horton's, Dr. William C. Williams, now of Vanguard University, was, as Horton recalls, one of his best Hebrew students. At the time Williams was at CBC, the school was offering only two years of Hebrew. Williams wanted more, so Horton tutored him for a third year. After CBC, Williams went on to serve God in ministry as a professor, writer, and translator of the Bible.

Another promising young student, William (Bill) Menzies, first became acquainted with Stanley Horton when Bill arrived for his freshman year at CBI in September 1949. Bill took Horton for several classes in the course of his three years and had great respect for this "young, shy faculty member," as he remembers him.[28] At one point during Bill's first year, he began to get that restless feeling; he just had to go out and change the world. After all, the Lord was coming soon! "I didn't think I could stay in Bible school long enough to finish," he remembers, "because the world needed me." Since Bill respected Horton so much, he chose to consult with him over others. He went into Horton's office and explained his predicament. Bill recounts: "I still remember that very quietly in his humble, gentle way, he said, 'Bill did God call you to CBI?' And I said yes. He said, 'Well, you know, if you were completing what God had called you to, and if the Lord came before you graduated, don't you think He'd be pleased with you?' And I paused, I remember, and it registered that I was doing what I should do." After all, as Horton pointed out, Jesus put His apostles through three and one-half years of training! So Bill decided to continue school.

Making it through that crisis moment at CBI as a young freshman thanks to the encouragement of Stanley Horton, Menzies not only graduated and served as commencement speaker but also went on to become "one of the most highly-regarded educators in the Assemblies of God."[29] This young man who just had to go out and change the world certainly did so in countless ways—yet more equipped to the task because of a levelheaded, Spirit-directed teacher, with whom he would eventually serve as a colleague and colaborer on numerous projects. Years later, in a volume commemorating Horton's lectures at Asia Pacific Theological Seminary and in the *Faces of Renewal* Festschriften in honor of Horton's seventieth birthday, Menzies would write of him:

> Early on, I recognized in this gentle man a rare combination of serious scholarship, spiritual passion, and Christlike humility. . . .

A special gift of Dr. Horton's is the ability to write plainly, simply, and directly. His humility comes across even in his style of writing. There is no pretense, no "gilding of the lily" to create special effects—just unvarnished proclamation of truth as he sees it. The transparency of his character is evidenced by the fact that his message has not wavered over the years. He profoundly encountered God as a young man and has lived consistently in the light of his personal Pentecostal experience. . . .

Few people have contributed as much to the world of Pentecostal scholarship as has Dr. Stanley Horton. . . . one who has not only articulated Pentecostal theology clearly and persuasively, but who has lived a transparently clear life that is an authentic reflection of his message."[30]

His quiet manner and practical wisdom helped me greatly in those formative years. His commitment to scholarship demonstrated to me that piety and intellect could—and should—go together. I have never forgotten the model this youthful instructor set before me.

Years later, I was asked to join the faculty of the school from which I had graduated. Stanley and I were now colleagues; in fact, we worked together for many years, first at Central Bible College and in more recent years at the Assemblies of God Theological Seminary (then known as the "Grad School"). During these years my dear friend time and again displayed not only patience in times of crisis, but restraint and tolerance. His spiritual and intellectual maturity continually served as a source of inspiration and as a corrective to my own temptation to impatience and judgment.[31]

Godly Colleagues

Because of Horton's faithful commitment to higher education and his remarkable number of years within the field, there were other former students of his who later became his colleagues at CBC and/or AGTS.[32] One young man, Charles Harris, was Horton's student at CBI, his pastor at Bethel Assembly, and his colleague at CBC. In all those contexts, Harris had the highest respect for Horton:

> Some of the students at CBC thought he was dull . . . but I've never in all my years understood that. Because if you cared for what the man was saying, you couldn't [help] but listen to and hang onto every word he was saying! He could give you not just the facts from Scripture, but . . . "soul food"! Gifts of the Spirit—words of wisdom, words of knowledge—would be implanted in your soul and bear fruit.
>
> We had men like Myer Pearlman and E. S. Williams, and they wrote those little booklets. I used to say, any book you see by these guys, buy it. Because there's soul food there. The brothers would say, we need this and that [theological booklet]. But few could write well. Then [along] comes Dr. Horton. And he could write. And he's given us more than booklets! He doesn't lose people with theological jargon, either. . . .
>
> I remember one time there was a guy who . . . had a too-great sense of his own self-importance, and he said to Dr. Horton, "My, I'll bet it must get quite wearisome writing on that low level." He thought Dr. Horton's writing wasn't sophisticated enough! He had no idea.[33]

Horton was blessed by many other godly colleagues over the years. Glenn Reed, called into ministry while in medical school, had a very friendly demeanor and was a great encourager to

Horton. Another colleague, Robert Cummings, was a Presbyterian seminary graduate who had been a missionary to India, specializing in translation. He had discovered there that he needed something more to meet people's needs. His wife received the baptism in the Holy Spirit, and then Robert recognized that the gift of tongues was not gibberish but real language sounds.[34] His messages at CBC on the meaning of the Cross were particularly inspirational to Horton.

Another colleague, Elmer E. Kirsch, had been Horton's student in 1949, his second year of teaching at CBI. Kirsch eventually became vice president for academics at CBC during the time Horton was a senior professor there. He remembers Horton as an "encouraging, helpful . . . excellent instructor" and always appreciated the fact that although he had advanced academic degrees, Horton did not "speak or teach in a way that left students behind. Students admired and deeply respected him." During Kirsch's years as vice president for academics, he recalls Horton as exhibiting the same "helpful and God-like character that I remembered from years earlier. I found him consistently to be the ideal of a warm Christian gentleman, always willing to . . . give support. His excellent scholarship and gifts in writing are a lasting legacy to the Evangelical Christian community."[35]

One longtime colleague, David Drake,[36] came to CBI in 1950 and was there until 1992, serving as registrar and teaching English composition, journalism, New Testament history, and literature. Having heard of Horton before, from his years in New York state, David appreciated Horton's messages in chapel and always loved to hear him speak. "I knew to go to him as my theology man," he recalls. "When I came across questions . . . he was my pillar and post. He knew the facts. He was a tremendous help to me."[37] David appreciated Horton's persistent and consistent learning and that he was "always digging in." He admired that Horton was a skillful writer, always producing important materials and

Stanley M. Horton, CBC, 1977
(Used with permission from CBC.)

on so many different levels. "You never had to be embarrassed or worry about his theology," David recalls. Horton was "not a loose gun. Not at all."

Impressed by Horton's knowledge and skills, David would ask him questions down through the years. But he was particularly struck by Horton's humility and graciousness:

He'd take the lowliest place, never seeking any recognition. He never got upset over things. He'd just ride it on out calmly. He never stood up to argue against things. He'd express his opinion, such as dealing with those in the Movement who were so skeptical of education. Stan proved that you can have both spirituality and academics. He never flaunted his education. He never tried to dominate or overly impress people. His spirit, that's what impressed. Stan never tooted his own horn. He never did and hasn't to this day. When he's called on he will respond, but he's not the kind that will step forward.

He was always compassionate, always courteous, always a gentleman, and not interested in trouble. I never had any problems with Stan. The dean would say who teaches what, and the registrar would say when and where. Stan would never question anything. "Wherever you want me is fine," he'd say. He was just very unusual in that way.

He was a fine spiritual leader. Even though he had so many things on his mind and so many things to do, he didn't seem to get frustrated about it. He just took it on its own time. He's been as solid as a rock.[38]

Spiritual Mentors

Horton's CBI/CBC years were a time of mentoring the younger generation and of working together with colleagues. At the same time, Horton accepted the mentoring and influence of others who greatly contributed to his own spiritual and personal growth.

In addition to Horton's Uncle Wesley Steelberg, another powerful spiritual influence during his life as a young professor was W. I. (William Irvin) Evans. Born in 1887 in Philadelphia, Evans was led to the Lord by his mother at age twelve. The family had been members of the Methodist Church, but after William's conversion, they began attending Christian and Missionary Alliance (CMA) services. In 1906, the same year as the Azusa Street Revival, Evans received the baptism in the Holy Spirit at a Torrey-Alexander campaign in Philadelphia in 1906. He was "so greatly moved upon that he shook like a leaf all during the sermon. After the service, he told his mother that he had experienced a marvelous infilling of the Holy Spirit."[39] Feeling a call to Christian service, Evans enrolled in the four-year course at the CMA Training Institute in Nyack, New York.[40] Following three more years of schooling, at Richmond University in Virginia, Evans pastored in Virginia, New York, and New Jersey. He began teaching at Bethel Bible Training School in 1916, where in 1923 he succeeded Frank Boyd as principal and gained a reputation as a "deeply spiritual man." While there he continued his studies, this time by taking courses at Biblical Seminary in New York. In 1929, Bethel merged with CBI, and Evans became CBI's third principal. After the school added a fourth year (and "seminary" to its name) in 1948, Evans became dean of CBIS when Bartlett Peterson[41] was made president.

Horton felt fortunate to serve under Evans. The dean's spiritual leadership in early morning faculty prayers (a half hour each morning before chapel) and in the chapel service that followed was, according to Horton, "inspired by the Holy Spirit." He had quite an influence on the young instructor[42] because of his encouragement of prayer and of the gifts of the Spirit, as well as his example of being a lifelong learner and judging Pentecostal experience in light of the Scriptures.

From time to time the Holy Spirit would move over the student body in an unusual way. The chapel service, which was the first hour, would be extended, sometimes even into the evening. One service Horton remembers as being a powerful move of God with a tremendous time of repentance was when Adele Flower Dalton[43] preached. When chapel would go long like this, Dean Evans would refer to that time as the "classroom of the Holy Spirit." Evans consistently encouraged both students and faculty to respond to the Spirit's leading. Horton tells how on one occasion the Spirit brought a few words to his mind and impressed upon him to speak them to the students: "The president and the dean were about to close the service, but I stepped forward and asked permission to

CBI faculty, 1953. l to r: W. I. Evans, Stanley M. Horton, J. Roswell Flower, Frank Boyd, Richard Brown (Used with permission from CBC.)

speak. When I went to the pulpit it felt like stepping into an electric field. Words the Spirit continued to give me poured out of my mouth. Students began running forward and falling on their knees. Some received the baptism in the Spirit at that time."

On another occasion a student made a statement that was obviously unscriptural and shocked both students and faculty. The Spirit gave Horton a word of wisdom that cooled everyone down and also helped the student. During another extended chapel, a student from the nearby Baptist Bible College had come into the service and started to argue with the students. One of the students brought the young man to Horton, who asked what his questions or objections were. Horton recalls: "He would make a statement. I would look to the Lord, and the Spirit would bring a Scripture to my mind. I would open my Bible, hand it to him and say, 'Here, read this.' He would then make another statement. Again, I would open my Bible, and ask him to read. This continued for quite a few minutes. Finally, he said, 'I guess it is in the Bible.'"

These were powerful times that lasted as long as W. I. Evans was dean. On Saturday, May 15, 1954, Evans went to be with the Lord at age sixty-seven, following his second stroke. On the night before his passing, the dean attended a worship service presented by the Revelation classes and based on the Book of Revelation.

Many remarked about the exuberance with which he praised and worshipped the Lord at that service. . . . The scripture and songs used during the service expressed the joys of being with Jesus and our Dean was in ecstasy throughout the service. Little did anyone realize that he would be with his Savior the next morning.[44]

The loss of Evans was a severe blow to the CBI family. His spiritual influence as a mentor profoundly shaped future generations. Carl Brumbeck, both a historian and an Evans protégé,

183

looked upon Evans as "chiefly responsible for the school's spiritual well-being. Until his death in 1954, his presence impacted the character of the institution tremendously."[45]

Biblical Archaeology Society

In addition to Old Testament and Hebrew, another of Horton's academic passions during his CBC years was biblical archaeology. His love for this field of study was closely connected to its usefulness in proving the validity of Scripture "to the many skeptics . . . attempting to disprove the Bible."[46] In 1959, when Dean Bob Cooley returned from a four-month Israel trip where he participated in an archaeological dig in Dothan with the Wheaton Archaeological Expedition, he and Horton worked together to begin the Biblical Archaeology Society of CBI. The organization was later referred to as *Athar Quadeemi* (Hebrew for "my ancient site" or "my place of antiquity") and eventually just the Archaeology Club.[47] Student interest in archaeology had been rising over the previous years, and after Cooley's expedition, students wanted to get more involved in its methodological aspects.

The monthly meetings—open to all students for the modest dues of fifty cents per year—served to stimulate "student interest and participation in archaeology,"[48] enlighten students about archaeological developments in the field, and help them appreciate its apologetic usefulness. Cooley went back to the Middle East in 1960 and 1964, and brought back purchased artifacts from each of those trips, building a significant collection in Evans Hall at CBC.[49] Horton went to Israel on a 1962 tour and eventually became faculty sponsor for the group after Cooley left CBC. Student members, Horton as the sponsor,[50] fellow faculty,[51] or outside guests[52] would present at the monthly meetings; often presenters would show films or slides on relevant topics such as archaeological excavation techniques and reconstruction of broken artifacts. The group was small but saw a steady annual growth.

Also as a result of his interest in Old Testament and Jewish Studies and his desire to make that meaningful to students, Horton conducted a number of Passover Seders on campus. One time, about a hundred people gathered for the service. Horton showed slides from the Samaritan Passover he had witnessed while in Israel (with actual animal sacrifice) and lectured on the meaning of Passover and the elements of the Seder meal. "This is the biggest event that we have had this year," said the young Gary B. McGee, president of the organization that year. McGee played the part of the "youngest son" who asked the "four questions" during the Seder.[53]

Throughout the 1960s, the *Athar Quadeemi* club, in addition to classes and chapel services, served as a context where CBC students learned about their Jewish roots and ways to improve Jewish-Christian relations. In 1964, Rabbi Solomon S. Bernard, director of the Department of Interreligious Cooperation of the

Stanley Horton conducting a Passover Seder at CBC, 1966 for a hundred in attendance at the Archaeology Club. At left is his wife Evelyn; at right is Gary B. McGee, playing the part of the "young son" who asked the traditional "four questions" of the Seder. (*The Centralite*, April 7, 1966)

Anti-Defamation League of B'nai B'rith came from New York City and lectured at CBI, Drury University, and Evangel College, particularly on the significance of the Jewish holidays. Rabbi Myron M. Meyer of Temple Israel in St. Joseph, Missouri, visited CBC March 14–15, 1966. He spoke in the morning chapel service on "The Synagogue—Its Character and History," to a theology class on "The Jewish Doctrine of Man," and to a music class on "Music in the Bible." Rabbi Meyer's campus lectures were conducted under the auspices of the Jewish Chautauqua Society, to foster a better understanding of Jews and Judaism through education. Also with the Chautauqua Society, Rabbi William J. Gordon, director of the B'nai B'rith Hillel Foundation at Washington University in St. Louis came to CBC on March 21, 1968. He spoke in chapel on "What Every Christian Should Know About Judaism," in Hebrew classes on the sacrifice of Isaac, and in a typology class on "Jewish Sources."[54]

The club was inactive for several years. Eventually, it was revived by a Jewish believer, Philip Rothberg, who also wrote several articles for *The Centralite* on messianic topics such as the *brit milah* (circumcision), keeping *kashrut* (kosher), the Jubilee year, and the festivals of Hanukkah and Purim. Every other Monday evening the group would show slides, and Horton would lead a discussion. His daughter, Faith, then a student at CBC, served as secretary-treasurer of the group during this time.[55]

Bible Lands Tour

In 1962, Dr. Joseph Free of Wheaton College invited Horton to accompany him for a Holy Land tour and archaeological dig that would last four months. This was the first of his many international trips. Free, Horton, R. Laird Harris of Covenant College in St. Louis, and Bastiaan van Elderen of Calvin College in Grand Rapids, Michigan, were slated to serve that spring on the faculty of the Near East School of Archaeological and Biblical Studies in Jerusalem in conjunction with the tour.[56]

To raise enough money for his fare and expenses, Horton spoke in a number of churches across the country. CBC did not have a sabbatical program at that time, so he took a leave of absence for the spring semester. The following is Horton's own account of their journey:

On March 7, we took a ship out of New York City (the *S.S. Independence*) and went through a storm with thirty-foot waves. I didn't get seasick, but the smell when I left my stateroom was terrible. We stopped for a day at one of the Canary Islands and then at Madeira and Gibraltar. I was surprised to find how the British had hollowed out portions of the great rock at Gibraltar, using various portions of the rock for rooms, offices, and storage. From there we went to Naples and visited the Isle of Capri and then Pompeii at the foot of Mount Vesuvius. It was interesting to see the excavations, the restored homes, patios, pools, and even some paintings. The street corners had stepping stones to cross the street, and ruts made by chariot wheels were between them. The stepping-stones were necessary because people threw garbage into the streets for the dogs and pigs. (No wonder foot washing was important in Bible times!)

We took a bus to Rome, enjoying the Amalfi-Sorrento drive along the coast and having lunch in an eleventh-century monastery. Then we visited the Catacombs, the Coliseum, St. Peter's Basilica, the Vatican Library, and the Sistine Chapel. Brother Thomas Brubaker and I found the local assembly, and the pastor took us around and showed us some more of the sights of Rome.

After a week in Rome we flew to Cairo, visited the step pyramid, the Great Pyramids and the Sphinx, the old city, and the alabaster mosque. Inside the Great Pyramid I was amazed to see how the great blocks of stone were polished so they fitted together too tightly for the thinnest piece of paper to go between them. Then we took the train south up the Nile to Luxor where we visited Karnak (the ruins of ancient Thebes) and crossed the Nile to see the Valley of the Kings. We went down into many large tombs that had been robbed in ancient times but still had paintings on the walls with colors kept bright by the extreme desert dryness. I never felt so thirsty in my life before that. We went into King Tut's tomb, which was smaller and had only his outer wooden sarcophagus in it. Back in Cairo we went through a large room full of artifacts taken from his tomb. His innermost coffin was solid gold. The next one was gold plated and covered with diamonds and other jewels.

While in Luxor we did no tours during the middle of the day. So another man and I went into the town and found a Coptic church. A fifteen-year-old boy wanted

Stanley Horton (front, center) in Egypt at the Pyramids in 1962
Bible Lands Tour

to practice his English on us, so he took us through the church. There were about ten million Coptic Christians in Egypt at that time. They have a cross tattooed on their wrist, partly to discourage intermarriage and partly to make sure they get a Christian burial. He asked me why I didn't have a cross on my wrist. I told him we didn't do that in my country, but I had Christ in my heart. He said he had Christ in his heart too. (Later I heard there had been quite a revival in some of the Coptic Sunday Schools). Then I opened the Arabic Bible chained to the pulpit and asked him to read from Acts chapter 2. I tried to explain to him about the baptism in the Holy Spirit, but it became too much for his English. He said, "Why don't you speak Arabic?" I could not, but have prayed that someone else would come and teach him.

From Egypt we flew to Lebanon and went inland to see some great temples built by a Roman emperor who was trying to restore paganism. Then we took a bus to Damascus where we walked on the street called Straight [Acts 9:11] and saw the house where tradition says the Apostle Paul received his sight. We visited the ruins of cities on the east side of the Jordan and then visited Mount Nebo, Petra and Solomon's seaport. At Petra we had to ride a horse in through the narrow canyon into the city. Each horse was led by one of the Arab villagers there. We went up on both sides of the city to see. On one side there was an Edomite altar, and on the other side there was an enormous building cut into the rock. At Solomon's seaport the Jordanian King had commissioned one of his army officers to take us into that area. He also made arrangements for us to take a trip down the Gulf of Akaba into Saudi Arabia. And on the beach there I picked up seashells and brought them back with me. After those two full weeks in Arab Bible lands, we finally came to Jerusalem where we spent ten days. I swam in the Mediterranean, the Sea of Galilee, the Dead Sea, and the Red Sea on that trip!

At Bethlehem we visited the Church of the Nativity (built over the traditional place of Jesus' birth) and spent an evening with a Christian family who owned written records dating back for over a thousand years. They said according to tradition their ancestors were converted in Samaria by Philip. The Church of the Nativity was like so many Catholic shrines with all kinds of art and other things covering up everything so it didn't give a good idea of what it was like in NT days. I thought it was interesting that the main entrance was partly blocked up so that men on horseback couldn't ride in.

I taught a class on the Mount of Olives and visited many Holy Land sites, proceeding on to Dothan to take part in archaeological excavations. Classes were to begin on the Mount of Olives on April 9 at the Jerusalem school. In the spring term students spent half of their time on the dig in Dothan and the other half in class work and field trips. We found a Canaanite clan tomb used before 1400 BC. Every burial was accompanied by a jar of food, a jar of oil, and a lamp. One of the oil lamps we found was sevenfold, with seven lights in one lamp. This meant something to me because Dr. Pfeiffer at Harvard had said that one of the reasons he believed Moses did not write the Pentateuch was because it mentions a seven-fold lamp. In his opinion Moses' day was too early for seven-fold lamps. He seemed to think there had to be an evolutionary development of lamps. But this lamp definitely came before Moses' time.

We also visited Amman and had an interview with King Hussein of Jordan in his palace. After Dr. Free left I stayed three weeks longer; I visited an Assemblies of God church in west Jerusalem, went to more archaeological sites, stayed in a kosher hotel in Tiberias, half-way up the hill from the Sea of Galilee, took a boat trip across the Sea, walked north to the ruins of Capernaum, walked south to archaeological sites, and then took a bus to Nazareth. Walking through a pine grove on the hill north of Nazareth, I felt the presence of the Lord and thought surely Jesus as a boy had walked on that hill.

From Haifa I took a one-class ship to New York. On a Sunday during our journey, I had the privilege of preaching in the ship's chapel. As we were going through the Azores, the captain died of a heart attack. The first mate had been with him for years and was too broken up to conduct the burial at sea that the captain had requested. So at dawn I had the privilege of reading the ceremony and leading the crew in prayer. Then the captain, wrapped in sailcloth and weighted with anchor chain was slipped off a board into the ocean. I had opportunities to talk to people on board about the Lord after that. [57]

Society for Pentecostal Studies

Eight years after Horton's Israel trip, the Society for Pentecostal Studies (SPS), an "organization of scholars dedicated to providing a forum of discussion for all academic disciplines as a spiritual service to the kingdom of God,"[58] was formed—thanks to the collaborative efforts of Dr. Horace Ward (Church of God), Dr. Vinson Synan[59] (Pentecostal Holiness), and Dr. William (Bill) Menzies (Assemblies of God). Bill served as its first president in 1970 and editor of its journal, *Pneuma*; he recalls that at the Assemblies of God seminary where he was then on faculty, there was little interest in SPS. Few were supportive at all, but—as Bill recalls—"Stan Horton [still then at CBC] quietly helped me and encouraged me when very few people did. He went out of his way to attend the meetings and participate. He saw the value of such a society, and in that, he was ahead of his time. He quietly put his oar in and was helpful. I think he had a spirit of helpfulness!"[60]

A usually meek and gentle man, Horton's support for SPS in its pioneer days was a display of "courage and conviction," in Menzies' opinion. He notes:

> When many were reluctant to identify with an unproven association, Dr. Horton lent his influence and strength to this new creative venture, for in it he saw a possible forum wherein serious biblical and theological study might begin to flourish in the various charismatic traditions. Believing that sincere Christian scholarship should never be insular or suspicious, and that good teaching must be firmly based on serious biblical study, he has always encouraged those who would continue to study, learn, and grow, both academically and pastorally. With his gentle personality, completely free of anti-intellectualism and authoritarianism, he has steadfastly encouraged a scholarly and spiritually sensitive exploration for truth. [61]

Joining SPS shortly after it was formed, Horton served as president from 1979–80. That year the society met at Oral Roberts University in Tulsa, Oklahoma, and Horton's presidential speech was published in *Pneuma*.[62] Even now at age ninety-two, Horton attends the annual meetings and enjoys the interaction with other Pentecostal scholars and scholars of Pentecostalism. The year he served as first vice president, he was in charge of getting the program together for the annual meeting (then in Vancouver, Canada). He was able to get several Canadians to take part in the program, including theologian Roger Stronstad.[63] During their time together, Horton

"If we would please God, let our hearts and our mouths be so full of praise to God and encouragement to our brother, that we will have no room for either criticism or pride or anything else that might hinder the work of God."—Horton ("Criticism," *The Scroll*, February 4, 1954, 2)

encouraged Stronstad to continue to write, which he has done, making significant contributions to Pentecostal literature.[64] He also persuaded Dennis Bennett—an Episcopal priest and pioneer leader in the Charismatic movement from Seattle with whom Horton had often corresponded—to be the SPS banquet speaker that year. He also became closely acquainted with Vinson Synan and other leaders of various Pentecostal and Charismatic groups.

In 1988 at the annual SPS meeting, Horton was presented with a Festschrift entitled *Faces of Renewal: Studies in Honor of Stanley M. Horton.* The book contained chapters from sixteen contributors and a brief biographical sketch by the book's editors, Paul Elbert and William Menzies.

Perhaps Horton's most significant contribution to SPS was the role he played in racial healing during the years of the society's formation. His conversations at that time with Bishop Ithiel Clemons and later with Leonard Lovett (at that time dean of C. H. Mason Seminary in Atlanta)[65] became a link that helped bring Church of God in Christ (COGIC) brothers and sisters on board. Clemons had relayed the story of his interaction with Horton to his young associate Lemuel Thuston, who eventually became a COGIC bishop. As Thuston recalls:

COGIC had been very reluctant to participate in SPS. They had been excluded from the Pentecostal Fellowship of North America (PFNA) and had experienced a series of other disappointing wounds. Dr. Horton collaborated with Bishop Ithiel Clemons and was very aggressive in convincing him to come on board with them for SPS. This connection between Horton and Clemons became the link for much of the Pentecostal scholarly world in terms of SPS. COGIC probably would not have been open to the risk of that kind of united collaboration had it not been for Stanley Horton. This is a very underrated and I think obscured chapter in the history of Pentecostalism in our time. This connection has been so essential in having a comprehensive and a very inclusive feature in SPS—the likes of which, on an organizational level, has not been revisited since Azusa! With SPS, there has been a sustained organizational level of inclusivity. And Horton was largely responsible.[66]

The End of a Season

On April 14, 1973, the local newspaper[67] noted Dr. Horton's quarter-century as a faculty member at CBC. The college honored him for his service at a faculty dinner in the school's cafeteria. In the fall of that year, Dr. Horton was to begin teaching part-time in the Bible Department of the new Assemblies of God Graduate School while retaining his association with CBC for the rest of his teaching hours. The year prior, Horton—now father of a twenty-six-, twenty-four-, and seventeen-year old—had authored *Desire Spiritual Gifts* and *Tongues and Prophecy*; he had written the *Adult Teacher* for twenty-one years, and was working on a book on the Holy Spirit. Who would have thought that some of his most productive years for the Kingdom lay ahead?

Endnotes

[1] When Horton joined the faculty, CBI was CBIS, Central Bible Institute and Seminary. It became CBC after 1965. (See chapter 7 for a description of the evolution of Assemblies of God graduate and seminary education.)

[2] "Horton Extended Honor," *The Scroll*, February 18, 1949, 1. "Reverend Stanley M. Horton, instructor of Hebrew and Old Testament, has been extended the honor of membership into the Society of Biblical Literature

and Exegesis. This society has been in existence since 1880 and includes Bible Professors from outstanding Universities such as Princeton and Johns Hopkins. They publish a monthly magazine which edits research articles from the Bible and Biblical Manuscripts by outstanding Biblical Professors."

3   "Instructor Horton Teaches Own Book in Local Assembly," *The Central-ite*, February 29, 1956, 1.

4   Ibid.

5   Ray Peters, interview by author, May 17, 2008.

6   G. B. McGee and E. J. Gitre, "Horton, Stanley Monroe," in *The New International Dictionary of Pentecostal and Charismatic Movements*, rev. and expanded, ed. Stanley M. Burgess and Eduard M. van der Maas (Grand Rapids: Zondervan, 2003), 772–3.

7   As told to Dilla Dawson (Research and Development, GPH), e-mail to author, July 31, 2008.

8   See chapter 8, "Man of Theological Integrity," by Ray Gannon.

9   William Menzies, interview by author, April 10, 2008.

10 Ibid.

11 Ibid.

12 "My Testimony," *The Scroll*, May 19, 1950, 2, 5.

13 One of the ways Horton encouraged students to fall in love with the Word of God was through his column, "Kwiz Korner," in CBI's campus publication (printed October 16, 1954, through January 13, 1955). Instructor Horton would ask questions for which students would have to give the Scripture references. Students were to submit their answers, and then the correct answers would be printed in the next issue along with the names of the students who turned in the most "nearly correct" answers. For example:

What's My Name? (1) I was the champion long-distance runner of the Bible (Elijah, I Kings 18:46); (2) I slew a king with a wet blanket (Hazael, II Kings 8:15); (3) My chief interest was the Department of Agriculture (Uzziah, II Chron. 26:10); (4) I blamed women for the drunkenness of my time (Amos, Amos 4:1); (5) I was encouraged by being told that the worst was yet to come (Jeremiah, Jer. 12:5). (Oct. 29, 1954, 2.)

Identify with the correct city: (1) Dates; (2) The best carpenters; (3) A seaport outside Palestine built by an Israelite; (4) The chief Canaanite chariot city; (5) Mentioned more times in the Bible than any other city except Jerusalem.

Give Scripture References for: (1) A universal tendency toward the type of divagation exhibited by the genus *Ovis*. (Isa. 53:6); (2) Desiccated skeletal remains (Ezek. 37:1, 2); (3) Cracked reservoirs for the most universal solvent (Jer. 2:13); (4) Utterance from a flaming heart (Ps. 39:3); (5) Headgear representing deliverance (Eph. 6:17) (November 12, 1954, p. 2, the first column with Horton's picture)

Name the proper people, places and books by unscrambling (Nov. 20, 1954, p. 2): 1. Nebanshrice 2. Udonsmice 3. Urolsnice 4. Odarmice 5. Ekdelzhmice 6. Odaalice 7. Hhtrice 8. Ondaamice 9. Utilsvice 10. Talcseessice. Answers (Dec. 11, 1954): Sennacherib, Nicodemus, Cornelius, Mordecai, Melchizedek, Laodicea, Cherith, Macedonia, Leviticus, Ecclesiastes

Other issues included naming rivers and hometowns of famous biblical characters.

[14] Dan Betzer, e-mail to author, June 9, 2008. Dan's father had a barbershop at 1717 North Grant in Springfield, where Horton used to get his hair cut. On page four of CBI's campus publication *The Scroll* for October 16, 1954, there is a picture of Dan's father and an ad for the Betzer Barber Shop, just under Horton's "Kwiz Korner" column.

[15] Don Meyer, e-mail to author, September 2, 2008.

[16] Robert Cooley, interview by author, August 28, 2008.

[17] See *The Centralite* article "Cooley Leaves on Tour; Spittler Interim Dean," February 18, 1959. Cooley encouraged Horton to go on the 1962 Holy Lands Expedition tour.

[18] Horton's ninetieth birthday book is full of letters from former students now in ministry, as well as family, friends, and a multitude of colleagues with whom he has worked over the decades. The impact of his life and ministry has extended literally around the globe and to a multitude of generations, even in his own lifetime. See Appendix B for a selection of those letters.

[19] The following story is taken from my interview of Spencer Jones as well as from the testimony portion of his sermon at Bethel Assembly in Springfield, Missouri, on August 3, 2008. See also "Spencer Jones Pastors Tampa St. Assembly," *The Centralite*, January 23, 1970, 1. This article reported that Jones planned to enter inner-city ministry after graduating. It recounted his popularity on campus and his friendliness, greeting new students "with a Christian smile, handshake, and 'How are you, brother?'" and said that "his Christian love radiates as he recognizes all believers as his Christian brothers or sisters." Spencer saw his life's purpose as living and working for Jesus. "Anytime I can find work to do for Him, I want to do it with my whole heart," he said. Spencer was elected vice president of the student body for the 1971–72 school year. See "A New Look in . . . Student Government," *The Centralite*, May 26, 1971.

[20] Mittelstadt and Paugh, in "The Social Conscience of Stanley Horton," *Heritage,* January 2009, 17, 18, describe in detail Horton's life-changing interaction with Jones that played a vital role in racial healing at CBC at that time. In researching their article, Mittelstadt interviewed Rev. Spencer Jones on November 9, 2007, in Springfield, MO. The audio version of this interview is available through the Flower Pentecostal Heritage Center.

[21] Southside Tabernacle was founded by Rev. Thurman Faison.

[22] Mittelstadt and Paugh, 18.

[23] Bishop Lemuel Thuston, telephone interview by author, September 12, 2008.

24 There had been a survey on campus years earlier about interracial marriage; some professors and students were very against it. Frank had not taken the survey.

25 Frank began as pastor at Tampa Assembly in 1971.

26 See Appendix B of this book.

27 One grateful CBC student waxed poetic in his admiration by crafting the following acronym for "DR. STANLEY HORTON," engraving it for him on a brass plate: **D**evoted, **R**espected; **S**criptural, **T**eacher, **A**nointed, **N**oteworthy, **L**oving & **E**nriched; **Y**ielded to **H**oliness, **O**bedience, **R**ighteous, **T**ruths in **O**ld and **N**ew Testaments.

28 "Though Horton was not demonstrative and certainly not assertive, on spiritual occasions at high tides in the chapel, when we had revival meetings and there was a sense of God's presence, I remember times when he would stand to speak with tremendous authority and power in the chapel. This seemed so out of character compared to his normal mode of behavior. But he was very sensitive to the leading of the Spirit. God used him in remarkable ways at critical times. At those times, a courage that was latent manifested itself. One such time, in 1950 or so, a new translation of the Bible came out, the Lamsa version that Oral Roberts unwittingly had promoted, that purported to be a translation from Aramaic and all. Brother Horton went through it and got up in chapel one day and said, 'This is Nestorian Christianity; this is not a new revelation. This is actually a representation of ancient heresies.' Out of his knowledge he was able to show that translation for what it truly was" (William W. Menzies, interview by author, April 10, 2008).

29 "Doris Dresselhaus Menzies Autobiography," Flower Pentecostal Heritage Center, http://ifphcseeninprint.wordpress.com/2008/01/23doris-dresselhaus-menzies-autobiography/ (accessed June 7, 2008). Menzies did an M.A. at Wheaton and a Ph.D. in religion at the University of Iowa (1968), pastored two churches, returned to CBI in 1958 as professor of Bible and church history, authored numerous books, including the Assemblies of God history *Anointed to Serve* (1971), and traveled the world while holding teaching and administrative positions at Evangel College (now Evangel University), the Assemblies of God Graduate School (now Assemblies of God Theological Seminary), California Theological Seminary in Fresno, California, and Far East Advanced School of Theology in the Philippines (now Asia Pacific Theological Seminary). Menzies was cofounder and first president of the Society for Pentecostal Studies (1970–1971). One of his nine books, he coauthored with Horton, *Bible Doctrines: A Pentecostal Perspective* (GPH, 1993).

30 Stanley Horton, *Reflections of an Early Pentecostal* (Baguio City, Philippines: APTS Press, 2001), i-ii.

31 Paul Elbert and William Menzies, eds., *Faces of Renewal: Studies in Honor of Stanley M. Horton Presented on His 70th Birthday* (Peabody, MA: Hendrickson Pubs., 1988), xviii.

[32] Such as Ben Aker and Gary B. McGee. Horton joined Aker, McGee, and John Katter for the fall 1977 faculty lecture series on the inerrancy of Scripture. (See "Biblical Inerrancy Examined: Fall Faculty Lecture Series, Nov. 14, 15, 16, 17," *The Centralite,* November 10, 1977, 1.) Horton's topic was "Inerrancy: The Role of Archaeology." This article commented on Horton's concern that there were some with credentials with the Assemblies of God—even those with considerable influence—who had taken a "soft view on inerrancy." Horton warned that church history had shown "that a soft view is the first step toward a weak view, and finally a denial of the Scriptures." Examining the archaeological aspect of inerrancy, Horton urged his listeners to remember that the Bible does claim inerrancy and, second, that many problems in the biblical text have been fully resolved through archaeological discoveries. Therefore, rather than throwing out inerrancy due to problems, the church just needs to "hold steady. The answer will come." The hope of those conducting the series was that "a more healthy and correct view of the Scriptures [w]ould be held by all who will come with open hearts and minds and a teachable spirit."

Another CBC faculty series Horton participated in was the fall faculty series on sin (Nov. 12–15, 1974) taught by Horton, Thomas Harrison, Gerald Flokstra, and Ronald Wright. Horton's part in the series was on the origin of sin. See *The Centralite,* November 14, 1974, 1.

[33] Charles Harris, interview by author, May 6, 2008.

[34] When Robert began to seek the Lord to baptize him, he felt God was asking him to give up his tennis. Then after he received the baptism, the Lord told him he could have his tennis back! God wanted him, not the tennis. But for Robert now, tennis was no longer a means of getting attention to himself or letting the world around him know who he was. For him now, Christ, not tennis, was central. In later years when he was at CBI, when new students would brag about their tennis, older students would match them up with Cummings and Frank Boyd. (Boyd at age fifty won the college tennis championship when he went for further studies at a California college.) The new students would begin their game looking very confident; they looked quite different when they left the court in total defeat!

[35] Elmer Kirsch, e-mail to author, October 6, 2008.

[36] See picture of David Drake, *The Scroll,* September 23, 1950, 3, with other faculty. Drake was also elected to *Who's Who in Education.* (See, *The Centralite,* December 14, 1955, 1.)

[37] David Drake, interview by author, May 6, 2008.

[38] Ibid.

[39] "The Evans Story," *The Cup,* Springfield, MO: Central Bible Institute, 1955, 18. Evans often would tell students at CBI that during the time he was seeking for the baptism in the Holy Spirit, he experienced a marvelous spiritual blessing that involved "holy laughter." He would often reach a certain spiritual experience where he would laugh and laugh.

One of his teachers told him that he was "stuck" on a particular plateau spiritually and he needed to "go higher" to receive the Baptism with the evidence of tongues. Eventually, he did. (See also Horton, *Reflections*, 51.)

[40] "Nyack's founder is widely recognized as one of the foremost figures in the American missionary movement. Dr. A. B. Simpson resigned a prestigious New York City pastorate to develop an interdenominational fellowship devoted to serving unreached people. Simpson's view was shared by a wide group of men and women, including mainline church leaders, laborers, and theological scholars. This ever-growing alliance was bound together by a desire to inspire the church to fulfill its Great Commission of world evangelization.

"An important step towards making their vision a reality was the founding of a training school for missionaries (the Missionary Training Institute), the first Bible college in North America. This school was the forerunner of Nyack College. Thus, from its beginning in New York City in 1882, Nyack has been devoted to the concept of education as preparation for service. After purchasing 28 acres on a picturesque hillside, in 1897 the school moved to the village of South Nyack, New York. In 1956 the school was renamed Nyack Missionary College and then in 1972 changed to Nyack College to reflect the total program of the college. . . .

"The Christian and Missionary Alliance, the sponsoring denomination, was formed in 1887 when Simpson, while starting the Missionary Training Institute, founded two organizations, the Christian Alliance (an interdenominational fellowship of Christians dedicated to experiencing the deeper Christian life) and the Evangelical Missionary Alliance (a missionary sending organization). The two merged in 1897 and became The Christian and Missionary Alliance. The Christian and Missionary Alliance recognizes ATS as the denomination's official seminary in the United States." "Nyack History," Nyack College, http://www.nyackcollege.edu/content/NyackHistory (accessed June 28, 2008).

[41] Peterson was the first full-time president of CBI. Under his ten-year service as president, the school underwent significant changes, including accreditation and the adding of a fourth and fifth year. In addition, a school for the deaf was launched and the flight school—begun in 1946 so students could take the gospel worldwide—continued to grow, as did enrollment. Upon Peterson's resignation in 1958 to serve as secretary-treasurer of the Southern Missouri District Council, Rev. J. Robert Ashcroft became the president of both CBI and Evangel College. *A Souvenir Album Commemorating Seventy Years of Excellence* (Central Bible College, Springfield, MO: Western Printing, 1992), 5, 7. In March of 1958, J. Robert Ashcroft was nominated to serve as president of both CBI and Evangel (*The Centralite*, March 15, 1958, 1). Five years later, on July 1, 1963, the schools separated because both colleges were growing and the "combined program [was] too heavy for one president" (*The Centralite*, December 12, 1962, 1).

[42] However, Evans' views about the Assemblies of God beginning a liberal arts school (Evangel) did not sway Horton. Evans was not in favor of anything that might take away from the purpose of CBC. "If they want a liberal arts college, let them put it over there [pointing toward where Evangel is today]," he said. Horton, however, believed it was good to have a Christian liberal arts college and was glad his sons attended there.

[43] Adele Flower Dalton was the daughter of J. Roswell Flower and Alice Reynolds Flower. She served in Latin America as a missionary, returning to the U.S. in the 1950s where she married Roy Dalton. The two then served together as missionaries in Spain, until Roy's death only ten years after they were married. Adele served in Spain for another eight years and then returned to the United States to work in the editorial office of the Department of Foreign Missions. She worked tirelessly to promote missions, authored numerous articles and was instrumental in preserving historical missionary records (see McGee, *People of the Spirit*, 415–7). The Flower Pentecostal Heritage Center was named in honor of the J. Roswell Flower family.

[44] "W. I. Evans With Jesus," *The Scroll*, May 20, 1954, 1. On the day Evans died, he rose early "for his daily devotions as usual . . . went back to bed and went into a coma and did not regain consciousness" (Ibid.). CBI's 1955 yearbook was dedicated to Dean Evans. It contained a poem by L. B. Richardson, general presbyter, a recounting of Evans' life story.

[45] *Central Bible College, Springfield, Missouri: A Souvenir Album Commemorating Seventy Years of Excellence.* Western Printing, 1992, 2.

[46] "Diggers Dig Horton," *The Centralite*, January 24, 1964, 1.

[47] See CBC's yearbook, *The Cup*, 1966–68,1970.

[48] "Athar Quadeemi," *The Cup*, 1966, 124. See also "Athar Quadeemi," *The Cup*, 1967, 83.

[49] Although previous artifacts were purchased from antiquities shops, following the 1964 excavations, Cooley brought back forty crates from the Dothan dig (artifacts Jordan let him have as part of the license agreement). All of that collection is now at Wheaton in the Dothan exhibition.

[50] After Horton's 1962 trip to Israel, he would show slides to the group from his "Bible Lands Tour," specifically the archaeological dig at Dothan where Dean Cooley had earlier worked with the Wheaton expedition. Upon his return, Horton spoke to the club on the method of pottery dating and familiarized them with artifacts from Cooley's collection.

[51] Horton, Cooley, Donald Johns, and Russ Spittler presented at this first symposium, coinciding with the one hundredth anniversary of the publication of Darwin's *Origin of Species*; they met to discuss Christian "versus contemporary views of science regarding Genesis 1–11." "First Symposium Discusses Creation," *The Centralite*, November 18, 1959, 3.

[52] For "Archaeology Day" in 1972, Dr. R. L. Harris was the speaker. He was one of the founding faculty members of Covenant Theological Seminary. Harris was not only a teacher and a church leader, but an

author as well. His works include *Introductory Hebrew Grammar*, the prize-winning *Inspiration and Canonicity of the Bible*, and *Your Bible and Man—God's Eternal Creation*. He was editor of *The Theological Wordbook of the Old Testament* and a contributing editor to the *Zondervan Pictorial Encyclopedia of the Bible*, and has written articles for the *Wycliffe Bible Commentary* and *Expositor's Bible*. He also served as chairman of the Committee on Bible Translation that produced the New International Version of the Bible.

[53] This event was on April 5, 1966. The four questions are as follows: (1) Why is it that on all other nights during the year we eat either bread or *matzah*, but on this night we eat only *matzah*? (2) Why is it that on all other nights we eat all kinds of herbs, but on this night we eat only bitter herbs? (3) Why is it that on all other nights we do not dip our herbs even once, but on this night we dip them twice? (4) Why is it that on all other nights we eat either sitting or reclining, but on this night we eat in a reclining position? Subsequent Seders were held, as for a while this became an "annual event." *Athar Quadeemi* members were admitted free; all other participants paid fifty cents. ("Horton Conducts 'Model Seder'," *The Centralite*, March 3, 1967, 1.)

[54] Several articles in *The Centralite* reported on these important meetings: "New York Rabbi To Speak Here," February 5, 1964, 1; "Rabbi Bernard Visits Campus," March 6, 1964, 1; "Jewish Rabbi Speaks on Jewish Concepts," March 19, 1966, 1; and "Gordon To Speak On Jewish Theme," March 15, 1968, 1.

[55] "Archaeology Club Comes Back," *The Centralite*, December 17, 1974, 3.

[56] See "Dr. Stanley Horton: CBI Professor To Bible Lands As a Teacher," *Springfield* (Missouri) *Daily News*, February 17, 1962, 2, and "Dr. Horton to Join Near East Faculty," *The Centralite*, February 14, 1962, 1.

[57] Stanley M. Horton, original written response to "Life Chronicles" questions provided to him by author, 2006.

[58] "The purpose of the society is to stimulate, encourage, recognize, and publicize the work of Pentecostal and charismatic scholars; to study the implications of Pentecostal theology in relation to other academic disciplines, seeking a Pentecostal world-and-life view; and to support fully, to the extent appropriate for an academic society, the statement of purposes of the World Pentecostal Fellowship.

"The society publishes *Pneuma: The Journal of the Society for Pentecostal Studies* and an occasional newsletter. The society also holds an annual meeting for members and friends. Each meeting includes plenary sessions related to a particular theme, numerous paper sessions organized by discipline-based Interest Groups, worship, fellowship, and networking opportunities." "Mission & Goals," Society for Pentecostal Studies, http://sps-usa.org/about/home.htm#HISTORY (accessed April 11, 2008).

[59] Former general secretary, Pentecostal Holiness; dean emeritus and Distinguished Professor of Church History, Regent University School of Divinity.

[60] William Menzies, interview by author, April 10, 2008.

[61] Elbert and Menzies, eds., *Faces of Renewal*, xix.

[62] See Stanley M. Horton, "Presidential Address," *Pneuma*, vol. 3 (Spring 1981): 48–53. Horton's other SPS writings include "The Old Testament Foundations of the Pentecostal Faith," *Pneuma*, vol. 1 (Spring 1979): 21–30 (recorded, SPS, Atlanta, Georgia, 1976); "Eschatology and the Holy Spirit" (SPS—1992): A1–A22; "Response to Douglas Jacobsen's 'Knowing the Doctrines of Pentecostals: The Scholastic Theology of the Assemblies of God, 1930–1955'" (presented at the twenty-third annual meeting of SPS, Guadalajara, Mexico, November 11–13, 1993. This response was not included in the published SPS book for 1993). The SPS archives are at the David du Plessis Center, Fuller Theological Seminary.

[63] A Canadian Pentecostal Bible scholar and theologian, Stronstad is associate professor in Bible and theology at Summit Pacific College (formerly Western Pentecostal Bible College) in Abbotsford, British Columbia.

[64] See Stronstad's *The Charismatic Theology of St. Luke* (1984), *Spirit, Scripture and Theology* (1995), and *The Prophethood of All Believers* (1999).

[65] See Leonard Lovett, *Kingdom Beyond Color: Re-Examining the Phenomenon of Racism* (Philadelphia: Xlibris Corporation, 2007).

[66] Lemuel Thuston, telephone interview by author, September 12, 2008. Lemuel's father told him that when he had wanted to come to CBC in the late 1930s, early 1940s, that CBI was segregated. He had wanted to attend CBI but was "not allowed." Thuston told his son that he "knew it was because he was black" and that this reality at CBI was "common knowledge" at the time. Though no formal proof exists that this was official policy at CBI at the time, a handful of other African-Americans have relayed a similar story. The elder Thuston eventually went to a Nazarene school, where he became that school's first African-American graduate in 1954. It was Lemuel's knowledge of Horton's cooperative interaction with Clemons that played a role in Lemuel coming to Springfield (known for its history of racism), to CBC, and to an Assemblies of God school. Horton's behavior gave him hope for CBC's future.

[67] "25-Year Mark: CBC Honors Dr. Horton," *Springfield* (Missouri) *Daily News*, April 14, 1973, 9. At the time of his twenty-five year mark, Horton's teaching assignment included Theology V, Hebrew, Pentateuch, Man's Biological Environment, Isaiah, and the Minor Prophets. Before that time he had also taught Pentecostal Truths, History of Missions, New Testament Survey, Apologetics, and Science.

CHAPTER 7

"Now Therefore Give Me This Mountain"

Horton's Pentecostal journey continued full speed ahead throughout the end of the twentieth century and on into the twenty-first with the strength and spiritual fervor of Caleb.[1] He continued to teach, preach, write, travel, undertake major editorial projects, and serve as a godly example to his family and all those around him—always with a sense that he was simply doing what the Spirit was leading him to do.

Assemblies of God Graduate Education: The Early Years

Throughout that journey, Horton found himself squarely within the context of Assemblies of God higher education. As a Pentecostal college and seminary student from 1933 to 1945, a multidegreed Assemblies of God educator from 1945 to his formal retirement in 1991, and an author who contributed prolifically to Christian educational resources on many levels into the twenty-first century, Horton's faithful commitment to the cause of "knowledge on fire"[2] helped at key points to propel the evolution of Assemblies of God higher education.[3]

With the outpouring of the Holy Spirit and the founding of the General Council of the Assemblies of God in 1914, the early founders were so convinced of the Lord's imminent return that their greatest priority was to evangelize and win souls. The thought was, "You only need the Bible to do that; you don't need an education." Yet on the other hand, some of the founding principles of the Assemblies of God involved training for ministry. So there was a tension between evangelism and education that went back to the early years. In the 1930s, it began to focus on general education.

The evolution of Assemblies of God *graduate* education began in the mid-1940s when missionary Maynard Ketcham and missions educator Noel Perkin began to talk about the need for a master's degree program and graduate studies for missionaries. This move served as a great impetus behind CBI being named Central Bible Institute and Seminary (CBIS), so it would be ready to offer that kind of education. The emergence of the chaplaincy as a result of World War II was also a factor. An important part of Assemblies of God organizational programatics resulted from the fact that the government required a seminary education for the chaplaincy. This was also the era when Sunday Schools were developing, and the value of education was beginning to be appreciated by the Assemblies of God community.

By 1948 when Stanley Horton arrived in Springfield, the school had taken on the name CBIS, added a fourth year, and planned to add a fifth year for the M.A. degree. At this time, the school was looking for accreditation with the American Association of Bible Colleges (now Association for Biblical Higher Education). However, the accreditation organization made CBI discontinue the M.A. program because they said the graduate program would have to have a different faculty than the undergraduate program, and the name was changed back to CBI.

In the late 1950s, Stanley Horton, Robert Cooley, and Donald Johns served on the graduate school committee, which began to provide direction to a graduate program. The years 1957 and 1958 saw the establishment of the so-called fifth year program, with the vision that the graduate program at CBI would grow into a seminary program on that campus.

Horton, Cooley, and others taught the graduate courses to twenty or thirty students at a time,[4] some of whom achieved significant academic and ministry careers. William C. Williams, now professor of Old Testament at Vanguard University, consulted on a number of Bible translations and contributed to reference works such as *The New International Dictionary of Old Testament Theology and Exegesis* and *The Evangelical Dictionary of Biblical Theology*. Another student, George W. Westlake, Jr., went on to do a doctorate and pastored various churches, including Sheffield Family Life Center in Kansas City, Missouri—a superb model of an inner-city, intercultural church. George reflects on the impact Horton had on his life, from his CBC days to the present:

Having accepted Jesus Christ at age 19, and serving in the Korean War in the US Army from age 20 to 22, where I had started preaching and teaching the Bible, going to Bible College in 1954 I had the idea I pretty well "knew it all." After only one day in Brother Horton's Old Testament Survey class I was very aware I knew nothing at all.

I had been connected in the army with a lot of Christians who thought in order to be a good, anointed preacher you could have no formal education. When I heard Brother Horton teach, then preach in chapel, I knew they were wrong.

He became one of the three strongest influences in my life because of his brilliant scholarship, his anointing, and his humble attitude. I took every class he taught, including three years of Hebrew, even though there were only two of us in the third year, and was able to sit under his teaching at the graduate level.

I had the privilege of substituting for his first year Hebrew class on Thursdays while he took the train to Kansas City to complete his doctorate, and I also read the draft of his doctoral dissertation.

He taught me to challenge traditional biblical inter-pretation, to be a careful exegete of Scripture, to never stop learning, and to continue to depend on God for the anointing of the Holy Spirit. He is one of the two individ-uals whom I felt God wanted me to follow as examples. Because of that influence I have had the privilege of not only pastoring for over 50 years, but teaching in our own Bible College and on the adjunct faculty of many of our Seminaries and Bible Colleges in the US, Europe and Asia. The impact he made on my life is beyond measure.

It has been my privilege to have him as a friend and confidant for all these years as he has ministered in the various churches I have pastored. The most recent: he taught a class on Isaiah in our church Bible College at age 90 and ministered in our church of 5,000. He is still as sharp as ever. I am so grateful to God He allowed me to sit at the feet of this great man of God.[5]

Another student, Larry Hurtado, was doing his B.A. during most of the time that the fifth year program was underway and took some master's classes in the spring of 1965 before the pro-gram was no longer offered. Horton was his professor between 1961 and 1965 and his colleague from 1966 to 1968 when he taught at CBC. Eventually Larry went on to become professor of New Testament language, literature, and theology at Edinburgh University Divinity School and director of the Centre for the Study of Christian Origins. Also head of the School of Divinity, he has authored eight books and numerous articles. Reminiscing about being Horton's student and colleague, he recalls Horton's sense of humor as one of his finest qualities:

Dr. Horton . . . was a gentle, very honorable, and very learned member of the faculty. . . . I do remember him fondly. One thing in particular that wasn't so often noticed, I think, was his quiet but lively sense of humor. I recall one sleepy afternoon in late spring in a course on the OT (he wasn't actually a very lively lecturer, and that plus the warm weather and afternoon time slot combined to put many in the class in a drowsy state). I just caught him making the note that there were two Hebrew words used in the Genesis creation account, the one meaning to fashion or build, and the other meaning to create (more from scratch). He then observed with a twinkle in his eye, "So, then the account says that God 'created' (Heb. *bara*) man, but 'built' (Heb. *asa*) woman!"

On another occasion, at a CBC homecoming buffet dinner, he was standing in a line with former students. One of them had obviously led a life of generous eating, and his former classmate was teasing him about piling too much food on his plate, warning him about calories. The corpulent guy responded, "I'll take authority over those calories. I could do that couldn't I, Dr. Horton?" And Horton responded slyly, "Yes, if you fast and pray."[6]

Because of financial stresses, the graduate program at CBC eventually ended at the close of the 1964–65 school year, to the great disappointment of the students and those professors who had served on the committee as an integral part of the program. However, the conversation regarding ongoing graduate studies even separate from CBI/CBC lingered.

AGGS/AGTS

In 1958 C. C. Burnett became national education secretary at Assemblies of God headquarters, succeeding J. Robert Ashcroft, both of whom had been at CBI.[7] In his role, Burnett desired to revive the graduate school idea but to make it separate from CBI because at the time the relationship between CBI and Evangel

College was not the best. Burnett played a key role in the establishment of the Assemblies of God Graduate School (AGGS), as it was called then—and not only to just "do it," but rather to do it well. Horton remembers that when the first committee was formed to discuss the graduate school, many there wanted to "do it as cheaply as possible. But C. C. Burnett came along and said, 'No, let's do this right.' "[8]

Thus, in 1971, ten years after the concept of a "graduate school of theology and missions [had been] originally approved by The General Council in Session at Portland Oregon,"[9] the General Presbytery,

> after lengthy and prayerful consideration . . . accepted a recommendation presented jointly by the Executive Presbytery and the Board of Education that the school be implemented. On May 18, 1972, the General Presbytery adopted a preliminary constitution and bylaws and authorized establishing the school at the International Headquarters in Springfield, Missouri. The school was incorporated in December 1972.[10]

On September 4, 1973, AGGS held its first classes.[11] This was an exciting time, because the conversation about the role of advanced education to prepare ministers had been decades long, and now the vision was coming to fruition.[12] Such a venture would require not only scholars trained in the field, but those with a full commitment to Pentecostal spirituality. Horton taught at the graduate school only part-time for its first five years because of his ongoing full-time duties at CBC. As one of the earliest and most-degreed scholars in the Assemblies of God, however, he was a logical pick by 1978 to serve on the graduate faculty full-time, even though he was then sixty-two years old—an age that only those who did not know him might consider "near retirement."[13]

With "nostalgic qualms" about leaving CBC after having served a thirty-year tenure there and beloved by both students and colleagues, Horton's decision to transition to full-time faculty at the grad school did not come frivolously but rather only "after weeks of prayerful contemplation."[14] When the school wrote, asking him to serve in a full-time capacity, they requested a response within two weeks, but his "strong affirmative" came six weeks after the initial request. He resigned from CBC in May of 1978 though he continued to teach one class per semester there through 1984. "This was a time of diligently trusting God and seeking the leading of the Holy Spirit," he recalls. "I continued to have good relationships with family and friends, and things did become a littler easier financially, too. God was giving me a settled confidence in Him and in the ministry He was laying out before me. I felt it was important to take every opportunity for service to the Lord. God kept me in Springfield. Several times I had had offers to go elsewhere at a much higher salary, but God would never give me a green light to do so." Clearly, God had prepared Horton for the contribution he could make to and through Assemblies of God graduate education and wanted him right in the midst of that process.

For some in the Assemblies of God, that process was fraught with peril. But others saw God's hand in using graduate education to more effectively prepare servant leaders to reach a changing world. In the years leading up to the establishment of the graduate school, the debate had been focused around whether it should be called a "seminary" or a "graduate school." The term "seminary" was emotional at that time; it brought up fears about intellectualism and the danger of education as the Assemblies of God contrasted itself to the liberal mainline denominations.[15] "Graduate school," according to Cooley, refers more to an academic theology, whereas the focus of a "seminary" is on practical theology, i.e., education for ministry. As Cooley notes, "They really should have been more fearful of 'graduate school' because that was more of an academic, liberal arts focus. Seminary takes the academic theology and contextualizes it in a more practical way."[16]

C. C. Burnett had to struggle with that tension between academic theology and application for ministry. Thus, at the time, the school pursued accreditation with North Central Association rather than with the Association of Theological Schools (ATS). When the school became the Assemblies of God Theological Seminary (AGTS) in August of 1984, they then pursued ATS accreditation and—as Cooley put it—"got the school on the right track."

In this way, the evolution of Assemblies of God graduate and seminary education—all of which provided the underpinning for the establishment of AGTS—involved several steps: (1) the expression of missionaries, the rise of the chaplaincy, and the rise of Sunday Schools, which all provided a foundation in the 1940s; (2) the founding of Evangel College in 1955; (3) the graduate program at CBI in the late 1950s; (4) the establishment of AGGS in 1972; and (5) the name change to AGTS in 1984.

Stanley Horton stood squarely in the midst of this entire evolution. The fact that he was a product of the early Pentecostal revival did not deter him from education. In fact, it was his obedience to the leading of the Spirit and the call of God to pursue higher education that resulted in his arrival at CBIS in the 1940s not only with an undergraduate degree, but also two graduate degrees from Harvard and Gordon. More than anyone else— and even more so as he pursued his doctoral degree in the mid-1950s—Horton became for students during that time a model of advanced education and an example of one who did not lose his faith in the process. He was able to demonstrate a unique and powerful blending of education, spirituality, and leadership to a generation of younger students such as William Menzies, Anthony Palma, Russ Spittler,[17] William MacDonald, Donald Johns, and Gary B. McGee, who in the 1950s and 1960s pursued their doctoral studies and went on to contribute to the life of the church in education. In Cooley's words, "Dr. Horton was a central figure, a workman in that entire process."

What the Bible Says about the Holy Spirit

In 1975, during the time when Horton was teaching part-time at the graduate school and was still full-time at CBC, he traveled to Brussels, Belgium, at the invitation of George Flattery,

Stanley Horton on the set of the PTL Club with Jim Bakker and Henry Harrison, 1977, to discuss his new book, *What the Bible Says about the Holy Spirit*

then with International Correspondence Institute (ICI), now Global University, to write a study guide on the Holy Spirit for a college-level course.[18] ICI was bringing scholars to live and work at their new building in Brussels in order to write full-time, for they needed courses completed quickly. Flattery told Horton he could use any text he wanted for his study guide on the Holy Spirit. But since Horton had been gathering material for three years to write a book on the Holy Spirit, he told Flattery that if he would let him come for the twelve weeks of summer, he would put the book manuscript together *and* write the study guide as well. The text was finished within seven weeks, and the study guide five weeks later. Horton totaled twelve to fourteen hours of work each day to complete the text. After supper, he and the other writers would go out in the nearby King's Woods for a bit of reprieve and then come back and write some more. He enjoyed the additional ministry of teaching classes, but "the highlight of his trip was the way the Spirit of God worked in the services in which he spoke and the moving of the Spirit throughout Belgium and Germany."[19]

Being a product of the Azusa Street Revival and having witnessed the sweet move of God's Spirit throughout his life, it is no surprise that Horton since his earliest days as a student of the Word[20] has had such a strong interest in pneumatology.[21] But writing *What the Bible Says about the Holy Spirit* was no mere academic exercise for Horton. As the saying goes, "The best sermon is the one you've lived," and the pages of this book clearly resonate the Pentecostal life of the author. The book was to serve as a biblical theology of the Holy Spirit, to help people grasp the biblical background of the Pentecostal movement and how Pentecostals need to apply what the Bible says about the Holy Spirit and His gifts. This volume, Horton's first major book, has played a role in the spread of Pentecostalism in developing countries, helping disciple those who have come into a Pentecostal experience. He looks back on this book as his most meaningful written contribution, since it has been translated into more languages than any of his other works[22] and has been in use for decades.

The Complete Biblical Library and Full Life Study Bible Projects

After completing *What the Bible Says about the Holy Spirit*, Horton was asked to write a number of other books—some at the request of Berean School of the Bible and others as a part of the Complete Biblical Library project, a sort of amplified version of a set of commentaries. Ralph Harris, head of the Assemblies of God Church School Literature Department during the time Horton was working for them, had the original idea for the project and was then joined by Thoralf Gilbrant from Sweden[23] to put it together. The first commentary was published in 1987, and the final one in 2000. They asked Horton to write several of them[24] and also serve as national editor, which involved approving all that was written and distributed in the United States. His commentary on the Book of Acts for the project was published in 1987, followed by Matthew and 1 & 2 Thessalonians in 1989, Revelation in 1990, Isaiah in 1995, Genesis in 1996, portions of 2 Kings in 1997, Daniel and Amos in 1999, and Lamentations in 2000.

During this same time—while maintaining his teaching load at the Assemblies of God Theological Seminary—Horton worked with Don Stamps on the *Full Life Study Bible*, later called the *Life in the Spirit Study Bible* (published in 1990, 1992, and 2003), editing all of Stamps' notes, writing some notes himself, and preparing the Greek and Hebrew word studies throughout the text. Stamps was a Nazarene missionary in Brazil who had received the baptism in the Holy Spirit and was, as a result, dismissed from the Nazarenes. While still in Brazil, he saw the desperate need for sound teaching and wanted to work on a study Bible to address that need. Acquainted with the Assemblies of God, he had learned more about them there and had connected with Loren Triplett, head of the Division of Foreign Missions (now Assemblies of God World Missions). As Bill Menzies, who served as cochairman for the project, recalls:

> Loren stopped me in the hall one day at headquarters and said, "Bill, I'd like you to work with Don Stamps and help him get this project together." Don wanted to put notes in a study Bible for the Portuguese people. Now I didn't believe in putting notes in a Bible, but Don had reported that the Brazilians wouldn't buy any books except for the Bible. Well, Stan as the premier theologian in the Assemblies of God became the chairman . . . .We worked on that for a number of years. We spent a lot of time, met in various venues with different people. He was always a joy to work with. He always had positive things to say. He was nonconfrontational. He would try to steer things in a

Horton holding a copy of the Fire Bible (Life in the Spirit Study Bible in Portuguese). With Horton, Ronaldo DeSouza, Manager of CPAD: Casa Publicadora das Assembléias de Deus in Brazil

gentle way. He wasn't adamant or demanding this or that. He was a congenial colleague to work with. Don Stamps certainly respected Dr. Horton's wisdom.[25]

The team worked throughout the 1980s. Initially Stamps would send his comments to Dr. Horton to edit, but eventually those involved with the project brought Stamps to Springfield so the team could more rapidly complete their work. They published the New Testament notes first and then the notes for the Old Testament. But Don's cancer was getting worse. He died two weeks after he finished writing the comments on Malachi.

Next to his book on the Holy Spirit, Horton viewed this project as his most rewarding and significant contribution: translated into many other languages—and dubbed the "Fire Bible"—it has been used around the world.

"Literally Global"

Horton's impact on the lives of students in his classes and readers of his works stretches from 1945 to the present; it is now multigenerational, multinational, and multilingual. Those he has taught have taught others who have transmitted their knowledge and passion for the Word to yet others. Sitting one day in the city of Dushanbe, the capital of Tajikistan, Dr. Mark Hausfeld, Assemblies of God World Missions Central Eurasia area director, was visiting with an AGWM missionary who had had Stanley Horton as a professor. They were discussing Old Testament theological truths they had both learned from Horton at AGTS back in 1982. Similar scenes have been repeated dozens if not hundreds of times across the globe, as the impact of Horton's influence through his teaching and writing has been "literally global."[26]

"Already Legendary"

One student of Horton's now affecting others around the world is Dr. Craig Keener. Prolific author,[27] Bible scholar, and professor of New Testament at Palmer Theological Seminary, Keener first took Hebrew at CBC with Stanley Horton in the fall of 1978.

He recalls how he and his classmates were all "in awe" of Horton because he was "already legendary by then, including his love for the Lord and His church, and the great labors of love he expended on his research."[28] Craig remembers how Horton was patient with him as a student of Hebrew at CBC, and then again with his "only slightly improved" Hebrew when Craig was

Horton with AGWM Central Eurasia Area Director Mark Hausfeld and his wife Lynda after Hausfeld's inaugural address as the 2007–08 J. Philip Hogan Professor of World Missions, AGTS, October 10, 2007 a graduate student at AGTS from 1984 to 1987. In a letter to Horton in celebration of his professor's ninetieth birthday, Keener wrote of his appreciation for the doors that Horton's "humble service of scholarship" opened for "other generations of Pentecostal scholars first trained or interested in institutions he served so faithfully."[29] Regarding Keener's once-challenging Hebrew, he assured his esteemed professor: "You will be happy to know that at the doctoral level, reading nine pages a week of Qumran texts in Hebrew, I did finally begin to get Hebrew. Now I often read Hebrew biblical narrative in my devotions, so your labor on me did not prove in vain! (I hesitate to confess that Hebrew poetry is still a bit rough for me.)"[30]

"Preserving Me for Ministry"

Horton's influence was not limited to the classroom or the textbook. Some of his greatest lessons and spiritual gifts to others were in the most unexpected places. Phil Duncan, pastor of King's Chapel in Springfield, Missouri, also sat under Horton's teaching at AGTS, graduating in 1979. Throughout Duncan's years of pastoring, Horton's books greatly blessed him, but the effect of Horton's teaching and writing were eclipsed by a profound act of kindness Horton showed Pastor Duncan in 2000:

You waited through a line of at least 400 people (men half your age gave up) during the visitation the night before my son's funeral. You pulled me aside for just a few seconds to share what you understood from your studies about what the Bible says about suicide. There is nothing anyone could have said that was as important for me to hear as what you said, and there is no one who could have said it with . . . your credibility. As I think of your willingness to go through what you did just to share those things with me my eyes fill with tears again.

You were instrumental in preparing me for ministry and perhaps, that night, instrumental in preserving me for ministry.[31]

"He Made All the Difference"

A recurring theme when one speaks with Horton's students is that they would not be doing what they are doing today were it not for him. Some moment of clarity shared, some instance of kindness shown, some word of encouragement given—all of these things done in the graciousness of Christ and the sweetness of a Spirit-led life made all the difference. John Houser, senior chaplain at Kirkland Correctional Institution in Columbia, South Carolina, was one such individual.

> Arriving in Springfield . . . to attend the Assemblies of God Graduate School . . . turned out to be more of a daunting challenge than I could have imagined. . . . Many . . . could not understand or comprehend the call God had placed upon my life. I was not . . . a seasoned . . . minister. I was just a businessman called to serve Christ. . . . [But] there were those professors who went out of their way to encourage me. . . . One such professor was Dr. Stanley M. Horton. He . . . even helped me meet and even exceed the educational standards for graduate study. . . . Dr. Horton . . . made Old Testament Theology, Biblical Aramaic, and Hebrew understandable to one who came from the mountains of Appalachia. During the past 22 years, Barbara and I have served in both the military chaplaincy and institutional chaplaincy. Literally thousands of men and women have accepted Christ, recommitted their lives to the Lord, were baptized in the Holy Spirit, and received sound Christian teaching. This ministry to which God called me may never have come to fruition without the encouragement and nurture of great men of God such as Dr. Stanley M. Horton.[32]

Sometimes it was the little things Horton did that made all the difference. As Dennis Jameson, academic vice president at Trinity Western University, recalls:

> It is with great fondness that my wife and I remember our days at AGGS and my favorite professor. Fresh out of college we arrived at the "Grad School" the day that Dr. Burnett passed into glory. We quickly learned from fellow students that your courses were among the best and I enrolled in every one that I could fit into my schedule. As newlyweds and first semester students from California, Marlene and I felt quite alone in Springfield. On one [occasion] eating out in a cavernous cafeteria, we saw you and your wife walk into the room. [I was q]uite sure that you had no idea who I was and before the evening was over you came to our table and introduced your wife to "Dennis Jameson from California—one of my new students." A small gesture of kindness, but one that became part of my family's lore. As an academic, I have tried to remember and retain the spirit of that small courtesy . . . "A professor knows my name!"[33]

A (Very Tired) "Hero of the Faith"

And in case such an overwhelming show of love and appreciation for him, especially on his ninetieth birthday, might tempt one to think of Horton as Superman, the following account proves that he was indeed human: Dr. Larry Asplund, now of Portland Bible College and Healthy Congregations Ministry, fondly recalls his days at AGTS. One of his earliest memories is of Dr. Horton being there to greet him and make him feel welcome. He enjoyed the Old Testament courses he had with Horton, which richly contributed to his understanding. He saw him as a "hero of the faith . . . a personal role model . . . an important mentor and spiritual father [who] will always have an important place in my heart." Laudatory remarks notwithstanding, however, one of Larry's most poignant memories harkens back to a side of Horton that those outside his classroom would never have seen:

> Dr. Horton had been out all week for a very busy time of ministry. He was obviously exhausted when he came to class, so he lectured while sitting at his desk. Soon he began to talk more and more quietly. Then his words became a bit disjointed and his head began to bob. Then he was fast asleep. All of us students, realizing his need for sleep, slipped silently out of the class and didn't see him again until the next week![34]

Given the kind of herculean schedule Horton maintained over the decades, his occasional nodding off in class as a result of working half the night is a scene more than one former student has recalled with a smile!

If You Stay Long Enough . . .

Because of his longevity and stamina in ministry, both at CBC and again at AGTS, some individuals who were once Horton's students—Ben Aker, Anthony Palma, and others—eventually became his colleagues. Roger Cotton, professor of Old Testament at AGTS, recalls how blessed he felt both to have been Horton's student and fellow graduate professor. On the occasion of Horton's ninetieth birthday, he wrote to him:

> You are the leading influence on my career in teaching Old Testament. Because you presented such a living understanding of the Old Testament I was inspired to want to study it more and help others hear God's message through it. One reason I went to AGTS was so that I could study more under you and I was greatly enriched. I

love your answers to the issues because they bear witness with God's Spirit within me. They make the best sense in the context and give the best picture of God. You made the Bible fit together the way I believe God intended it. Furthermore, as everyone will agree, you always presented what you believe with humility and gentleness. You admitted when someone had a good argument, you did not get defensive, and you avoided exaggeration. You were aware of the scholars' approaches but you spoke and wrote in very down to earth, clear, relevant to real life, words. I always enjoyed the illustrations you gave from your own life experiences. They always fit. I am very encouraged by your life because you are consistent with what you teach and you are always learning and growing in the Lord. . . .You are a wonderful testimony for the Spirit-filled life and teaching ministry. You model a true sensitivity to the Holy Spirit. Your family is a good testimony, as well. I want to thank you for helping me as a young teacher and for patiently answering my questions over the years.[35]

In 1976, Horton also made an impression on another young man, James Hernando, who would eventually return to teach New Testament at AGTS. Recollecting his years studying with Horton, Jim writes:

I remember being most impressed with his knowledge of the Hebrew Bible. No matter what verse we referred to, Dr. Horton would methodically turn to the page in his *Biblia Hebraica* and just start reading. We were amazed! But what impressed me the most was his love of the Word and the profound insight he brought to our minds from the Scriptures. His class on Old Testament Theology is where I first saw the "big picture" of

God's plan of salvation. It inspired me and gave me a love for God's Word. I wanted to be the kind of teacher that had the same effect on students that he had on me. . . . Dr. Horton modeled what it means to be a "humble scholar," regarded as oxymoronic by some. In spite of his enormous knowledge of the Scriptures, he never came across as being a know-it-all. What's more

Stanley Horton with AGTS Mace after Commencement

he never made anyone feel stupid for their comments or contributions in class, no matter how ill-informed. He was respectful of our stumbling efforts to think theologically and biblically. I am profoundly grateful that the Lord let me study at AGTS (then AGGS) under Dr. Horton. He has blessed our fellowship with his scholarship and writing, but his legacy will live on in countless students he has impacted through the character of his life. He did so by having a focused life in service to the Lord and His church. I'm sure he has slowed down some at 90 years old, but the embers of his heart and devotion to Christ burn as bright as ever. Thank you, Dr. Horton, for touching my life. I will never forget you or your contribution to my life and ministry.[36]

In 1987, after Horton had taught full-time at AGTS for nine years, the seminary awarded him with the title of "Distinguished Professor of Bible and Theology." He then served as chairman of the Bible Department from 1987–88 and again in 1990.

"Retirement"

In 1991, when Horton was seventy-five years old, the school decided that its three professors over seventy years of age must retire. They held a banquet for the retirees; Stanley was delighted that even his sisters Esther and Ruth from California were able to attend. Friends and colleagues from CBC and AGTS were in attendance and presented him with a book of letters. One long-time CBC colleague, David Drake, gave Horton this letter:

Stanley Horton in AGTS
Library, ca. 1980s

March 7, 1991

Dear Dr. Horton:

1948 was a big year for Central Bible Institute (now college). It was the year of accreditation, adding a fourth year, and the incoming of a number of new teachers. I heard the names of J. Robert Ashcroft, Cordas Burnett, O. Cope Budge, Carl Erickson, and STANLEY HORTON.

There were many comments about each of the new faculty, but when word was received that Stanley Horton was coming, we began to ask, "Who's he?" Then the information came filtering in. "He's a brain!" "He's a bookworm with an I.Q. of 186." "He has more degrees and language skills than we have ever seen around this place!"

Some of us were frightened, thinking that perhaps it was true that [since] CBI was now going to be a college, emphasis would be on academics, and the long heritage of spiritual preparation for ministry was in grave danger. We had all been warned that this new emphasis would be the end of CBI, as we had known it.

I love it when Paul Harvey says, "Now the rest of the story—"

Stan, your coming to CBI was one of the greatest things that could ever have happened. You demonstrated from the first that spirituality and academics can go together when Christ is kept at the center. Your knowledge and skills, together with your self-effacing spirit of humility, and your desire that Christ be exalted in all things has over the years made you one of the most valuable assets of Central Bible College. Without a doubt, you have become "Mr. Theology" for the entire fellowship of the Assemblies of God.

As a prolific writer, Bible teacher, lecturer, and one who would do whatever his hand found to do, Stan, you have excelled. No one can tell the countless thousands of young people and adults you have influenced. Your name has become a household word to Pentecostals, worldwide, and the last word when theological issues of the Assemblies of God needed an answer.

Personally, I feel very honored to have worked with you and known you as a personal friend over these more than forty years. You are "rock solid" in your theology and in the hearts of your friends. As you take this step called "retirement" I know that you will keep busy till Jesus comes. We wish for you a most blessed and rewarding future without perhaps so much constant pressure as you have borne through the years.

Cordially,
David B. Drake[37]

Upon retiring, Horton received the title, "Distinguished Professor Emeritus of Bible and Theology."[38] The year he retired, his book, *The Ultimate Victory: An Exposition of the Book of Revelation,* was published.

Having learned a few lessons along the way from teaching thousands of students over the years, Horton says that if he could give advice to professors and teachers today, he would tell them:

> Prepare with prayer and in-depth Bible study. Have more available in your class preparation than you will probably use. When the students ask questions treat them with respect and answer in a way that will bring you back to the subject at hand. Remember that when one student asks a question there are probably several others who have the same question in their minds. Be available for students to come to you with their problems—and don't think you have all the answers. Be ready to send them to others who might better be able to help them. Remember, too, that God will get hold of some of your problem students, change them, and give them a greater ministry than your own.[39]

The Pentecostal Textbook Series

After retiring from AGTS,[40] Horton was given an office at Gospel Publishing House where from 1991 to 2000 he served as general editor for the Pentecostal Textbook series, Logion Press. The mission of Logion was to provide textbooks from an evangelical/Pentecostal perspective to help "facilitate the education and discipling of college and seminary students, pastors, and other serious students of the Bible."[41] Perfectly suited for this role, given his seventy-five years in the Pentecostal world and forty-six years in Pentecostal higher education, Horton was able to contribute to the effort of providing textbooks by Pentecostal scholars in order to "ensure continuing education that is Pentecostal."[42]

While at Logion, Horton revised and expanded *Understanding Our Doctrine*, a work by William Menzies, into *Bible Doctrines: A Pentecostal Perspective*[43] (1993) and served as general editor for *Systematic Theology: A Pentecostal Perspective* (1994). In this work, Horton and nineteen other Pentecostal scholars built on Gary B. McGee's first chapter on the historical background of Pentecostal theology to present a "fresh defense of the faith." This important work was the Assemblies of God's first systematic theology since E. S. Williams' 1953 work.[44]

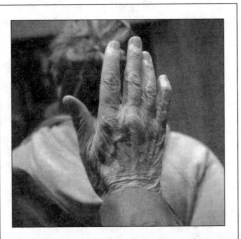

Horton's hand while he was praying, Day of Renewal, September 16, 2004

On September 16, 2004, Stanley Horton stood in the chapel of the Assemblies of God Theological Seminary for the "Day of Renewal" service. Hands raised in worship to God, Horton was oblivious to the snaps of the seminary photographer taking pictures for the school's magazine, *Rapport*. "I happened to be sitting behind him with my camera and started thinking about how cool it was to see the hand of the scholar who had written so much, upraised in worship like that. A picture of fiery scholasticism." –Jennifer Hall, AGTS Promotions Coordinator

Though in the midst of such lofty endeavors, Horton remained the gentle, humble, hard-working man he had always been. Glen Ellard, book editor at Gospel Publishing House, said of his time working with Dr. Horton on the Pentecostal Textbook series:

In my work with him I found him to be a quiet man. He would answer questions when asked, but he didn't seem to engage in small talk. Even so, he had a ready laugh, he

225

wasn't intimidating, and he was easy to work with. He seemed to be more focused on the reader than on himself as a writer. That is, he didn't mind being questioned about some aspect of a manuscript he had written. If he agreed that a change was in order, he simply okayed it. And he would as soon as not accept my recasting as put forward his own. Dr. Horton was one of the few writers over my twenty-plus years who regularly acknowledged the book editing staff of GPH by name. . . .

I recall his recognition of my fiftieth birthday. We worked in the same building, and the Book Editing staff had sent out an announcement and suggestions of how my birthday might be commemorated: 50 of anything. I got a miscellany: rubber bands, paperclips, hole-punch "confetti," some rolls of pennies. Dr. Horton was the most generous. He gave me 50 first-class stamps.[45]

Stanley Horton, picture for
Today's Pentecostal Evangel,
mid-1990s

Even though in his eighties during this time, Horton continued to produce written works seemingly with the strength of Samson. While simultaneously working on the Complete Biblical Library project, he produced *Our Destiny: Biblical Teachings on the Last Things* (1996) as well as his commentaries on *1 and 2 Corinthians* (1999), *Isaiah* (2000), and *Acts* (2001) during his time at Logion. Around 2005, GPH began to handle the Bible-Soft[46] program and included five of Horton's books on the PC Study Bible software (*Systematic Theology,* his Logion commentary on

Acts, *1 & 2 Corinthians*, *Bible Doctrines*, and *What the Bible Says about the Holy Spirit*). How times had changed from the days when Horton's mother Myrle helped fold *The Apostolic Faith* newsletters at the Azusa Street Mission as a girl. But the message remained the same.

Pentecostal "Answer Man"

In 1949, one year after arriving in Springfield, Missouri from the East Coast, Stanley Horton began writing for the *Pentecostal Evangel*. He published in forty-one out of the last fifty-nine years[47] since that time, a remarkable feat considering his myriad of other responsibilities. In 1992, the *PE* asked him to participate in a Question and Answer column for the magazine. Horton did not come up with the questions; instead, the *PE* staff would always send questions to him as inquiries arose. He has written in the Q&A column every year since it began, except 2003–05 when his wife was ill, and continues to this present time.

Ken Horn, editor of *Today's Pentecostal Evangel*, regards Horton as having been the "unofficial theologian" of the magazine for decades. Not only has this Answer Man "helped teach and guide our readers through his numerous articles and regular columns [but] he has also acted as theological advisor on many occasions. Many years of the *Evangel* bear the imprint, seen or unseen, of Dr. Horton."[48] Hal Donaldson, former editor-in-chief of the *Pentecostal Evangel*, has read Horton's writings over the course of the last thirty years. Not only have Horton's insights helped shape Donaldson's theology and perspective on life, but those of "thousands—perhaps millions"[49] as Hal puts it, because of Horton's contribution to the *Evangel*.

"Now Therefore Give Me This Mountain" (Joshua 14:12)

When God called Stanley Horton in 1940 to teach, He didn't necessarily specify which continent, and that's a good thing, because by the time he was ninety, Horton had gone to twenty-five countries[50] and every continent except Australia to teach in missions settings. Missionaries had always impressed Horton. "When I was a boy, every time a missionary would come and speak to us, I would go the altar and ask the Lord to call me to the mission field," he recalls. "But He never did! He called me to teach. Not until my old age did God give me wonderful opportunities to be on mission fields to see what He was doing."

Those opportunities began first with Horton serving as guest professor at the Near East School of Bible and Archaeology, Jerusalem while on his Holy Land tour in 1962. Then from 1980 onward, Horton was privileged to go overseas to teach and minister from time to time at theological schools for ministers in training. In each place he went to teach, he also ministered in churches. These were short-term trips, anywhere from three to five weeks during the summer, and he would travel to these countries alone.[51] After he left the seminary in 1991, he made trips at different times in the year because he could arrange his other work around them. He had a short-term missions account he would put money into, or sometimes he'd let some of his former students who were pastors know about an upcoming trip, and they would send money toward it as a missions trip.

Horton went several times to Southern Asia Bible College in Bangalore, India and to Madurai, India; he also went to the Far East Advanced School of Theology (now Asia Pacific Theological Seminary) in Manila and Baguio, Philippines.[52] Additional teaching opportunities resulted in Horton's traveling to Canada; Vilnius, Lithuania; Taichung, Taiwan; Berea Bible School in West Berlin, Germany; throughout Brazil (Pinda, Rio de Janeiro, Sao Paulo, Belém do Pará, Recife, Curitiba, Abreu e Lima, Campo Grande, and Cuiaba); Seoul and Pusan, South Korea; the East Africa School of Theology in Nairobi, Kenya (1982); Moscow, Russia (1994);[53] Continental Bible College in Brussels, Belgium (1997); Wicklow, Ireland (in 1999) where

Horton with Dr. Bill Menzies at the 2nd Annual Pentecostal Lectureship Series, Asia Pacific Theological Seminary, Baguio, Philippines, 1994

Horton ministering in Belém do Pará, Brazil in 1995

Horton with a group of his students in India

Horton in Dublin, Ireland with AGWM Missionaries Gary and Wilma David-
son, founders of St. Mark's Church. John Wesley preached at this church in
the late eighteenth century, and as a result Horton's ancestors came to faith.
St. Mark's is now an AG congregation.

they had a Bible College in a former castle twenty miles south of Dublin, and Oaxaca, Mexico (in 2000). On his most recent international teaching trip, he returned to Singapore (in 2007 at the age of ninety-one). "I found the students anxious to learn," remembers Horton, "and they treated me with great respect. Worshipping together with them in the chapel services was always a time of blessing for me."

Many of these trips were in made in connection with Horton's former students. David Plymire, son of the famous missionary Victor Plymire,[54] first heard Horton speak back in the summer of 1946 during a camp meeting in New York where he was with his missionary parents. In 1949 David came to CBI, taking Horton's Old Testament survey class. Years later when David and his wife Wardella were missionaries with China Radio in 1987, Horton came to Taiwan and ministered to all the pastors and the Bible school there. Plymire says of Horton that he "touched many from both east and west."[55]

Besides being able to touch lives as he ministered around the world, Horton himself was encouraged by their stories of having persevered in the faith. The father of one of Horton's students in Moscow was pastor of an underground church. When the student was a small boy, officers had come to arrest his father. They would not let the boy's mother give her husband a final hug good-bye, but the boy scooted between the officers' legs and jumped into his father's arms. His father then was taken to prison for a time. When Horton met this young man in Bible college in Moscow many years after this incident, the young man relayed his great joy to Horton that he could study for the ministry and preach God's Word freely. Being able to help him train for ministry was a rewarding experience for Horton.

Though he thoroughly enjoyed all these travels, Horton was most happy about his trips to India. He had studied India since his high school days, writing papers on this country in his history and English literature classes. He traveled there a number of times to minister in different parts of the country. In 1980, the first church he preached at was David Mohan's church, which had about 8,000 then but seats 65,000 now. "I'd like to see that church when it gets finished in 2009," Horton dreams at age ninety-two. "When it's finished, it will be the largest auditorium in India." He rejoices that everywhere he went in India in past years, new congregations exist now. Not long ago, he preached at the dedication service for a new church in Bangalore.

Some of Horton's students in India eventually came to the United States to study at AGTS. One of his finest was David Balasingh. Originally from Sri Lanka, David was on his way to the United States one time when his plane was delayed in Paris, causing him to arrive in Springfield a day late. At the same time that David was trying to get to Springfield, Horton was returning from preaching in Illinois, and the two just happened to get on the same plane in St. Louis. As Horton walked down the aisle, there was one seat left—next to David! This was fortunate, because David had not been able to contact anyone, and no one knew to meet him at the airport. Upon arrival in Springfield, Horton helped David get settled into an apartment and obtain furniture.

After receiving his M.Div. from AGTS, David returned to minister in India, then eventually came back to the United States to get his doctorate from Trinity Evangelical School. Today David is back in India training hundreds of young leaders and doing evangelistic work all over India and Southern Asia. In October of 2008, he wrote Dr. Horton, his professor and role model, thanking God for his great contribution to his life. David Balasingh perseveres in the work despite great persecution, in which many believers are laying down their lives; as he travels, he speaks of Horton as the "saint scholar"[56] he strives toward being one day.

Evelyn's Homegoing

Sometime in 2001, Evelyn grew weak, and Stanley finally had to take her to Maranatha Lodge nursing home where she lived for over three years. Her homegoing in October of 2004 at age eighty-one brought a major change in Stanley's life. He has had many friends, but also has mused, "My wife is the only best friend[57] who lasted over the years, and I do miss her greatly."

Mark Brown, now an Assemblies of God missionary to the Philippines who was a student at CBC long after Horton retired, remembers how every week he and his friend would go to Maranatha to join the residents for their dinner. Then they would have a chapel service for the residents whom they could wheel down to the meeting room. Mark knew he could count on one couple always being there—the Hortons.

> Every week was like their date together. Even when one time she [Evelyn] was too weak to attend, he made his way down from her room and that was an encouragement to us. Stanley was faithful to his wife. It says a lot about his heart and love for her when he drove from his house almost every day to be with her. After the service my friend and I would probe him on our theology and would proudly take our answers back to the dorm to amaze our friends. With a gracious smile and calculated answer he would take his time to appease our inquisitive minds. That is my professor from Maranatha Village.[58]

Stanley was faithful to the beautiful Evelyn he had met at church one Sunday in the fall of 1941. When she passed away, the two were just two weeks short of having been married fifty-nine years. Reflecting on his marriage, Stanley recalls that probably one of the challenges of being married was that he had to learn to accept his wife for the person she was (not trying to change her) and accept how she liked to do things. "The best thing," he says, "was our love for each other and our loyalty to each other. Evelyn was very faithful and expected me to be the same. We got along just fine." Horton's advice for young couples today was first given to him by Kenneth Haystead, whose parents Stanley stayed with when he lived in Sacramento. "When Evelyn and I were newly married, Ken told me, 'Do not try to change your spouse. You might destroy the very thing that drew you to her and made you love her in the first place. Accept each other and pray with each other, trusting the Lord to help you adjust to each other as you follow the Holy Spirit's guidance.'" And that, it seems, was just what they did.

Pressing On

Although physically Horton has slowed down a bit as he has entered his tenth decade of life, there has been no lapse mentally or spiritually. He continues to make significant contributions to the kingdom of God—preaching, teaching, and writing—but mostly through the Christlike example of the gracious and kind spirit he exhibits naturally to all those with whom he spends any time.

Whether his continued mental acuity is the result of godly living or due to having tackled crossword puzzles most of his life—and now he enjoys the added benefit of the *New York Times* puzzle on his computer—Horton is thankful. He has wondered at times why he has enjoyed such mental health while his brothers—both as smart as he—suffered from dementia in their later years. "Obviously, God had a plan," his son Ed muses. And so the father, grandfather, great-grandfather, writer, teacher, and Assemblies of God sage keeps pressing on, making the most of every opportunity set before him.

In 2004, Horton published "Spirit Baptism—A Pentecostal Perspective" in *Perspectives on Spirit Baptism* and continues to write for *Today's Pentecostal Evangel* and other publications. In 2006 at the age of ninety, he flew to Dallas to present a twenty-five-page paper, "The Inspiration and Authority of the Old Testament," to a group of eighty students working on their master's degrees through Southwestern Assemblies of God University. The following year he taught the Book of Isaiah for a twelve-day session in February and March at the Sheffield School of the Bible in Kansas City where his former student, Dr. George Westlake, Jr., is pastor, and then again he taught on Isaiah in May at the Assemblies of God Bible College in Singapore.

"People ask me, aren't you worried that he'll die?" says Horton's son Ed. "And I say, well where do you want him to die, sitting in a chair at Maranatha or in Singapore doing missions work? No brainer there for me. As long as he can go and wants to go, I'm saying go. I just as soon he pass away somewhere else doing what he loves than having to sit in a chair." And so Horton goes. Whether it's a trip overseas or a trek across the United States to attend the Society for Pentecostal Studies, Horton is ready. Redeeming his airline bonus miles recently, Horton accompanied his son on a trip to Boston where he visited his brother-in-law Frank, who just turned ninety-six. "He hadn't seen Uncle Frank in about six years," Ed says. "So we went to Frank's, and there they were, a ninety-two-year-old and a ninety-six-year-old, exercising together, showing each other the exercises they do in the chair." Apparently, exercise has contributed to Horton's good health—he often goes to the fitness center to walk a mile or more on the treadmill and pull weights!

Being with people has helped him, too. When the time came for him to move from his home on Prospect Street to Maranatha Village, one of Horton's longtime colleagues, Gerald Flokstra, was there to help. Also a former student, Gerald had Horton in 1954 for Old Testament Survey and a few other classes. He joined the staff of CBC in 1966 after having been a pastor in Connecticut and initially served as librarian—bringing the collection from 14,000 books to 144,000 during his tenure. "That was what God called me there for," he recounts. After several years, though, because of his master's in history from Vanderbilt and his master's and doctoral degrees from Gordon, Gerald eventually served full-time as an assistant professor in the Bible Department.

He and Horton were more than colleagues; Gerald has always considered Stanley a mentor and friend.

Dr. Horton has also enjoyed the friendships he's made at Maranatha. Even when Evelyn was still with him, he enjoyed the noon dinners at Maranatha's Community Center. A good place to enjoy the rich fellowship of friends he's known for decades, this context also provided the opportunity for Stanley to meet two new friends—Del and Kay Bonner—who would become quite dear to him. Del and Kay lived at Maranatha for a year or so before enrolling in the meal plan. Prior to that, their involvement in social activities there was limited to the once-a-month meetings or to chapel services. Soon after they began going to the community center for the noon meal, however, they noticed, as Del remembers, an "unfamiliar man sitting alone at the back table having his lunch." Del asked his wife if she knew who that man was. She did not. As Del recalls:

One of my pet peeves is seeing someone eating alone when there are others nearby paying no attention to what I consider a "Christian obligation of community love." So, although I had finished eating, I took my coffee and sat down at his table.

I introduced myself and asked if I could join him. He seemed delighted and said, "Please do." I guess we talked for half an hour about everything and nothing. We just spent the time talking and getting acquainted with each other. As he finished eating I asked him if he would be back for lunch the next day and if so, would he join us at our table. He accepted.

For the next several days we dined together. I still had no idea who he was, nor did Kay. About a month later our neighbor asked us if we knew who we were eating with. I said "Stanley Horton." She said, "No, 'THE' Dr. Stanley Horton." She then explained his stature in the Church and that many people here referred to him as Mr. Assemblies of God.

Strangely, that was not as important to me as his friendship. He is such a genuine and humble person that I guess I kind of look to him as an extension of my Dad, who was also my best friend. I knew that he was still grieving over the loss of his wife and I wanted to lessen that grief if I could.

I try not to take advantage of Dr. Horton's biblical knowledge, (not more than once a day anyway), unless I disagree with a point in a sermon. Then I will seek his advice.

Dr. Horton has become a very dear friend who shows genuine concern for the welfare of his friends and neighbors. Kay and I love him very much. (And he also laughs at my jokes, no matter how many times he has heard them.) P.S. Kay says that her claim to fame is that she can beat Dr. Horton at Mexican Dominos. But now that his four-year-old great-grandson has beaten him, she's not as good as she thought she was.[59]

A similar situation took place when Horton attended General Council recently and got into a conversation with a seventeen-year-old girl. He told her he was a teacher, so this girl began to ask him some deep theological questions. Horton was surprised at her understanding and at the questions she was asking. After their conversation, she got up and left, walking over to speak with some of the people she'd come with, and asked them, "Who is that man?"

"Why, he's the rock star of theology in the Assemblies of God!" was their answer.[60]

Thus, Horton's days are filled with friends and family. He spends time with his children and grandchildren, uses his new Webcam to video chat with his great-grandchildren, and speaks weekly with his two sisters who live in California. Unable to garden anymore because he's at Maranatha, he still enjoys his son's award-winning roses and enjoys each lovely autumn in Missouri. He reads the Bible daily, and when he's not writing and editing,[61] preparing messages, or preparing to teach guest lectures, he reads various types of other books. C. S. Lewis has been one of Horton's all-time favorites; he first read *Screwtape Letters* and then Lewis' other theological books, which helped him as a young man understand biblical themes and find answers to his theological questions.

Not having ever tired of the fellowship of God's people and the presence of the Lord after ninety-two years, Horton most enjoys his times in Sunday School and church. On Sunday mornings, he attends Central Assembly with his family, and on Sunday evenings Bethel Assembly where he and Evelyn raised their children and ministered for decades. He also finds good fellowship at the chapel at Maranatha and at the monthly David Lewis Ministries meetings, of which he has been a part for many years.

When Stanley is alone, he reads, corresponds by e-mail and Facebook, talks on the phone, and of course—prays. "I pray regularly for America," Horton recounts. "My greatest concern about America is on one hand the increasing vulgarity, profanity, and open sin, and on the other hand the need for revival. I feel bad about the paganism, the increase of immorality, the increase of the spread of Islam, and the fact that terrorism is not going to cease until Jesus comes. I know that only a move of the Spirit will answer the needs of our society."

Horton also continues to serve on the Commission on Doctrinal Purity.[62] First appointed to the Commission October 15, 1985, he now serves as a resource member. Bill Menzies, who served together with Horton on various General Council committees over the years—such as the "Doctrines and Practices Disapproved" committee—also worked with Horton on the Commission on Doctrinal Purity and recalls that Horton was always "congenial, helpful, and edifying."[63] Horton's meek spirit did not prevent him from taking a stand against modifying the Assemblies of God's position about divorce and remarriage, however. Like E. F. Hutton, when Horton stood to speak on the floor of the 35th General Council in Miami Beach in 1973, everyone listened. The main change put forward was that the Assemblies of God would allow credentials for ministers who were divorced and remarried *before* coming to faith.

Horton understands why the change has become necessary— that so many were divorced and remarried before they were saved and do now have a ministry and have proven themselves. But even though his name is on the modified version that allows this,[64] he's "still not too happy with what they're doing now," and his sentiment remains the same:

> I just don't want it to go any further than they've gone with this. My personal view is with what is written in the *previous* position paper, that ministers could not be credentialed at all if they'd been divorced and remarried.
>
> The main argument is a practical one. But I still have a problem with it because of the Scripture about being the husband of one wife. I checked back through what historical records I could find, and polygamy was never common except among kings and the very wealthy people. And that was true of the population in general in the Roman Empire.
>
> Regarding polygamy in the OT, God just tolerated that. Jesus said it was for the hardness of their hearts that He allowed divorce. And I think it's because of the hardness of their minds, too, that it was such an accepted thing in the ancient culture. It's become accepted in our culture too, but I still think in a lot of cases it's not really necessary. I can understand if a man becomes violent, then the wife has the right to leave. And of course Jesus did make an exception, so did Paul. So I agree that there can be exceptions.[65]

For this issue and others that continue to challenge believers today, the Assemblies of God and the Pentecostal world at large will continue to look not only to the teachings and writings of Dr. Stanley M. Horton for wisdom and biblical insight, but to the behavior and gracious speech of a man who has lived his life as one led by the Spirit. Though times change and books go out of print, the hearts and minds of those he has influenced for God's glory—and those they in turn will influence—will always remain. Of all that God has allowed him to do throughout his ninety-two years, Horton considers his major achievement in life to have been just simple obedience to the Lord. "I want to take whatever doors the Lord opens," he says with a smile, "and be satisfied with what I have."

In 1950, just two years after coming to Central Bible Institute to serve as a professor, Horton shared his personal testimony with the students in the campus paper. His words penned at age thirty-four provide an apt summation and characterization of his life:

> But above all my heart is thrilled as I think of the constant consciousness of the hand of God on my life. He has been my tender shepherd and constant guide ever since Christ came in when I was six years old. Dad finally yielded to my pleas for water baptism, and that experience was indelibly imprinted on my mind. Six years old—but I knew Jesus was real, and I have never been able to doubt it from that day to this.[66]

"Now may the God of hope fill you with all joy and peace in believing, so that you will abound in hope by the power of the Holy Spirit" (Romans 15:13, NASB).

Endnotes

1 "Then . . . Caleb . . . said unto [Joshua], . . . And now, behold, the LORD hath kept me alive, . . . I am this day fourscore and five years old. As yet I am as strong this day as I was . . . Now therefore give me this mountain, whereof the LORD spake in that day; . . . Hebron therefore became the inheritance of Caleb . . . because that he wholly followed the LORD God of Israel" (Joshua 14:6,10–12,14, KJV).

2 A catchphrase on the AGTS campus, understood as a part of the seminary "DNA," it was coined by Del Tarr, seminary president of the 1990s. (See http://www.agts.edu/rapport/2005summer/pdf/agts2005summer_rapport.pdf, 2.)

3 I am indebted to Dr. Robert Cooley for his description of the evolution of Assemblies of God higher education in the early years; much of the material in this section is paraphrased from our discussion. (Robert Cooley, interview by author, August 28, 2008.) (Assemblies of God constituents and leaders have certainly advanced in their thinking since the time Evelyn's pastor in Boston spent his entire sermon speaking against higher education simply because he knew Stanley was present in the congregation.)

4 Sixty-five students were enrolled in the "fifth year" program altogether between the years 1957–65, and forty graduated from the program before it was discontinued.

5 George W. Westlake, Jr., e-mail to author, September 24, 2008. Two other students in this program were Francis Thee, who went on to do a doctorate and teach at Northwest University, and Louise Walker, a missionary in South America who worked with ICI and helped Horton on *What the Bible Says about the Holy Spirit* while she was in Brussels.

6 Larry Hurtado, e-mail to author, September 10, 2008.

7 "New Education Secretary Appointed," *Pentecostal Evangel*, May 4, 1958, 21. Burnett was vice president of CBI from 1954–58. At the time Burnett accepted the post of national education secretary, Ashcroft was president-elect of CBI and Evangel.

8 Stanley Horton, interview by author, August 29, 2008.

9 General Council was held in Portland, Oregon, in August 1961. It was there that the vote to begin plans and studies "for the development of an A/G graduate school," began formally, "as the need and desire for upper-level training throughout our movement were becoming apparent" ("Grad. School Might Be For You," *The Centralite*, March 26, 1976, 3).

10 "History and Location," AGTS 2008–2009 Academic Catalog, 62–63. http://www.agts.edu/catalog/catalog2008_2009.pdf (accessed September 3, 2008). "The Executive Presbytery was authorized to serve as the Board of Directors of the Assemblies of God Graduate School. Thomas F. Zimmerman, general superintendent, was elected to serve as president. In August of 1984, by action of the Executive Presbytery and the General Presbytery, the school was renamed the Assemblies of God Theological Seminary. In December 1985, Dr. G. Raymond Carlson,

general superintendent, was appointed president, a position he held until 1986. Dr. H. Glynn Hall served as president from 1987–90. Dr. Del Tarr served as president from June 1990–1999. On July 1, 1999, the Board of Directors appointed Dr. Byron D. Klaus, who currently serves as the seminary's fifth president."

11 "Graduate School . . . Opening Set For Sept.," *The Centralite*, December 15, 1972, 1–2. Cordas C. Burnett, D. D., was executive vice president. Originally a pastor and evangelist ordained in 1937, Burnett was a graduate of CBI, Notre Dame, and Southeastern Bible College in Birmingham, Alabama. He had taught at CBI from 1948–52, served as vice president of CBI from 1954–58, held the position of Assemblies of God secretary of education from 1958–59, and was president of Bethany Bible College from 1959–72. Originally located on the fifth and sixth floors of the new addition to GPH, the school's tuition was only twenty dollars per hour with the total cost of the program slated to be around nine hundred dollars. The graduate school planned to offer a 36-hour M.A. in Bible and one in missions science.

"Grad School . . . More Faculty. Dean Johns Named," *The Centralite*, February 26, 1973, 2–3. The school planned to have thirteen faculty members for its first year, including Anthony Palma and Del Tarr. Three individuals had been assigned to teach earlier, in December of 1972.

"Looking at the A/G Graduate School," *The Centralite*, May 17, 1974, 2. "The present enrollment of 64 is a sign that there is a desire for a graduate school with a Pentecostal theology which recognizes the importance of declaring the whole counsel of God, including a proper emphasis on the person and the work of the Holy Spirit as revealed in the Word of God.

"The school seeks to provide a very practical professional orientation designed to assist students in acquiring the characteristics and skill which will prepare them for places of leadership and teaching ministries in Bible colleges at home and abroad, with a special emphasis on Biblical preaching. Academic excellence, a spiritual environment, and a missionary and evangelistic emphasis are also important objectives of the school."

In February 2009 AGTS received full endorsement from ATS to offer the Ph.D. in Intercultural Studies—the first independently offered Ph.D. by any AG educational institution (AG NEWS #1651: February 20, 2009).

12 "Grad. School Might Be For You," *The Centralite*, March 26, 1976, 3. By 1976, three years after it had opened, the grad school had achieved a 300 percent increase in enrollment.

13 Though Horton *was* retired from the seminary at age seventy-five, now at age ninety-two—thirty years from the time he first went to the grad school—he is still in demand.

14 "Faculty Labors and Promotions," *The Centralite*, December 14, 1977, 1.

15 "Graduate School . . . Opening Set For Sept.," 1. Burnett explained that a seminary was a three-year program (for those who'd graduated from a liberal arts college), but a graduate school was a one-year program (for those who had graduated from a Bible college).

[16] Robert Cooley, interview by author, August 28, 2008.

[17] Russell P. Spittler, now provost emeritus and senior professor of New Testament, Fuller Theological Seminary, Pasadena, California, was on the faculty as an assistant professor in Bible at CBC from 1958–62. He received his Ph.D. from Harvard in New Testament and Early Christian Origins. In February of 1974, Spittler (then dean of Southern California College in Costa Mesa, now Vanguard University) took part in the CBC alumni lectureship on "Theology, Culture, and Social Issues." He spoke in the Thursday and Friday chapels that week, forming the basis for two evening panel-forums dealing with biblical holiness. Spittler and Horton served on a panel for the alumni lectureship—along with G. Raymond Carlson, Stewart Robinson, and Del Tarr, to discuss divorce. See "Russell Spittler Chosen As Speaker," *The Centralite*, December 17, 1974, 1.

Called upon as a theologian to deal with the issue of divorce and remarriage, Horton has repeatedly addressed this issue. Even in 2008 in his position on the Commission for Doctrinal Purity, he continues to provide counsel regarding this topic.

[18] "Horton, Aker: Teachers Travel During Summer," *The Centralite*, October 17, 1975, 1.

[19] Ibid.

[20] In 1970 Horton took part in a CBC faculty series on the Holy Spirit, along with Charles Harris and Edmund Tedeschi. Horton's component was "Holy Spirit in Guidance." See, "Faculty To Present Series on the Holy Spirit," *The Centralite*, October 23, 1970, 1.

[21] See Charles Stephen Danzey, "The Holy Spirit in Christian initiation in the theologies of Donald Gee, Stanley M. Horton, and J. Rodman Williams: Reformed influences in Pentecostalism" (Ph.D. diss., Southwestern Baptist Theological Seminary, 1995), abstract. "Since its beginnings in the first decade of the twentieth century, Pentecostal pneumatology has moved away from a strong Wesleyan-holiness theological orientation toward a theology of the Spirit substantially influenced by Reformed theology. Although Wesleyan-holiness influences persist to the present day, the tenets of Reformed evangelicalism and traditional Reformed theology have been incorporated into current mainstream Pentecostal theology. The movement toward a modified Reformed pneumatology is illustrated in the theologies of Donald Gee, Stanley M. Horton, and J. Rodman Williams. . . . Stanley M. Horton's pneumatology indicates a further shift toward Reformed theology within mainstream Pentecostalism. Horton interprets Pentecostal distinctives in the broader context of evangelical theology. His doctrine of the work of the Spirit in regeneration, water baptism, and sanctification, and the doctrine of conditions for receiving Spirit-baptism, illustrates a movement in Pentecostal theology toward a more christocentric and theocentric pneumatology."

[22] This book has been translated into French, Spanish, Chinese, German, Korean, Portuguese, and Tamil. Similarly, Horton's *The Book of Acts* (1981) has also been translated into several languages.

[23] A Swedish firm put up the money to get the project started. They had done a similar project in Sweden and decided to do a more extensive one in the United States.

[24] Gregory Lint served as executive editor for the Old Testament portion of the project. Gilbrant was international editor for both the Old and New Testament portions.

[25] William Menzies, interview by author, April 10, 2008.

[26] Mark Hausfeld, letter to Stanley Horton on the occasion of his ninetieth birthday, May 6, 2006.

[27] See Dr. Keener's Web page: http://drkeener.googlepages.com/home. "Craig S. Keener is especially known for his work as a New Testament scholar on Bible background (commentaries on the New Testament in its early Jewish and Greco-Roman settings). His popular-level *IVP Bible Background Commentary: New Testament* has sold over four hundred thousand copies. Craig Keener is author of many books (with over half a million sold), including three commentaries that have won awards in *Christianity Today*. His commentaries include *A Commentary on the Gospel of Matthew* (Eerdmans, 1999), *The Gospel of John: A Commentary* (2 vols., Hendrickson, 2003), *Revelation* (Zondervan, 2000), *1–2 Corinthians* (Cambridge, 2006). Other books include *Gift & Giver: The Holy Spirit for Today* (Baker, 2001), *Paul, Women & Wives* (Hendrickson, 1992)."

[28] Craig Keener, letter to Stanley Horton, May 6, 2006.

[29] Craig Keener, e-mail to author, August 2, 2008.

[30] Ibid.

[31] Phil Duncan, letter to Stanley Horton on the occasion of his ninetieth birthday, May 6, 2006.

[32] John Houser, letter to Stanley Horton on the occasion of his ninetieth birthday, May 6, 2006.

[33] Dennis Jameson, letter to Stanley Horton on the occasion of his ninetieth birthday, May 6, 2006.

[34] Larry Asplund, letter to Stanley Horton on the occasion of his ninetieth birthday, May 6, 2006.

[35] Roger Cotton, letter to Stanley Horton on the occasion of his ninetieth birthday, May 6, 2006.

[36] James Hernando, letter to Stanley Horton on the occasion of his ninetieth birthday, May 6, 2006.

[37] Letter given to author by David Drake, May 6, 2008.

[38] Each year at AGTS, the "Stanley M. Horton Award," based on excellence in the writing of the seminary paper for the course, "Theological Studies Seminar," is awarded to a deserving student. In 2008, the winner of this award was Jeffrey D. Green with his paper, "Torah and the Disciple of Jesus" (http://www.agts.edu/encounter/article.2008_winter/green.htm).

[39] William Menzies, personal interview by author, April 10, 2008.

[40] Stanley M. Horton, original written response to "Life Chronicles" questions provided to him by author, 2006.

[41] See http://colleges.ag.org/faculty_resources/logion/index.cfm for a list of textbooks in the Logion Press series.

[42] Horton, *Reflections*, 37.

[43] Considering the Assemblies of God's "theological evangelicalization" after aligning with the NAE, Douglas Jacobsen in a 1993 SPS paper, characterized Horton's theology—and that of Assemblies of God leadership with him at the time—as adopting "evangelicalism's contextual definition of the Christian faith as battle against liberalism" (Douglas Jacobsen, "Knowing the Doctrines of Pentecostals: The Scholastic Theology of the Assemblies of God, 1930-55," in *Pentecostal Currents in American Protestantism*, 90–107, ed. Edith L. Blumhofer, Russell P. Spittler, and Grant A. Wacker, 101. Urbana and Chicago: University of Illinois Press, 1999. This paper was originally presented at SPS in 1993). Horton responded to Jacobsen's paper at SPS, then later in his book, *Reflections of an Early American Pentecostal* (81), stating:

"It was never my intention that we should be fighters. Rather, I have had in mind the failures of the fundamentalists and evangelicals to stop the tide of liberalism by their books and arguments. *I want people to see that the line is drawn at the point of the supernatural. Instead of depending on arguments and evidences, important though they may be, we need to promote the Pentecostal message of the Holy Spirit's power and the fact that the God who came down into the stream of human life and history in Bible times still is active through the Holy Spirit today* (italics mine). He still confirms the Word of God with signs and wonders."

Jacobsen, referring to Horton's *Into All Truth* (1955), said that Horton would only see the Bible—rather than the history of the Pentecostal movement—as the source for teachings that Pentecostals would consider fundamental. However, in reflecting on Jacobsen's critique, Horton commented that now he would refer to both as sources. He sees importance in the role Pentecostal history plays in shaping fundamental teachings but says that those teachings still must be biblically based (Stanley Horton, interview with author, 2008).

[44] Two issues of *AG Heritage* provided excerpts from McGee's chapter. See: "The Pentecostal Movement and Assemblies of God Theology: Exploring the Historical Background" (Winter, 1993): 10-12, 27-28 and "The Pentecostal Movement and Assemblies of God Theology: Development and Preservation Since 1914" (Spring 1994): 24-28, 31. Subsequent editions of *Systematic Theology* came out in 1995 and 2007. Horton's chapter was on eschatology, "The Last Things."

[45] Glen Ellard, e-mail message to author, May 19, 2008.

[46] The PC Study Bible with Horton's five books is available from: www.GospelPublishing.com. Not long after the software was released, some individuals from BibleSoft came to interview Horton. He told them how much he liked the PC Study Bible and how easy it was to use. Because of what he had said about the program in general, Jim Bakker—

who had made an agreement in 2008 with BibleSoft to produce a smaller version with some of his materials and other versions of the Bible on it—used Horton's comment to advertise that version.

[47] 1952, 1954, 1956–59, 1961, 1963, 1968–69, 1992–94, 1996–97, 2004, 2006–07.

[48] Ken Horn, Facebook message to author, July 19, 2008.

[49] Hal Donaldson, letter to Stanley Horton on the occasion of his ninetieth birthday, May 6, 2006.

[50] Horton also traveled and ministered in Canada, Jordan, Lebanon, Italy, Greece, Egypt, France, Netherlands, Switzerland, Malaysia, Japan, and extensively throughout the United States.

[51] Evelyn usually didn't go with Stanley because they couldn't afford it. She did go to Israel with one of her sisters on a tour, and then later on a tour of the capitals of Europe. She also attended the World Pentecostal Conference in London one year and joined Stanley in Switzerland for the same conference years later.

[52] "The work at Asia Pacific Theological Seminary (APTS) began around 1971. Leslie Hurst was the field director and invited Bill Menzies to serve as a consultant for what was then called FEAST—Far East Advanced School of Theology. Bill would teach block courses at the extension in Manila, and then around 1984 he accepted an assignment for one year to teach and serve as president at FEAST in Manila. Not too many years after that he was invited to go back. He had made a commitment to help Del Tarr establish California Theological Seminary in Fresno, CA, then in 1988 Bill and his wife Doris were commissioned to go serve as regular missionaries. In 1989, he was installed as president at FEAST. Right away they changed the name to APTS. Menzies served in that capacity until 1995, officially retiring in 2000 because of Doris' health.

"APTS had established a lectureship in 1993, and the second year they had it, Horton was their invited guest. Because he had written some substantial theological volumes, they were apprehensive about how he'd be received, as a man of such stature. But he disarmed everyone; he simply recollected Azusa and his experiences growing up as a Pentecostal. He was wonderfully received. As a result APTS published his lectures in a volume called *Reflections of an Early Pentecostal*. The students responded very well to his very positive, warm demeanor." William Menzies, personal interview by author, April 10, 2008.

[53] While in Moscow, Horton preached at the English-Speaking Assembly, where a number of businesspeople visiting the country and also well-educated Russians would attend. At one service where there were about 250 people he prayed with several to receive the baptism in the Holy Spirit. One Russian man who "really got blessed" said to Horton afterwards, "Did you put the Holy Spirit on me?" "No," Horton told him, "Jesus is the One who baptizes in the Holy Spirit. Keep seeking Jesus!"

[54] Victor Plymire was also the uncle of Assemblies of God General Superintendent George O. Wood. See George O. Wood, "Resolve to

Persevere," *Pentecostal Evangel*, May 23, 2004, 20. Also available at: http://www.ag.org/pentecostal-evangel/Articles2004/4698_wood.cfm. See also, "Papers of Victor Guy Plymire," Billy Graham Center Archives of Wheaton College, http://www.wheaton.edu/bgc/archives/GUIDES/341/htm (accessed October 27, 2008).

[55] David and Pat Plymire, letter to Stanley Horton on the occasion of his ninetieth birthday, May 6, 2006.

[56] David Balasingh, e-mail to Stanley Horton, October 13, 2008.

[57] Though Horton has made the acquaintance of thousands of people throughout his life, Evelyn truly was his "best friend." Relative to the question of who Horton's dearest friends were, David Drake, a colleague of Horton's for decades, commented, "I don't think he had time to sit down and relax and play a table game. He would attend functions, but there wasn't a social friendship type thing. He wasn't in any sports or games. He was just perpetually pouring out. He was a man everybody admires, and yet he was in his own realm, just great. A good, reliable friend, but not a 'buddy.' He was always good with the students. He'd take time with them, and rush off to work at headquarters." Others have commented that because Stanley was so intensely focused on his work and always so busy, he didn't really have the time to get to know people—or they him—on a deeper level.

[58] Mark Brown, letter to Stanley Horton on the occasion of his ninetieth birthday, May 6, 2006.

[59] Del Bonner, e-mail to author, May 20, 2008.

[60] Derreld Wartenbee, personal interview by author, May 6, 2008.

[61] In his role as a member of the board of Israel's Redemption ministry, Horton undertook in 2008 the project of editing Dr. Ray Gannon's five-hundred-page dissertation, "The Shifting Romance with Israel: American Pentecostal Ideology of Zionism and the Jewish State," in order to provide a popular version.

[62] The Commission on Doctrinal Purity was established in 1979. In November of 1997, the Executive Presbytery in session appointed him as a resource member. He was then appointed to fill an unexpired term ending November 2003. In both 2003 and 2007, he was again appointed as a resource member. Shelly Mackey, e-mail to author, June 11, 2008.

[63] William Menzies, interview with author, April 10, 2008.

[64] See the "Divorce and Remarriage" position paper. The modified version is available at http://ag.org/top/Beliefs/Position_Papers/index.cfm.

Even at age ninety-two, Horton continues to serve on the Commission on Doctrinal Purity, since the General Superintendent has asked the Commission to review and evaluate all the position papers. The group will have quarterly meetings through the next year, and Horton will probably be assigned one or more of the papers to review. So far they have only told him that he'll be asked about anything involving Hebrew.

[65] Horton, interview by author, May 26, 2008

[66] "My Testimony," *The Scroll*, May 19, 1950, 5.

CHAPTER 8

Man of Theological Integrity

Raymond L. Gannon

A quiet and unassuming Pentecostal saint, the intellectually brilliant yet soft-spoken Stanley M. Horton has been spartan in his disciplined readiness to do every good work with all humility of mind. He has always exercised his massively strong intellect and giant spirit to better equip others to serve. The kind and gentle demeanor of this spiritually great one has accompanied his preservation of multiplied tens of thousands of Pentecostal saints by protecting the vulnerable against theological plunder. His life is a perpetual model for Pentecostal piety and the pattern for resolved commitment to biblical truth.

Lois Olena's biography of Stanley Horton's life has exhibited his saintly self-sacrifice and proven scholarship that have accompanied and greatly influenced the twentieth-century expansion of the Pentecostal movement from its earliest days to the present. Dr. Horton's contribution to the formulation of Pentecostal doctrine has been carefully done with all faithfulness to the Hebrew and Greek of the Holy Scriptures. He has labored long decades with keen devotion to important biblical detail often missed in other camps. He has courageously defended the Assemblies of

God against the antagonists that have been critical of the sustained classical Pentecostalism enjoyed in the Assemblies of God.

Stanley Horton's multiplied numbers of books, Sunday School materials, and hundreds of articles, as well as his sound theological leadership in the classroom and chief editorship of the Pentecostal textbook series of Logion Press, have impacted not only Assemblies of God students, pastors, missionaries, and dignitaries but also thousands of Bible students of all nations (e.g., through Global University) and many Pentecostal denominations in the United States and Canada who share the Assemblies of God's gratitude for his work.

Two chief areas of theological concern for Horton in his writing and teaching have been the doctrine of the Holy Spirit (pneumatology) and the doctrine of the last days (eschatology). While his well-rounded theological input covered all the fields of Christian doctrine, including theology proper, Christ, salvation, Spirit baptism, the Church, and more, his expertise in the doctrines of the Holy Spirit and the last days has been particularly helpful to the Assemblies of God and the multitudes they have reached. His command of these doctrines is governed by his commitment to the revelation of the full gospel and his unwillingness to excise any truth from Holy Writ. Accordingly, he quietly challenges the traditional Christian theological dismissal of Israel and refutes the notion that God has two plans—one for Israel and a second for the Church. His astuteness enabled him to see beyond classical orthodoxy and capture the broader biblical perspective that recognizes the major role Israel must still play in salvation history. As a complement to his biography, this chapter will serve as an examination of these three main features of his theology.

The Stanley Horton Theological Distinctives

The student of theology will always see in Stanley Horton's theology that he is both Evangelical and Pentecostal in his persuasion. For the largest part, Horton follows the standard theological perspectives of the Evangelical world for both his doctrines of the last days and the Holy Spirit. For example, a careful analysis of his theology would display striking similarity to Lewis Sperry Chafer's eight-volume set on systematic theology. Yet Pentecostal survival in a theological world that gave no sanctuary to advocacy of Pentecostal Spirit baptism requires exhaustive reexamination of standard Evangelical theology.

There can be little doubt that Stanley Horton's most important text was *What the Bible Says about the Holy Spirit*,[1] first published in 1976. At the height of the Charismatic movement and in view of some the excesses increasingly apparent among new enthusiasts and critics alike, Horton offered his classical doctrine of the Holy Spirit in this text. His scholarly work is truly a biblical theology of the Holy Spirit that factors in historical events, word studies, and modern apologetics for classical Pentecostal positions; Horton richly and capably expounded the biblical texts in his advocacy of traditional Pentecostalism. This chief work has broadly served the Assemblies of God and greater Pentecostal movement well into a fourth decade now.

The Problems Stanley Horton Confronted

Evangelicalism, particularly in its frequent dispensationalist format, disallowed the very possibility of the baptism in the Holy Spirit or infilling with the Holy Spirit for Christians. Speaking in tongues was to be only a *Jewish* experience, not a Christian one. According to early Evangelical dispensationalist influences like John Nelson Darby (19th century) and Cyrus Ingerson Scofield (early 20th century), the Day of Pentecost actually occurred under the dispensation of Mosaic Law. In other words, the Pentecostal tongues-speaking experience was valid only prior to the birth of the Church and the commencement of the Church Age. Only when the Church Age concluded at the two-part Second Coming would *Jewish* tongues-speaking again be possible.

In this line of thinking, the Jewish rejection of God's appointed Messiah, Jesus, had resulted in the loss of Israel's kingdom of God opportunity. The Kingdom then being stripped from the Jews was given to the Gentiles, resulting in the birth of the Church (Acts 10). So during this parenthetical period identified as the Church Age, sandwiched between two different Kingdom offers to national Israel, there would be no need for Pentecostal-styled tongues speaking or other related manifestations of the Holy Spirit. The tongues-speaking experience the Jews had enjoyed near the climax of the dispensation of the Law—but lost when the Kingdom was taken from them—would resume only with Jewish repentance and the official embrace of Jesus as Messiah and Lord at the Second Coming, the moment of the second Kingdom offer. Until the Jews received Jesus at His return, according to this system of thought, the spiritual gifts had ceased. The manifestations of the Holy Spirit ceased at the same time the Church superseded Israel in God's program.

Earlier theologians than Stanley Horton had dealt with this theological problem for Pentecostals. Frank M. Boyd and Ernest S. Williams had both moved the birth of the Church to the Day of Pentecost in Acts 2, thus qualifying Christians to likewise share in the Pentecostal fullness. While many Evangelicals, and even Dispensationalists, were prepared to accommodate the conviction that the Church was born in Jerusalem on the Day of Pentecostal in Acts 2, they still contended that the Holy Spirit's manifestations of the 1 Corinthians 12 variety had ceased with the completion of the New Testament canon at the end of the first century.

In effect then, the Evangelical and Dispensationalist theologies had "book-ended" the time that the Holy Spirit could manifest in Spirit baptism as evidenced with tongues speaking. The first camp disallowed any members of the Church from participating in this distinctive Jewish experience. The second camp acknowledged the operation of the gifts in the first century but not after the Spirit's final inspiration of New Testament writings. Both camps could find no justification for Christian tongues speaking from the second through the twentieth centuries. Many were prepared to assign such powers to sinister, diabolical, or psychological sources.

Here is where Stanley Horton shines so brightly. Horton correctly assigns the birth of the Church to the inauguration of the New Covenant instituted by Jesus himself in Matthew 26:26–28, in fulfillment of the prophesied New Covenant of Jeremiah 31:31–34. It would be the members of the New Covenant who fifty days later would be filled with the Holy Spirit in Acts 2:4. The Holy Spirit's writing of God's law upon their "hearts" and "minds" and enabling them to personally "know the Lord" (Jeremiah 31:33,34) would be the heritage of the members of the New Covenant community for time without end.

Therefore, according to Horton's theology, the Jewish believers in Acts 2 were members of the New Covenant community. Their infilling with the Holy Spirit that issued forth in tongues speaking and related signs was the precedent and model for all future generations of those sharing in the New Covenant's multifaceted spiritual experience. It was then entirely legitimate for Bible institute students in Topeka and revivalistic church folk at Azusa Street or for Christians in any location or of any era to likewise share in this portion of their spiritual inheritance as born-again members of the New Covenant.

Stanley Horton's Pentecostal Uniqueness

Stanley Horton tracks carefully with most Evangelical or Dispensationalist theologians on the work of the Holy Spirit in the salvation experience and the Spirit's occupation of every believer for the purpose of ultimately transforming all believers into the very image of Jesus. Yet he breaks with classical Evangelicalism and Dispensationalism on the birthday of the Church. His astute recognition of the New Covenant community in

Matthew 26 suggests that believers of all times future can anticipate Holy Spirit baptism and the full operation of the Holy Spirit's gifts.

Admittedly, the birth of the Church is a matter of ecclesiology (i.e., the doctrine of the Church). Yet this aspect of ecclesiology has direct impact upon the doctrines of both the Holy Spirit and the last days. It raises the question of whether tongues speaking was to be the privilege of (1) Jews only, (2) Christians only, or (3) both Jews and Christians. It forces the issue of the relationship of Israel and the Church in God's economy, since the New Covenant prophesied in Jeremiah 31 and ratified in Matthew 26 was not made with Protestants or Catholics per se but rather with "the house of Israel and with the house of Judah" (Jeremiah 31:31). Have the theologians declared something that God has not? That is, has God established two different programs, created two different peoples, designed two means of salvation, for a universe forever divided between Jews and Gentiles?

Again, Stanley Horton, in spite of his quiet and congenial manner, was not afraid to post biblical truths in his writings that were rather unconventional and potentially problematic for classical Christian orthodoxy. He waved no red flag in challenge of traditionalists. He would not contend. He simply spoke and wrote the truth in love. Few seemed to have taken offense at his amazingly profound insights.

Although he was generally satisfied with the orthodox doctrine of the Holy Spirit, he offered perspective that afforded Pentecostals the right to think for themselves, to understand their identity and New Covenant privileges that other Christians might seek to deny them. In a similar manner, he stood back to see again all that God had promised Israel, the Jewish people, the progeny of the patriarchs. He discovered that what had been denied the Jewish people theologically had, in fact, not been denied them biblically.

Stanley Horton's Impact upon Pentecostal Theology

Stanley Horton's striking influence upon the distinctive Pentecostal doctrines of the Holy Spirit (pneumatology) and of the last days (eschatology) is inseparable from his doctrine of Israel. The ongoing activity of God among the Jewish people during the New Covenant era dramatically alters Horton's theology from being strictly Evangelical or Dispensational to being genuinely Pentecostal. Herein lies his massive importance to the shaping of Pentecostal theology. What follows now is the theology of "One Plan Stan," a theological perspective that reexamines the role of Israel throughout salvation history and refuses to relegate Israel's significance to a questionable past or an elusive utopian future.

Paramount to all consideration of the relationship between Israel and the Church is the target group for the New Covenant foretold by Jeremiah and made operational by Jesus (Matthew 26). Jeremiah wrote in 31:31–34:

> "Behold, days are coming," declares the LORD, "when I will make a *new covenant with the house of Israel and with the house of Judah,* not like the covenant which I made with their fathers in the day I took them by the hand to bring them out of the land of Egypt, My covenant which they broke, although I was a husband to them," declares the LORD. But this is the covenant which I will make with the house of Israel after those days," declares the LORD, "I will put My law within them and on their heart I will write it; and I will be their God, and they shall be My people. And they shall not teach again, and each man his brother, saying, 'Know the LORD,' for they shall all know Me, from the least of them to the greatest of them," declares the LORD, "for I will forgive their iniquity, and their sin I will remember no more" (emphasis mine).[2]

God's purposes for Israel are always universal, as displayed throughout the whole of Scripture. He has created Israel to be a blessing to all the nations of the earth (Genesis 12:3; 18:18) and to serve as a "kingdom of priests and a holy nation" (Exodus 19:5,6) for the benefit of all mankind. Plainly, God chose the Jews because He loved the Gentiles. But God's love for the nations in no way lessened or cancelled His loving commitments to Israel. And here in Jeremiah, after the severest of national calamities resulting from rebellion against God, God promises a New Covenant to Israel and Judah. Noticeably missing here is any reference to Gentiles or Christian fellowships. The New Covenant is made by God with Jews and Israelites. It is their covenant with God to enjoy. It is theirs to share with Gentiles as Paul registers in Ephesians 2. The Jews are not replaced in the New Covenant; rather, they share it with others as God has ordained from eternity past (see Romans 16:25,26).

The Integrity of God's Commitments: Israel's Ongoing Role in Salvation History

Stanley Horton always displays a keen awareness of God's abiding faithfulness to all His promises to the patriarchs, kings, and prophets of Israel. Just as recognized by Dr. Horton is the Lord's absolute unwillingness to adjust His revealed truth to accommodate the theological mistakes of past or present Christian teachers.

The promised children of Abraham are to play a leading and ongoing role in God's purposeful revelation of himself to mankind. Horton points up Israel's God-assigned redemptive role at the time of the establishing of the Abrahamic covenant.[3] Through Abraham's seed, Israel would play a central role in messianic redemption and related events from the patriarchal period to the present apocalyptic time (Revelation 7:1–8).[4] Through the chosen man of faith, Abraham, would come a chosen people to bless all the families, the multiplied millions, of the earth.[5]

Israel became that chosen people to accomplish God's redemptive purpose. To repeat, God chose the Jews because He loved the

Gentiles. God loved the nations that had chosen to forget Him. But like "a group of commandos might be called a chosen group. . . . Israel was selected for a purpose. . . . Through Israel, God meant to keep the truth alive and give witness to the world. Through Israel, He also offered an open door into the blessings of God."[6]

God's purpose has always been to use the chosen people to be His witnesses to the ends of the earth.[7] His love and grace were always to be inclusive of Israel and all mankind. All Gentiles prepared to commit their lives to the God of Israel were welcomed into the family of Israel—as the Hebrew Bible makes clear.[8] The prophets assured Israel of Gentile appreciation for the Jewish blessing of the nations (Zephaniah 3:19,20).[9]

Being the chosen people was no license to sin. A backslidden Israel may periodically go through seasons of divine chastening so that, indeed, God's plan to fully utilize Israel to serve as the conduit of blessing to all the families of the earth (Genesis 12:3) could be completely executed.[10] Israel needed to model God's holiness to mankind as an important ingredient of their international witness. God's intention to use Israel for the task of global redemption has never changed.[11] He will "still use His covenant people in His great plan to bless all peoples on earth."[12]

Of course, the only way Israel would ever be equipped to perform the divinely issued mandate of reaching all the nations with God's revelation and redemption would be as "[t]hey would receive power as a result of being filled with the Spirit."[13] They would be responsible to minister in the power of the Holy Spirit from the Day of Pentecost to the Second Coming, being the model for all future Kingdom team players, e.g., the Church universal.[14]

God's Response to Israel's Failure to Walk in God's Light: The Remnant

Unfortunately for Israel and all mankind, Israel has generally failed in their divine assignment. It was never God's purpose for Israel simply to survive or perpetuate their numbers. Related to

Israel's blessing of all the nations of the earth was their duty to execute their divine task of serving as a "kingdom of priests" (a nation of worshippers, interceding for other peoples and teaching the nations God's Word) and "a holy nation" (reflecting the holy character of the God of Israel). But too often Israel served not as "a light to the Gentiles" but more as a mirror, taking upon themselves the sins and evil ways of the Gentiles.

But in spite of Israel's repetitive failings, God would never give up on the Jewish people. He would never "replace" them with an alternate group but would seek to effect "the national salvation of Israel" on an ongoing basis. Until national salvation became a reality, however, God would always have a remnant of Jewish people ready to embrace His promises and discharge their Jewish mission. They would in reality worship God "in spirit and in truth."[15]

Those numbers of Jewish people who rejected God's Living Torah and refused to walk in the light of God in Messiah Jesus, usually the ethnic majority, were unable to please God since "without faith it is impossible" (Hebrews 11:6). Faithlessness in Jesus is an offense to God and an active hindrance to the proper execution of Israel's messianic mission. "The rejection of Christ by the Jews made it impossible for God to continue to use them as channels of His Spirit and blessing."[16]

But God would always have a remnant,[17] a faithfully obedient Jewish community who trusted God's promises as had Abraham, Israel's own father. Jeremiah understood that the Lord would always have a godly remnant of Israel within the larger nation who would love and serve Him no matter what (Jeremiah 30:11; 31:5–7).[18] Of course the apostle Paul made much of this same point in his theology of Israel in Romans 9–11.

Israel's blindness was partial and temporary. God would use Gentile Christians to provoke Israel to spiritual jealousy. Such envy for a vital relationship with God would compel Jewish unbelievers to put aside their given reasons for rebellion, genuinely repent, and ultimately become all God has desired of Israel from Day One.

Such was Paul's case in Romans 11. "God's purpose in judging Israel . . . is restoration. He will graft the Jews back in when they believe in Jesus. God's purpose is actually a full restoration and a full number.[19] When Christians come into their spiritual "fullness" (*pleroma*), Israel will experience revival and restoration leading to the Second Coming.[20] "Jews who were not living for God will be transformed and become real Israelites, honoring God and enjoying the rights and privileges He gives them."[21]

Has Israel Been Replaced by the Church in God's Plan of Salvation History?

Horton pointed up, "God offers a gift or calling and He does not change His mind and withdraw it just because some do not believe. Once they are given they are always available."[22] But in spite of this straightforward apostolic teaching, there have been from the middle of the second century to the present time a host of those who,

> have no room in their system for a literal restoration of Israel or the reign of Christ on earth, they take the prophecies of the Old Testament that relate to Israel, spiritualize them, and apply them to the Church. However, it is very clear, for example, in Ezekiel 36, that God will restore Israel for His own holy name's sake in spite of what they have done.[23]

Challenging the errant theologies of ancients, moderns, and postmoderns, Horton indicts them as they spiritualize Old Testament prophecies and have no room in their system for a restoration of national Israel or a literal reign of Christ on earth.

> They also believe that "[e]thnic Israel was excommunicated for its apostasy" and "Christ transferred the blessing of the kingdom from Israel to the a new people, the church."

They ignore the many Scripture passages that show God still has a purpose for national Israel in His plan.[24]

Horton reiterates again in *Our Destiny: Biblical Teachings on the Last Things* his distress that there are even modern tongues-speaking Christians who believe that

> the Church has replaced Israel in God's plan, and that the Old Testament prophecies dealing with the future restoration and glory of national Israel must be spiritualized and applied to the Church as "the Israel of God" (Galatians 6:16).[25]

He grieves the classical misinterpretations and directly related misapplications of Matthew 21 that have led to regretful Christian theological errors with associated tragic historical outcomes.[26]

Stanley Horton recognized that Gentiles share with Israel in the glories of the Messiah's reign. But he followed with, "But this does not mean the Church replaces Israel."[27] Even though we must painfully acknowledge that "some Jews rejected Jesus, Jesus did not reject Israel as a nation. He died for them. Their restoration will glorify God and let the world see how great is His love and faithfulness, how marvelous is His redemption."[28]

The New Covenant is for Jews . . . and Others

The restoration God desires "all Israel" to enjoy is not just a regathering to form a Jewish state in Zion but more importantly to spiritually restore backslidden Israel to himself. In order, however, for that spiritual restoration to be possible, God would need to make a New Covenant with Israel as prophesied in Jeremiah 31:31–34.[29] Spiritual rehabilitation for the larger international Jewish community is assured "after Israel returns to the land in unbelief" (Ezekiel 36:25–28).[30]

Even though Israel has repeatedly failed God, God has never failed Israel. God shall yet carry out His great and gracious plan for Israel.[31] The final victory for Israel is on the terms of the New Covenant, e.g., as ushered in by the Jewish Messiah Jesus in Matthew 26 and administered by the Holy Spirit (Jeremiah 31). All the blessings promised originally to Abraham will be fully implemented on the day "all Israel" puts their trust in Jesus.[32] And on the day Israel walks in the light of the Messiah Jesus, all humankind will benefit.[33]

There is no biblical basis for the dispensationalist supposition that the New Covenant with Israel and Judah (Jeremiah 31) is distinct from the New Covenant the Church enjoys (Matthew 26). "There is only one New Covenant, the covenant put into effect by the death of Jesus on Calvary's cross (Hebrews 9:14–15; 12:24)."[34] The New Covenant was made with Israel and Judah, not Baptists or Pentecostals. But all Christians are welcomed into the New Covenant faith community by virtue of their trusting in the work of God in Christ as He established the New Covenant with Israelites and Jews.[35] Many New Covenant Spirit-baptized Christians in our age are eager to boldly awaken the Jewish world to its "all Israel" New Covenant privilege in Christ.

The Holy Spirit's Empowerment for Israel

The Jewish people, Israel, have an ongoing, corporate calling of God to proclaim the fullness of His revelation to all humankind, and most certainly the richest expression of His personal revelation, that of Christ himself. To date, however, the majority of Israel remains gospel deprived and spiritually lifeless in sin. Such passive resistance to God's will for Israel leads to divine effort to effect their quick repentance and readiness to engage in the mission God has assigned them to execute, e.g., revealing Him to the alienated nations.

The godly chastening of an unfaithful Israel is to a divinely glorious end. Israel surely remains God's chosen people. He will blot out Israel's transgressions for His own name's sake and divine objective.[36] God's rebuke of Israel (through Christian witness, e.g., Romans 11) will result in a better day, one of "renewal, salvation, and prosperity."[37] The likening of God's outpouring of water on a dry and thirsty land (Isaiah 44:3) is compared to the coming outpouring of God's Spirit on the children of the spiritually parched chosen people. The New Covenant, personal and national salvation, and the infilling of the Holy Spirit are the glorious privileges of a regenerated national Israel.[38] The divine activity among "all Israel" will cause the nations to recognize the Eternal One, the Creator and Judge of all.[39]

Peter indicated that the outpouring of Acts 2 was for the Jewish men and the residents of Jerusalem of his very day.[40] Quoting Joel 2:28,29, he advised Israel, "this is that" (Acts 2:16, KJV) promised to the Jewish people for the duration of mankind's final epoch in the present order. With the coming of the New Covenant (Matthew 26) and the issuing of the Great Commission (Matthew 28), it was now clear Israel was responsible for evangelizing the nations in keeping with the Holy Spirit's revelation in the Hebrew Bible. The day of Israel's spiritual awakening was followed by the outpouring of the Holy Spirit in Pentecostal fullness "from on high" (Isaiah 32:15; Luke 24:49). The new outpouring of the Holy Spirit upon Israel thus began on the Day of Pentecost and remains available for "all Israel" from that day until this. But what Israel enjoyed on the Day of Pentecost in Acts 2 will be even more richly experienced in the Spirit-filled State of Israel.[41] "Modern Israel still awaits that day."[42]

Israel's New Covenant Pentecostal Relationship with the Church

As earlier pointed out, Peter's address was directed to the Jewish men and the inhabitants of Jerusalem.[43] He "then declared that what they saw and heard (Acts 2:33) was a fulfillment of Joel 2:28–32."[44] This was the beginning of the last days and approaching the culmination of all things, e.g., salvation history. This would be accompanied by Israel's execution of her destiny to impact all nations for God and the climactic restoration of national Israel. What could possibly interfere or hinder the culmination of all things?

It is at this point that Horton establishes that the Church was already in existence prior to the Day of Pentecost: "Hebrews 9:15, 17 shows that it was the death of Christ that put the New Covenant into effect."[45] Resurrection life was breathed *(ruach, pneuma,* spirit*)* into the first members of the New Covenant on that first Sunday. But in fact, the inauguration of the New Covenant in Matthew 26 officially ratified the beginning of God's new relationship with Israel.

The fact that "God's purpose for the Church is the same as that for Israel"[46] is spelled out very precisely in 1 Peter 2:9,10. While some want to drive a wedge between God's people, Israel and the Church, by suggesting Joel 2:28–32 was only for the Jews and not fulfilled on the Day of Pentecost, "both Joel and Peter indicate a continuing fulfillment from the Day of Pentecost until the end of the age."[47] In fact, the natural sense of biblical narrative is that the people of God, Israel and the Church, are to function alongside one another in harmony until we see the culmination of all things in prophetic fulfillment of the Hebrew Bible; "end-time events will have fulfillment that involves both Israel and the Church. Clearly, God will be faithful to His promises to national Israel without splitting Israel and the Church into two peoples and two plans."[48]

Israel (currently represented by the faithful remnant among the Jews) and the Church (represented by the universally "grafted in" [Romans 11:23] Gentile believers) are the One People of God, both exercising faith in Jesus and partaking of the same Holy Spirit under the same New Covenant. This unity between Israel and the Church does not lessen their ethnic or group distinctives as, for example, God's purpose for national Israel will always include the Promised Land.[49]

Peoples of all ethnic and cultural stripes, including Jewish, cry out "Abba, Father" in the spirit of adopted children. Together Jews and Gentiles are heirs and joint-heirs with the Jewish Messiah, sharing the heritage of faithful children of Abraham, basking in the glorious reality of the Son of God.[50] "God's purpose to bring everything together in Christ was first seen as Christ's blood brought Jews and Gentiles together so that they became 'one new man,' one new body in Christ."[51]

Accordingly, the apostle Paul adamantly declares in Romans 11:17–25 that there is only one olive tree. The "olive tree" is Israel, onto which Gentile believers have been grafted. But when the "broken off" Jewish people, individually and corporately, are successfully provoked by Christians to spiritual jealousy, they can be immediately regrafted and begin to engage in their God-given mission.[52] The remnant serves as the "earnest" of the end-times "salvation of *all Israel,*" when national Israel experiences full messianic redemption (Romans 11:25,26).

In another metaphor, apostolic teaching insists the "wall of partition" (Ephesians 2:14, KJV) has been obliterated through the work of the Cross. Divinely abolished, it does not exist anymore. Two groups of humanity, by virtue of their membership in the same New Covenant, are now to work together in carrying out the divine purpose.[53] After the Cross, what had been a great mystery was revealed: Jews and Gentiles have been united into the one people of God in the Jewish Messiah and are fellow heirs of God's promises.[54] The powerful representation of formerly alienated peoples—Jews and Gentiles—functioning in unity and peace is as rich a testimony today as in the first century.[55]

The dividing barrier has been successfully removed by the Cross. The Church needs to see what God sees. It is the blood of Jesus—His blood of the New Covenant—that forever brings Jews and Gentiles together into "one new man" (Ephesians 2:15) in Christ.[56] Yet Horton clearly notes that "the Church is never called sons of Israel, nor is it ever divided into tribes. . . . The New Testament does recognize the Jews as the Twelve Tribes."[57] In the New Jerusalem the twelve gates bear the names of Israel's tribes while the foundations are marked with the names of the twelve apostles. The richest display of Israel and Church unity in Christ as the one people of God will be eternally celebrated.[58] "[B]oth Jews and Gentiles will join in perfect worship and in the blessings of the Spirit."[59]

The Climax of Salvation History

Stanley Horton stated, "Clearly, God will be faithful to His promises to national Israel without splitting Israel and the Church into two peoples and two plans."[60] Neither does the Hebrew Bible indicate a need for a long delay between the first and second comings of Messiah Jesus.[61] All that is needed for Israel to see His soon appearing is for them to acknowledge Jesus with "Blessed is He who comes in the name of the Lord!" (Matthew 23:39). There is no required time gap, for God is event purposed, not time driven. The event is Israel's recognition of Jesus' kingship, which can happen any time the Church commits to successfully provoke Israel to spiritual jealousy.[62]

In the end, however, we find ultimate success, e.g., the twelve apostles ruling the twelve tribes of Israel in the patriarchal Promised Land with "all Israel" living in a restored Zion, cleansed from sin, and Holy Spirit baptized.[63] During the millennial reign of the Jewish Messiah Jesus from a revitalized Israel, the Jewish people will face no hindrances to perfectly executing their divine mission of proclaiming the gospel to all nations so that the rest of humankind will also have the privilege of embracing Israel's Davidic monarch and the true God of all creation.

Although the Jewish people shall return to the land of Israel in unbelief,[64] God forever rehearses His purpose to honor His covenant with them in which "they would be a peculiar (valued, choice, chosen, special) treasure to God, a kingdom of priests, or, as the New Testament puts it, a royal priesthood, and a holy (dedicated, consecrated, separated) nation."[65] No longer disqualified by unbelief in God's Anointed One, "all Israel" acknowledges that "God continues to fulfill His promise to the offspring of Abraham even to this day."[66] The Lion of the Tribe of Judah "brings fulfillment to the promises made to God's ancient people, Israel."[67] As Horton writes:

> God will restore Israel to her land and give her a spiritual restoration as well (Isaiah 54:11–14; 58:8; Ezekiel 36:33–38; 37:1–28; Zechariah 9:16). The desert will be restored to fertility and beauty (Isaiah 41:19,20; 51:3). Even the animals will be changed (Isaiah 11:6–9). The Holy Spirit will do a transforming work, and undoubtedly even the atmosphere will be cleansed from all pollution.[68]

The Gentile nations will recognize and love the Jews as the blessed, chosen people of God and the rightful heirs of the Promised Land. The evidence of God's abundant blessing upon them will settle any doubts as God indeed makes Israel a blessing to all peoples, all families of the earth.[69]

The chosen people are not only the seed of Jacob but also the work of God's hands. God purifies the nation of Israel, fully resanctifying them upon their repentance and faith in Jesus. The "holy nation" promised in Exodus 19:6 will fully exhibit God as "the Holy One of Jacob" (Isaiah 29:23) and stand in holy reverence before Him.[70] In place of rebellion and murmuring, the Jewish people now exhibit discernment and accept instruction.

In the present, God still wants to use the Church to proclaim the gospel in the power of the Holy Spirit to the whole house of Israel.[71] The Lord himself "will come, save, and transform them. Changed hearts and lives will be even more supernatural than the desert blossoming."[72] In that day, nations will restore Israel to its own land. Instead of nations taking possession of Israel, Israel will possess the nations, and the people of the nations will serve Israel. Their captors will be the captives, and Israel will rule over the despots who once oppressed them. God will still use Israel in His divine plan.[73]

One People of God: One Plan for the Ages

Horton has insisted, "God's purpose for the Church is the same as that for Israel."[74] There is only one "olive tree." It bears repeating that "God will be faithful to His promises to national Israel without splitting Israel and the Church into two peoples and two plans."[75]

The New Covenant prophesied by Jeremiah (31:31–34) and made fully functional by the Jewish Messiah Jesus (Matthew 26:26–28) was established not with Christian denominations but with "the house of Israel and the house of Judah" (Jeremiah 33:14). Yet the empowering of faithful Israel with Spirit baptism on the Day of Pentecost in fulfillment of Joel 2:28–32 had ramifications for both Israel and Gentile Christians. Not only for Israel, but for Messiah's Gentile sheepfold as well would the opportunity for a New Covenant relationship with God, eternal salvation, and the infilling of the Holy Spirit be available.[76] It is no wonder then that all God's people experience the climax of the ages together and in unity.

For the end, the Hebrew prophets envisioned the restoration of the nations to God, who would bring His peace to the entire globe.[77] The Jewish prophets looked ahead and saw restoration. God would bring peace, not only to Israel, but also to the whole world, as "many nations shall be joined to the LORD" (Zechariah 2:11, KJV).

With Jews and Gentiles sharing in messianic ministries and a common spiritual heritage even in the Promised Land, the absence of a middle wall of partition will be witnessed by the overwhelming evidence to unity of the "One New Man" in Christ. These fellow members of the same New Covenant are fully joined in perfect Pentecostal worship and the Holy Spirit's multiplied blessings.[78] Their common sonship to God will be manifestly celebrated.

So, What's the Eschatological-Pneumatological Delay?

Why the delay in Israel's redemption? Since Israel is to play this central and leading role in the international proclamation of the glad truth of the gospel, why doesn't Israel get on with it? When shall the "last days" come to their promised conclusion with the reign of Jesus upon the earth and His ruling Israel and all nations from Zion? When indeed shall the Holy Spirit be poured out upon "all mankind," not just segments of humanity? When shall the "survivors of Israel" (Isaiah 4:2) be fully reclaimed for their messianic destiny in the Promised Land?

To Stanley Horton, the Church and Israel are forever linked in God's program. God has one people and one plan for the ages. But that oneness and joint plan is too often ignored or disputed in Christian theological circles. Nowhere is the indictment more radically proven than when one observes classical Christian doctrines of the Holy Spirit (pneumatology) and the last days (eschatology). Orthodox Christianity, including many Evangelicals and Dispensationalists, override apostolic doctrine and prophetic biblical witness to the chief importance of Abraham's progeny, national Israel and the international Jewish world.

Dismissing the relevance of God's commitments to "all Israel" as having only spiritual and allegorical significance to the Church is often an unintended assault on God's integrity. Yet the effect is to make God's Word shallow and unreliable. Those who do theologically retain God's promises to Israel too often simply want to relegate fulfillment to the utopian future. But the negative impact upon the opportunities for the redemption of Israel are lost in either one of these "replacement" systems.

Restorationist Pentecostalism of the early twentieth century sought to honor the fraternal relationship with "all Israel" in ways often unimaginable to modern Christian circles.[79] But over the course of succeeding generations, the role of Israel in the last days, Israel's Holy Spirit experience past, present, and future, and the Pentecostal duty to proclaim the gospel to the Jewish world in the power of the Holy Spirit have become obscured.

Stanley Horton's doctrines of the Holy Spirit and of the last days never made these mistakes. He recognized the present interplay God has always intended for Israel and the Church. That interplay is possible only as apostolic Christians deliberately provoke temporarily backslidden Israel to spiritual jealousy in the demonstration of the fullness of the Spirit. Horton fully supports Jewish evangelism at the very present hour:

> The future miraculous salvation of Israel, however, does not mean that we should neglect seeking the salvation of Jews today. . . . Therefore, even though some Jews rejected Jesus, Jesus did not reject Israel as a nation.[80]
>
> His faithfulness would also be seen in giving them a new heart and a new spirit and in putting His Spirit within them (Ezekiel 36:26-27; 37:14).[81]

Horton, like the apostle Paul, recognized God's eternal heart of love for Israel and God's passion to infuse "all Israel" with the life of the Spirit.[82] God's desire to pour out His lovingkindness (*chesed*) upon Israel proclaimed in Ezekiel's day was reiterated in loving witness in apostolic times and is still God's intention for Israel at this present hour. May God's engrafted Gentile branches serve as conduits of God's love and mercy. Functioning as channels of God's grace, may the Pentecostals, with all Holy Spirit boldness, provoke "all Israel" to spiritual jealousy to receive everlasting life in Jesus in these last days.

269

Endnotes

1. Stanley M. Horton, *What the Bible Says about the Holy Spirit* (Springfield, MO: Gospel Publishing House, 1976).

2. All Scriptures quotations, unless otherwise indicated, are taken from the New American Standard Bible.

3. Stanley M. Horton, *Bible Prophecy: Understanding Future Events,* Spiritual Discovery Series (Springfield, MO: Gospel Publishing House, 1995, rev. ed., 2003), 24.

4. Ibid.

5. Ibid., 25.

6. Ibid., 27.

7. Stanley M. Horton, *The Book of Acts* (Springfield, MO: Gospel Publishing House, 1981), 21.

8. Horton, *Bible Prophecy,* 27.

9. Ibid.

10. Ibid., 88.

11. Stanley M. Horton, *Isaiah: A Logion Press Commentary* (Springfield, MO: Gospel Publishing House, 2000), 348.

12. Ibid., 95.

13. Horton, *Book of Acts,* 22.

14. Ibid.

15. Horton, *Bible Prophecy,* 28.

16. Stanley M. Horton, *The Promise of His Coming* (Springfield, MO: Gospel Publishing House, 1967), 66.

17. Ibid., 13.

18. Ibid.

19. Ibid., 66.

20. Ibid.

21. Horton, *Isaiah,* 334.

22. Horton, *Promise,* 67.

23. Stanley M. Horton, "The Last Things," in *Systematic Theology,* rev. ed., ed. Stanley M. Horton, 620 (Springfield, MO: Gospel Publishing House, Logion Press, 1995). Horton quotes here from the three-volume work on *Systematic Theology* crafted by former General Superintendent E. S. Williams, vol. 3, 224, 233.

24. Horton, *Systematic Theology,* 621–22.

25. Stanley M. Horton, *Our Destiny: Biblical Teachings on the Last Things* (Springfield, MO: Gospel Publishing House, 1996), 190.

26. Ibid.

27. Ibid., 191.

28. Ibid., 197.

29. Horton, *Bible Prophecy,* 29.

30. Ibid.

31. Ibid., 74.

32. Ibid., 29.

33. Ibid., 76. See also Romans 11.

[34] Horton, *Our Destiny*, 176.
[35] See Ephesians 2.
[36] Horton, *Isaiah*, 35.
[37] Ibid., 250.
[38] Ibid., 483.
[39] Ibid., 35.
[40] Horton, *Book of Acts*, 37.
[41] Horton, *Isaiah*, 334.
[42] Ibid., 250.
[43] Horton, *Book of Acts*, 37.
[44] Ibid., 38.
[45] Ibid., 31.
[46] Stanley M. Horton, *The Ultimate Victory: An Exposition of the Book of Revelation* (Springfield, MO: Gospel Publishing House, 1991), 27.
[47] Horton, *Our Destiny*, 177.
[48] Ibid.
[49] Horton, *Systematic Theology*, 630.
[50] Horton, *The Promise*, 63.
[51] Ibid., 85. See Ephesians 2:13–16.
[52] Horton, *Our Destiny*, 175–76.
[53] Horton, *The Promise*, 85.
[54] Ibid., 85, 86.
[55] Ibid., 87.
[56] Ibid., 85.
[57] Horton, *Ultimate Victory*, 112. See Luke 22:30; Acts 26:7; James 1:1.
[58] Horton, *Systematic Theology*, 636. See Galatians 3:28; cf. Ephesians 2:11–22.
[59] Horton, *Promise*, 16.
[60] Horton, *Our Destiny*, 177.
[61] Horton, *Systematic Theology*, 620.
[62] See the context for Romans 11:25,26 where "fullness" *(pleroma)* is not numerical (i.e., quantitative) but spiritually elevated to the fullness of Christlike redemptive character (i.e., qualitative).
[63] Horton, *Systematic Theology*, 630. See Luke 22:30 and Genesis 15:18.
[64] Horton, *Bible Prophecy*, 29. See Ezekiel 36:25–28.
[65] Horton, *Promise*, 11. See Exodus 19:4–6; 1 Peter 2:9–10.
[66] Horton, *Bible Prophecy*, 25.
[67] Horton, *Ultimate Victory*, 86.
[68] Ibid., 292, 293.
[69] Horton, *Isaiah*, 440. See also Zechariah 8:13.
[70] Ibid., 233.
[71] Ibid.
[72] Ibid., 265
[73] Ibid., 145.
[74] Horton, *Ultimate Victory*, 27.
[75] Horton, *Our Destiny*, 177.

[76] Ibid.

[77] Horton, *Bible Prophecy*, 76.

[78] Horton, *Promise*, 15, 16. See Isaiah 25:9; 62:10–12; 66:18; Jeremiah 31:31–34; Ezekiel 47:21–23; Zechariah 2:11; and Ephesians 2:14,15.

[79] For a thorough discussion of Pentecostal-Israel fraternity, see Raymond L. Gannon, "The Shifting Romance with Israel: American Pentecostal Ideology of Zionism and the Jewish State" (Ph.D. diss., Hebrew University of Jerusalem, 2003).

[80] Horton, *Our Destiny*, 196, 197.

[81] Ibid., 202.

[82] "God really wanted Israel to enjoy this new heart and new spirit in Ezekiel's day. . . . God still called them to repent, get rid of their rebellious sins, and make for themselves a new heart and a new spirit. He did not take any pleasure in bringing judgment and death, so why did they not turn back to Him and live (18:30–32)? That is, they could make a new heart and spirit for themselves by coming back to God and letting Him renew them by His Spirit. Horton, *What the Bible Says about the Holy Spirit*, 70.

AFTERWORD

The apostle Paul wrote to the Philippians (3:13,14), "Forgetting what is behind and straining toward what is ahead, I press on toward the goal to win the prize for which God has called me heavenward in Christ Jesus." But there were times when he did remember and remind others of his times of weakness as well as the signs and wonders that accompanied his ministry.

As I look back, I remember too many times of weakness and failure. I regret those times, but I remember also the love, grace, and faithfulness of God. He has never failed me.

I grew up surrounded by people who helped me and encouraged me to follow the Lord. I did not have a dramatic conversion like the apostle Paul or like so many of the people who testify on television today. However, my baptism in the Holy Spirit was more intense and glorious than anything I could have ever imagined or desired. After that, God more quietly led me but always in His own wonderful way. I still press on.

May the Holy Spirit inspire all the readers of this book to do the same.

Dr. Stanley M. Horton
Springfield, Missouri
November 2008

Appendix A

Fitting Tributes

If it were up to Stanley Horton, this appendix would not exist. Being the humble man he is, the premier Pentecostal theologian is not one to promote himself.[1] "He never looked at what he did as being for honor or recognition," recalls his daughter-in-law, Diana, "but he just felt led to keep expanding and doing and investigating. It was just his nature. He didn't do it for what the public was going to think, but because of what was inside him—it was his way to serve." As Horton would put it, "I just wanted to do what I felt the Lord wanted me to do."

Even with his own family, Horton never spoke about his work, obligations, honors, awards, or the like—unless they asked. The walls in the entryway of his apartment at Maranatha Village now contain a myriad of plaques and honors—items that were simply stored in a box for decades. "I never knew he had all those plaques," said his son, Ed, "until he moved to Maranatha!"

First Timothy 5:17 says, "The elders who rule [*proistemi*, stand before, preside, practice, maintain] well are to be considered worthy of double honor, especially those who work hard at preaching and teaching" (NASB). It is fitting, then, in this biography of one who has "stood well" before us these many decades, to show double honor—not only to tell the story of his life and to include here a list of his memberships in organizations to give added insight into his life, but also to show the many tokens of recognition others have bestowed upon him for his remarkable contributions to the furtherance of the kingdom of God.

Memberships

Life Member California Scholarship Federation Honor Society (awarded February 2, 1933), from High School ". . . by reason of his consistent and superior Scholarship and Service."

Life Member Phi Alpha Chi (Gordon-Conwell Honor Society) Phi Alpha Chi stands for the motto *Philoi Aletheias Christou*—"Lovers of the Truth of Christ."[2] This society is comparable to Phi Beta Kappa.

Member: Evangelical Theological Society

More important to Horton than the AG's entrance into the National Association of Evangelicals (NAE) in 1942 was the establishment of the Evangelical Theological Society (ETS)[3] in 1949. Horton joined the Society in 1951, not long after it was established. A May 5, 1957, article in *The Centralite* reported on his address to the ETS meeting in St. Louis on April 18–19 and his leading the opening devotions.

In 1963, the Midwestern Section of the ETS held its 8th general meeting at CBI. The April 18, 1963, article on the front page of the school's paper, *The Centralite*, "Evangelical Theological Meet at CBI," notes that membership included "professors or deans who have acquired a Master's degree or better in Theology of Bible." At that time, Stanley Horton, Theodore Kessel, Bob Cooley, Russ Spittler, and Bill Menzies were members. Distinguished guests presented papers and attended an "autograph party" on the last evening.

One of the most significant meetings to Horton took place later that year, the national meeting on December 28, 1963, in Grand Rapids, Michigan. In preparation for that meeting, Dr. Burton Goddard had asked Horton to arrange a Pentecostal-Evangelical dialogue.[4] William G. MacDonald, a CBI/C professor from 1963–66, presented an excellent paper on the baptism in the Holy Spirit, and Horton and Russ Spittler served on a panel. Horton recalls overhearing Dr. Kenneth Kantzer, then editor of *Christianity Today*, comment how well MacDonald's paper was received. Those in attendance were sympathetic to the Pentecostal viewpoint and truly wanted to know what they believed. The meeting dismissed late, and several even followed Horton and his CBI colleagues to their rooms where they all "continued to talk about the Lord and the Holy Spirit until after midnight."[5] Even the next morning at breakfast, a Baptist member was asking Horton how one receives the baptism in the Holy Spirit.

Dr. Bob Cooley, who in 1970 served as president of ETS, remembers how Pentecostals during that time were not fully welcome in the broader world of the Evangelicals. There had been quite a discussion about whether or not Pentecostals should be admitted into the NAE, but they eventually were. Both C. C. Burnett who became secretary and Thomas Zimmerman—the first Pentecostal to be elected as NAE president—were active early on. But in those days, Pentecostals were considered anti-intellectual. So ETS, as a professional academic society, was a context in which Pentecostals could defuse the potentially harmful effects of that image. Since Horton had a Gordon-Conwell and a Harvard degree, he was well respected for his scholarship, and this respect opened the door for other Pentecostals to join. Because Horton and others, like C. C. Burnett and Robert Ashcroft, launched out into the wider world, they were able to show that following Christ into all the world was far more important than being restrained by the boundaries of the General Council.

Member: American Scientific Affiliation

Member: American Association of Professors of Hebrew

Member: Near East Archaeological Society

Member: Society of Biblical Literature

Member: National Association of Evangelicals (served on the Theology Commission)

Life Member: Central Baptist Theological Seminary Alumni Association

Honors and Awards

(1954) *The Cup* (CBC Yearbook)—dedicated to Dr. Horton

(1970) Outstanding Educators of America

"This is to certify that Stanley M. Horton has been selected to appear in the 1970 edition of Outstanding Educators of America in recognition of contributions made to the advancement of education and service to community, state and country (John Putman, Director)"

"The Outstanding Educators of America is an annual program designed to recognize and honor those men and women who have distinguished themselves by exceptional service, achievements and leadership in education. . . . Nominations . . . are made by the presidents, deans . . . and other heads of . . . colleges."[6]

(1973, April 12) Central Bible College—Twenty-five Years of Dedicated Service

(1975) AG Honors Horton for His Writing Ministry

"A tribute to Stanley M. Horton in recognition of the outstanding contribution to the Assemblies of God through his writing ministry."—1975 Spring Communications Seminar, Assemblies of God

During a communication seminar of AG editors and writers at the AG grad school, General Superintendent Thomas F. Zimmerman presented Dr. Horton with a plaque "for his outstanding contribution to the Assemblies of God through his writing ministry." Zimmerman noted that Horton's "strict adherence to the principles which produced our movement shines through in his recurring emphasis upon the need to contend for the faith once delivered to the saints."[7] The article mentions Horton's twenty-five years of writing church school literature and says that Horton's name had become "known to hundreds of thousands of church school teachers and students around the world."

(1977) Adult Teacher Award from Sunday School Department To Stanley M. Horton:

Unique is the word for Dr. Stanley M. Horton who for 25 years has served as writer for the *Adult Teacher*, while at the same time presiding in the classroom at Central Bible College, and more recently at the Assemblies of God Graduate School. His name has become known to many thousands of Sunday school teachers and students in America and around the world.

AG General Superintendent Thomas F. Zimmerman presenting an award to Horton from the AG editors and writers, paying tribute to him for his "outstanding contribution to the Assemblies of God through his writing ministry" (*The Centralite*, March 19, 1975)

In addition to the *Adult Teacher*, he has authored ten books, written countless articles, and prepared many book reviews. Through his avocation of writing he has made a unique contribution to Assemblies of God literature.

Dr. Horton possesses a unique religious background. His early years in Los Angeles were spent among relatives and friends who helped pioneer Pentecost in California. His dedication to the principles which produced our Movement shines through in his recurring admonition to "contend for the faith once delivered to the saints."

This man has a unique educational background. Those acquainted with him know his deep immersion in the languages and customs of the Scriptures. But many do not know that one of his majors in higher education was science, a subject he has taught at Central Bible College.

In the quarterly Dr. Horton often opens up a rich treasure of meaning in one of the words or phrases of the original languages. In addition, his scientific background is often put to good use. He has checked the content of a high school course on the Bible and science.

Stanley Horton often serves on committees which hammer out doctrinal points for the General Council of the Assemblies of God. His understanding of the nuances of the original languages makes his contributions especially significant.

Also unique is the happy marriage of intellect and humility found in this man. In committee work he is not talkative, preferring to wait until he can make a significant contribution. But his quiet presence is felt, and often his precise interpretation of the Scriptures has helped the group reach a satisfactory decision.

Even on the few occasions when major changes have been necessary in his materials, Brother Horton has shown the humility of true greatness. Never once have the fires of resentment flashed. Never once has he flaunted his superior educational credentials.

Dr. Stanley M. Horton came to his work as professor and writer with fine educational and mental tools. He has honed those tools by personal application, and a desire to become a craftsman. Today, increasingly, he is using those tools to benefit multiplied thousands—and as he himself wants more than all else—to bring glory to God.

(1977, 1992 Editions) Inclusion in *Who's Who in Religion*

(1978) CBC—Thirty Years

> "With Deep Appreciation to Dr. Stanley M. Horton for thirty years of faithful and generous service: The unique combination of scholastic attainment, humility, and submission to the Holy Spirit, coupled with skillful teaching and writing ministries, have inspired his students and colleagues alike."—Central Bible College, 1948–1978

(1978) Stanley Horton Dorm (CBC)

> In November of 1976 the Board of Directors approved a new, 178-bed men's dorm, to address the housing problem due to increasing enrollment at the college. Groundbreaking ceremonies for the $810,000, three-level structure were scheduled for February 1977.
>
> The February 24, 1979, issue of *The Centralite* publicized that CBC had honored Dr. Horton as a "prominent Pentecostal scholar and longtime CBC faculty member by naming its newest dormitory the Stanley M. Horton Hall."

(1978–1979 Edition) Inclusion in *Who's Who in the Midwest*

(1979) Assemblies of God Graduate School Five Hundred Foundation

> "Stanley M. Horton is an active member of the AGGS Five Hundred Foundation. The purpose of this foundation is to provide continuing financial assistance for advanced-level ministerial education for pastors, missionaries, Christian educators, chaplains,

Horton (ca. 2007) with grandson Zachary Stilts
by the CBC men's dorm named in his honor in 1979

and other church-related ministries. The projection of this foundation is to provide 500 annual academic cost grants in the amount
of $2400 each to be used in the support of the Assemblies of God
Graduate School educational program. (January 1, 1979; T. F. Zimmerman, President; D. R. Guynes, Executive Vice President)"

(1987) AGTS—"Distinguished Professor of Bible and Theology"

"The Board of Directors of the Assemblies of God Theological
Seminary hereby awards the title of 'Distinguished Professor of
Bible and Theology' to Dr. Stanley M. Horton in recognition of
outstanding and distinguished service. (June 4, 1987)"

(1988) 70th Birthday Festschriften: *Faces of Renewal: Studies in Honor of Stanley M. Horton Presented On His 70th Birthday*. (Peabody, MA: Hendrickson Pubs., 1988).

Paul Elbert, physicist-theologian and New Testament scholar, serves
as an adjunct faculty in Scripture, Science, and Theological German at the
Church of God Theological Seminary in Cleveland, Tennessee.[8] Elbert became
acquainted with Horton through the Society for Pentecostal Studies (SPS) and
edited this Festschrift, which was presented to Horton at SPS in 1988. Horton
was also honored at the June 2, 1988, AGTS baccalaureate when Dr. Gary B.
McGee presented an honorary copy of *Faces of Renewal* to him.[9]

This book included biblical studies, historical studies, and contemporary studies. One article that was especially meaningful to Horton was McGee's piece, "Levi Lupton: A Forgotten Pioneer of Early Pentecostalism," since Levi Lupton was the principal of the missionary training school Horton's father had attended and graduated from. Dr. William Menzies also collaborated with Elbert to include an excellent biographical sketch.

Of the book, Elbert says: "Looking back on this effort, F. F. Bruce's jacket comment for *Faces*, that 'All who are interested in the theology and experience of renewal will find enlightenment here, while students of the Bible and church history will welcome its fresh perspectives on their special studies,' is harmonious with my perception that Stanley's pastoral and biblical studies were indeed festschrift worthy. Everything I had read from his pen convinced me that here was someone the Holy Spirit was especially working with to do God's work in a scholarly and sensitive Christ-centered manner."[10]

The following are excerpts from the biographical sketch:

During his truly evangelical career he has evidenced a rare combination of gifts and graces as a Christian leader whose humble piety, intellect, disciplined study, and keen sense of practical ministry have commanded our respect and admiration.

His spiritual wisdom and understanding, poured into the lives of thousands of students during forty years of classroom teaching, have had and continue to have a godly and steadying influence.

My . . . first contact with Stanley came through his written ministry, . . . I was immediately impressed by the sober pastoral concern and the emphasis on spiritual reality in his writings. His devotion to serving our Lord through a thoughtful application of his distinctive charisma of pastoral scholarship led me to a deep appreciation of this genuine and humble servant. His generous friendship as a colleague has always been warm and courteous and his interest in the scientific underpinnings of much theological discussion is always dynamic and progressive. I believe that his unfailing attention to duty, his life-long obedience to God's call, and his charismatic and sacrificial love of God's people enable us to recognize his true stature. . . .

As a person . . . Dr. Horton has lived out before us those qualities of Christian grace worth emulating. In addition to these personal graces, faithfully and unpretentiously shared, the Lord's servant has placed before us some important theological and biblical insights. These may well serve to chart a helpful course for younger leaders and thinkers to consider . . . for Stanley is not only a man of the Spirit, but a devoted student of Scripture. Equipped with a command of the biblical languages and insight into the scholarly literature of biblical studies, he has synthesized his biblical understanding and his fellowship with Christ into a thoroughgoing evangelical world view. His pen has perhaps fashioned the most significant theological affirmations in the classical Pentecostal tradition.

As Stanley approaches the sunset of a fruitful career of service it is indeed fitting that many of his friends, former pupils, and professional colleagues should seek to honor him with a collection of essays. And so it is with warm feelings of appreciation and thanksgiving for his ministry that we offer him this volume on his seventieth birthday. We believe him to be eminently festschrift-worthy and wish him and his wife, Evelyn, who is organist at their local church, many happy and peaceful years together.[11]

(1991) AGTS—Distinguished Professor Emeritus of Bible and Theology

(1991) Honorary L.H.D. (Litterarum Humanorum Doctor) from Faraston Theological Seminary

(1993) AGTS—Delta Alpha Distinguished Educator Award

(1996) 50 Years of Service (AG) for 50 Years of Ordained Ministry in the Assemblies of God (April 10, 1996)

(1996) Berean University—Named to the Royal Order of Berea

(2000) Assemblies of God—Christian Higher Education Award

(2001) Society for Pentecostal Studies—Lifetime Achievement Award

(2006) Sixty Years as a credentialed minister in Southern Missouri district (April 19, 2006)

(2006) 90th Birthday Celebration

In celebration of his ninetieth birthday, Dr. Horton was presented with a book full of greetings from friends and family. A selection from this book has been included as Appendix B.

(2008) The Dr. Stanley M. Horton Pentecostal Heritage Lectureship Series

Funded by an anonymous donor who had been greatly influenced by Dr. Horton's life and work, the annual lectureship series at Evangel University is intended to reinforce the importance of the Pentecostal doctrine and heritage of the Assemblies of God. For the inaugural event on April 3, Dr. William Menzies interviewed Dr. Horton about his Pentecostal

Horton at the AGTS President's Brunch, May 6, 2006.
Those in attendance sang "Happy Birthday" to Horton in honor of his
ninetieth birthday. Back, l to r: Pastor Charlie Arsenault; Dr. Steve Lim,
AGTS Academic Dean; Lil Arsenault; Yen Lim; Dr. Jim Hernando.
Front l to r: Victor Ostrom, Dr. Stanley Horton; Dr. Darrin Rodgers,
Director of the Flower Pentecostal Heritage Center

heritage. On April 4, his son, Dr. Robert P. Menzies, preached on "Acts 2:17–21: A Paradigm for Pentecostal Mission."

(2009) *Assemblies of God Heritage* magazine—Dr. Stanley Horton was featured on the cover article of the 2009 issue.

(2009) The Dr. Stanley M. Horton Scholarly Resources Endowment Fund

Through the Pillars of the Faith project, "AGTS has chosen to honor men and women who have dedicated their lives to serve Jesus Christ and have followed the call of God in ministry, missions and the training of ministers. We acknowledge their generous contribution to AGTS and its mission to shape servant leaders. The Pillars of the Faith initiative is a symbolic and meaningful way to honor these individuals.

"Persons being honored have been nominated by the president and approved by the Board of Directors in addition to meeting the following qualifications:

- Dedicated the majority of his or her life to significant full-time ministry in the AG.
- At least 65 years of age; a deceased person may be honored posthumously.

283

- An endowment gift of $25,000 or more to AGTS in honor of the minister.

These and future honorees will be acknowledged prominently on a pillar located outside the AGTS Prayer Chapel."[13]

The alumni of AGTS launched The Dr. Stanley M. Horton Scholarly Resources Endowment Fund campaign in the spring of 2009 to honor Dr. Horton through the Pillars of the Faith initiative and presented this honor to him at the AGTS graduation, May 2009. The endowment fund provides an annual scholarship of biblical-theological and Pentecostal history books for the C. C. Burnett Library in Dr. Horton's name. (See http://agts.edu/more/horton/)

AGTS "Pillars of the Faith"

Stanley Horton with his signature smile on the occasion of his ninetieth birthday

"My father told me recently that he still feels called to do whatever the Lord has for him to do, and that sense doesn't stop when you're seventy or eighty or ninety. It stops when God calls you home."

—Faith Horton Stilts

Endnotes

[1] Horton told his daughter a story once about someone in the 1960s or 1970s who actually took credit for some writing that he had done—and got a promotion instead of him. Irate when she heard this story, she remembers asking him, "Well, why didn't you, you know, do something about it?" Horton merely smiled and said, "Because I knew the Lord would take care of me, and it wasn't my place to do that. Anyhow, it turned out that he got that promotion, but he very quickly died out and was never heard from again. And I'm still here."

[2] "Gordon Faculty Online," Gordon College, http://faculty.gordon.edu/ns/craig_story/PhiAlphaChi.cfm (accessed September 6, 2008).

[3] "How Did the ETS Begin?" Evangelical Theological Society, http://www.etsjets.org/?q=faq (accessed September 6, 2008). "The impetus for this fellowship came from the faculty members of Gordon Divinity School, who proposed that conservative scholars meet regularly for biblical and theological discussion. As a result, sixty evangelical scholars convened in Cincinnati, Ohio, December 27–28, 1949."

[4] Horton, *Reflections*, 74.

[5] Ibid., 75.

[6] "Three CBC Teachers Selected to Outstanding Educators of America," *The Centralite*, October 2, 1970, 1.

[7] "A/G Honors Springfield Writer-Teacher," *The Centralite*, March 19, 1975, 1.

[8] http://www.cogts.edu/directory/p_elbert.htm

[9] "Special Book, Presentation Ceremony Honor Writer, Teacher Stanley Horton," *Pentecostal Evangel,* July 31, 1988, 25.

[10] Paul Elbert, e-mail message to the author, April 18, 2008.

[11] Paul Elbert and William Menzies, eds., *Faces of Renewal: Studies in Honor of Stanley M. Horton Presented On His 70th Birthday* (Peabody, MA: Hendrickson Pubs., 1988), xvii-xx.

[12] Audio of the April 3, 2008, Evangel University chapel service (Interview of Stanley Horton by William Menzies): http://www.evangel.edu/Students/SpiritualLife/ChapelAudio/files/2008_0403_DrHorton_DrMenzies_Interview.mp3.

[13] "Pillars of the Faith," Assemblies of God Theological Seminary, http://www.agts.edu/partners/pillars_of_faith.html (accessed September 6, 2008).

Appendix B

Selections from Dr. Horton's 90th Birthday Book

Presented to him May 2006, at his birthday celebration at Central Assembly of God, Springfield, Missouri

~Listed Alphabetically by Last Name~

Ben Aker, AGTS Professor Emeritus of New Testament Exegesis
"We were both young men, I more than you, when I first remember you. I was a student of yours at CBC in the mid-sixties and new to the Assemblies of God and to in-depth study of scripture. I am most grateful for your influence and friendship over this intervening time. . . . One event of note regarding your influence comes immediately to mind. Coming from a ranch in New Mexico, my background did not prepare me for public life. I remember the feeling of being overwhelmed when I was chosen to represent my senior class as commencement speaker. The sermon had to be completely memorized without the aid of notes. As my trembling body mounted the steps of the platform, I looked up and you were there sitting on the platform. You gave me that wonderful Dr. Horton smile and a nod of your head—I shall never forget that moment of encouragement. Our thanks are to you for the wonderful space you have filled in our lives and to God who makes it possible."

Zenas J. Bicket, AG Educator and Author
"It is indeed a great privilege to reflect on and share some of the blessings your life has been to ours over the years. It all began as a student in your classes at CBC. Your classes always conveyed your love for God's Word and your sensitive spirit toward students who were finding God's path for their lives. Then years later, it was a privilege to serve with you on the Doctrinal Purity Commission. You always had such a balanced and wise approach to the many difficult issues we were discussing. Now, in my retirement days, I admire your continued contribution to the Assemblies of God and the larger Kingdom in your excellent books and writings for various publications. I often find myself quoting appropriate

passages from many of your scholarly writings. May the Lord give you many more opportunities to use your gifted talents for the advance of the Kingdom of God. Rhoda and I appreciate you more than you will ever know."
John Philip Blondo, AGWM

"As a young man hungry to study the Word of God at AGTS in the 1980s, you impacted my life greatly. I will be forever thankful for your verse by verse exposition of Isaiah. You made the Word truly come alive. You inspired us with your burning desire to know Christ! Your illustrations made the Word so practical. You lived before us a life of humility before God! . . . Now it has been my joy to serve for 14 years as an Assemblies of God World Missionary to the Chinese . . . [and] as the Missionary in Residence at Zion Bible College. . . . Our students use your textbook for the Book of Acts. I am delighted to tell them that you were my teacher and a wonderful example of integrity in ministry."
Sam Brelo, AGWM Missionary to the Middle East (AGTS 1984–85.)

"I was greatly blessed by your teaching in and outside of the classroom. I appreciate your obvious love for Jesus. God used your classes to develop a love in me for His Word, but more importantly a love for the God of the Word. God used you in the development of my own theology. Please know that your teaching, in one form or another, has been passed on to Arabs and Jews in the Middle East where I have had the privilege to minister. . . . Thank you for being one of my mentors."
James K. Bridges, General Treasurer of the Assemblies of God (2006)

"I have admired your life and ministry and scholarly example to us all. You have been a role model for Pentecostal theologians and scholars in our Movement and around the world. We salute you!"
Rod R. Butterworth, CBC 1969, AGTS 1974

"I remember sitting just in front of you during a chapel service and hearing you cry out to God with humility and zeal during a time of worship and prayer. . . . I want to thank you also for your graciousness in being willing to write the foreword for my book *Walking With God.*"
Joseph L. Castleberry, Academic Dean AGTS (2006); President of Northwest University (2008)

"When I was a young child in A/G churches, I used to read your columns in the *Pentecostal Evangel.* As I grew up, it meant so much to me to know that an A/G scholar could graduate from Harvard and still be a faithful Pentecostal. It was your example—along with the very few who followed in your footsteps in those years of the 1960's and 1970's—that inspired me to dream of a first-class graduate education and to believe that I could achieve it. Though I was never in your classes, you were still my teacher—a shining example of faithful Pentecostal scholarship for me to emulate."
David W. Clark, President, Palm Beach Atlantic University

"I had the wonderful privilege of sitting in on one of your summer classes at CBC while I was a student at Evangel University. I was impressed by your intellect, humility, and spiritual depth. I have discovered in the intervening years this is a rare combination of gifts [for] a . . . professor."
Nita (Juanita) Colbaugh, cousin (Wesley and Ruth Steelberg's daughter; Elmer Kirk Fisher's granddaughter)

"Stanley, you were always the academic star of our extended family. We had high regard for . . . your wisdom . . . and your desire to know all that was to be known about the scripture. Most of all we honor you for your contribution to the Kingdom through your selfless dedication."

Glen D. Cole, Pastor Emeritus, Capital Christian Center, Sacramento, CA (2006);
Pastor, Trinity Life Center of Sacramento (2008)
"I remember well my early days at Central Bible Institute . . . in 1951. . . .
My life was greatly impacted, my vision forged, and my calling solidified. . . .
You have touched my life in a significant way, as well as the lives of many of my
contemporaries. . . . I love you in the Lord. Your humble spirit, your great intel-
lect, and your gracious walk with the Lord have inspired me many times over.
God bless you for being available to the Holy Spirit all through the years."

Bruce D. Coleman
"You . . . challenged me to think deeply about theological issues and not
settle for 'what everybody else thinks.' But your example also showed me how
to treat others who may hold different views. This has made all the difference in
enabling me to have meaningful relationships with many. . . . Your example also
has helped in developing relationships with believers with heritages other than
Pentecostal. I was encouraged to have dialogue rather than espousing legalistic
dogmatism. Carefully examining the texts has allowed me to hold unswervingly
to Pentecostal roots and evangelical theology while ministering these truths in a
spirit of meekness."

Thelma Cook, Bethel AG, Springfield, MO
"I well remember your Sunday School class at Bethel Assembly here in
Springfield. . . . You are admired by many for your study, insight, and love for
God's Word."

Charles and Esther Cookman
"We all stand amazed! We could never have guessed that from September
1945 until now, we would still be here to tell the story. Esther and I were some of
your first students at Metropolitan Bible Institute in North Bergen, New Jersey.
Thank you for putting the valuable lessons of God's Word into our hearts. We
have followed your career with avid interest. We wish to thank you for the contributions you have made to the family of God. God continue to richly bless you!"

Paul and Sigrid Cope, Springfield, MO
"What wonderful memories we have of you, your wife, and family. Sigrid
was in some of your classes during the 1958–59 school year at Central Bible
College. For seven years we were neighbors on Williams Street, 1965–1972. . . .
We have a deep respect for your commitment to higher education. Your expertise
in the Word and scholarly publications have contributed to the church in a unique
way. What a wonderful gift you have given!"

Lloyd E. Couch, Illinois Deaf Ministries
"I was one of your students . . . from 1956–59. You were one [of] my favorite teachers. . . . I still have my note books from those years."

Couples Class, Central Assembly, Springfield
The class which Dr. Horton is a part of each week wrote a warm letter of
appreciation for his life and work: "As you celebrate your 90th birthday, we are
honored you have chosen our class and have become a part of what we are."

Ken and Marcie Dahlager, Latin America ChildCare
"Thank you for the impact you have made on my life and on the lives of
thousands of others. I had the privilege of receiving a class on 'Teaching from
the Prophets' as a part of my masters program from the Assemblies of God
Theological Seminary. Your experience and insights gave the class tremendous
meaning. When we were missionaries in Costa Rica we used several of your
books at the Bible School. So your influence stretched to hundreds of people
there as well."

Fern (Green) DeGarmo (CBI in the 1950s)

"I was a reporter for the school newspaper and was asked to do an article on instructors' post graduate studies. You were one of those I interviewed, and I still remember. . . . I was impressed with your humble approach to the scholastic honors you had received."

Leon DeGarmo (CBI in the 1950s)

"I hadn't received the Holy Spirit Baptism and was baptized during a mighty visitation of God in chapel. You were there tarrying with me until I received. I've appreciated your teaching, writings, and especially your walk with God."

Gary A. Denbow, President, Central Bible College

"All of us at Central Bible College want to take this opportunity . . . to send you greetings and honor you for your many years of service to CBC. You came to Central Bible College as a young man in some very critical years. You know better than we the challenges that were faced by our Church at that particular time . . . challenges that could very well have splintered the Assemblies of God. However, you remained true. You taught theology and various books of the Bible in such a way that it gave students a firm foundation in biblical truth with which they could then eschew false doctrine and false theology. Throughout the years your teaching has been a hallmark of Central Bible College and the Assemblies of God Theological Seminary. Many of us have benefited from your books. I have never taught the Book of Acts in any of the stations where I've pastored without reference to your notes and your comments on various passages. I've also appreciated your study in 1 Corinthians. Your diligence to 'rightly divide the Word of Truth' has helped me in ministering to congregations both here and in the Philippines. We pay you honor and respect for your faithfulness to the cause of Christ, for your faithfulness to study the Word of the Lord, and for your faithfulness to teach the truths of the Gospel to men and women for almost sixty years."

Jim Dickinson, Pastor—Paisley Assembly of God, Paisley, Oregon

"I graduated in 1972 from CBC, and put off the required class you taught until my senior year. I have always regretted that decision, because after that class, I wished I had taken everything you offered. Your depth of insight, your vast knowledge, and your sense of humor have stayed with me after all these years. Thank you for the part you played in my education."

Roland and Judy Dudley, (Roland, President), Continental Theological Seminary, Brussels, Belgium

"We will always remember, with tremendous gratitude, the classes we took with you at CBC during our years 1962–1966. One can never forget those early morning Old Testament classes in the basement of Bowie Hall. I am one that saved class notes from those days of study and don't know how often I have, through the years, returned to them to glean additional insight and understanding from your lectures. Thank you for pouring into our lives. . . . Thank you for coming to CTS in Belgium on a number of occasions to teach in our Masters program. You have touched and impacted the lives of students from around the world in our classes at CTS."

Jerry Falley, Nixa, MO

"I remember meeting you for the first time at CBI in the classroom. You were serious about your class and it was easy to see that you wanted us to carry something away from those times together that would help us in future ministry. I loved your teaching and your grasp of biblical languages. Often you would speak in chapel. I remember your simple but anointed presentation of truth. It seemed

there was always a move of the Spirit following your preaching. Thank you for modeling anointed, Bible-based preaching. In so many ways, you have modeled Christian life and ministry."
Glenn Garrison, AGWM Missionary

"I was one of your students during 1967–70. I took every class I could from you. . . . You inspired me to love the OT. . . . I have taught OT in three different Bible Colleges, in the US, Taiwan. and the Philippines. My wife and I have been missionaries with AGWM since 1982."
Donald G. Gifford, Superintendent of the Indiana District Council of the Assemblies of God

"Dr. Horton as a teacher at Central Bible College impacted my life during the early 70's. Later I was greatly helped by his class on Divine Healing in extension education while obtaining my MA degree. On several occasions over the years I have phoned him to ask Biblical questions I needed help with. I have referred often to his written materials, especially his commentary on the book of Acts. I believe our Fellowship has been greatly helped by Dr. Horton's writings, helping us have Pentecostal textbooks for our undergrad and post-grad students. I have appreciated Dr. Horton's words on the General Council floor concerning Credentials & Marriage and Divorce and Remarriage. Thank you, Dr. Horton, for impacting not only my life, but the General Council of the Assemblies of God. Blessings!"
Don and Lorene (Yates) Gould, AGWM Missionaries, Paraguay

"It was our pleasure to have been under Dr. Horton's teaching . . . from 1955–57. . . . It was a great preparation for what we are doing now. We have been . . . in Paraguay for more than 30 years, and since retiring from full-time service, we have returned yearly for the past 6 years to teach in the ministerial level Bible Institute, teaching doctrine that we learned from Dr. Horton."
Jim Grams, CBI class of 1961

"My wife, Charlotte also took the class and together we want to say thank you for not only the classroom teaching but the wonderful messages you gave in Chapel. You brought such scholarship and balance to the Chapel services and your spirituality and integrity was an unbelievable blessing to students for so many years. Of course, those of us who went to the Mission Field tried our best to pass on those things we learned in your class. Hundreds of Brazilian and African Pastors heard me teach O.T. Survey and are now sharing with many thousands of others. You were the Faithful Man who passed it on to other faithful men and on and on and on it goes."
Jim and Jane Harris, Springfield, MO

"We have always held you in great esteem. We love your sweet, gentle spirit and admire your deep, deep knowledge of the Word and how you express it to all believers in the body of Christ. We can see your great love of the Lord and how you have aimed to build up the kingdom of the Lord by your life and words."
Scott Harrup, Associate Editor, *Today's Pentecostal Evangel*

"It was through my dad [Rev. Obie Harrup Jr.] that I first heard about you. He would talk about your Bible teaching with an admiration he reserved for few others. He shared with me that on several occasions he relied on you to answer some pressing questions he had. You visited our family while we were missionaries in Kenya in the 1970s. I remember your friendliness and that you were so approachable. Years later, I was privileged to sit under your teaching at AGTS. And here at the *Evangel* I have again been blessed by your wisdom as I've read your articles and interviewed you. Your latest interview in the *Evangel*

(August 14, 2005) was on the Second Coming. You wrapped it up by saying it would be wonderful if you lived to see Jesus return. I pray that you do."

John R. Hembree, Administrator, Harrison Christian School

"I claim you as my mentor. . . . Early in my education at Central Bible College I was blessed to engage your teaching. You opened my eyes to a yearning for the Hebrew Scripture. This 'bigger' part of God's Word is too often overlooked as irrelevant for Christians today. However, God has always been a God of mercy, love, and grace. These characteristics did not come into existence with the incarnation; Jesus bore them incarnationally as the true representation of who God has always been. You helped me understand this. Dr. Horton, I pray that your quiet grace is contagious. I have watched over the years as your diligence was not dependent on recognition. I applaud your determined efforts to give God your very best even when no one else is looking. . . . You have remained faithful to God in all seasons of your life and through many deep waters. I pray that God will reward your faithful service."

Ron Hembree, President of Cornerstone TeleVision Network and Good Friends, Inc.

"Thank you, Dr. Horton! You touched my life and gave me wonderful insight into God's precious Word! For years we have taken people through the Bible through our Quick Study program and Quick Study Guide. I thank you for helping me learn to love God's Word so that I, in turn, could share it with others!"

John and Faith Higgins, AG Church, Kolkata, India

"You are the epitome of the description: 'a gentleman and a scholar.' For years we knew of your scholarship through your writings. We were appreciative of a Pentecostal we could be proud of in the sphere of biblical/theological scholarship. God had also gifted you with the ability to take wonderfully complex truths and make them understandable to the ordinary member in the Church. Through your classes, your articles, and your books you have been the teacher to thousands, helping them to know God better and understand His ways. Your example of academic excellence has encouraged many young men and women to commit not only their hearts but also their minds to God and His service. In heaven you will share in the reward of the many you have inspired and motivated by your commitment. It was not, however, until you came to be with us at Southern Asia Bible College, Bangalore, India, as a visiting professor that we came to know you as a Christian gentleman. In fact, this was the first time we had ever met you, and we were a little nervous about entertaining such a renowned scholar in our home for several weeks. That concern soon vanished when we became acquainted with your gracious spirit. Your teaching blessed the college; your life enriched us tremendously. Sharing meals around the table, chatting in the evenings, visiting places in India . . . will be memories that we long cherish. Your Christian scholarship is preserved in the books you have written; your Christ-like example is preserved in the hearts you have touched."

Melvin, Louise, and Mariesa Ho

"We thank God that in His providence, He has allowed our paths to cross—from being first, 'distant' readers of your book *What the Bible Says about the Holy Spirit* in Malaysia to being friends of your family in Springfield, Missouri. As one of your many students, I remember well your commitment to scholarship and to precision and details, your patience with students, and your gracious humility both in and outside the classroom. You have the amazing ability of inspiring students to excel. . . . We were privileged to attend the Sunday School class that you taught. By then you had already been teaching there 30 years.

What incredible faithfulness, especially in the midst of your Herculean work schedule. We also learnt of your generosity to others in supporting their ministries and needs as well as the stewardship of your life and resources that Evelyn and you so effacingly displayed. . . . Most of all, how blessed we have been personally as a family. The investment of Evelyn's and your love and kindness in our lives . . . is one we shall never forget."

Richard L. Hoover, CBC Graduate 1972; Missionary to Brazil since 1977
"One of the highlights of my ministry was traveling with you to four of the major cities and A/G mother churches in Brazil and translating for you. I believe the year was 1995 and the Brazilian GPH had just released one of your books in Portuguese and brought you down here to assist them in promoting your written work among the Pentecostals."

Ken Horn, Managing Editor, *Today's Pentecostal Evangel*
"I want to express my deepest appreciation for you and your teaching ministry. It has been so meaningful throughout the years. . . . Your writings have always been most helpful to me. You are the theologian of our movement."

Ron A. Iwasko, President, Global University (2006)
"I first met you . . .when I enrolled at Central Bible College in 1965. . . . I was . . . anxious to learn all I could. Your course and your demeanor were such a great blessing and encouragement to me. . . . Your scholarship coupled with such a humble spirit has served as a wonderful inspiration and role model for me. Your teaching has helped ground me in the Word and in the Spirit. Thank you for all you do to promote Pentecostal scholarship and well-informed teaching and preaching. . . . Together we look forward to that day when we shall gather around the throne to rejoice to praise our great Redeemer with the loved ones who have preceded us. Because of you, multitudes will be there too."

Doris P. Johnson, veteran missionary to Brazil (widow of Bernard Johnson)
Terry and Beth Johnson, veteran missionaries to Brazil
"How well we remember your classes back in the early fifties, when Bernard and I both studied at CBI. Your skillful transmission of Biblical truths provided us with much needful insight to the depths of God's powerful Word. Our son was also blessed by your teaching ministries there in the late seventies, which eventually led to his involvement with the Brazil Extension School of Theology and the Brazil Advanced School of Theology. . . . Undoubtedly your greatest contribution to our beloved nation of Brazil, where I have labored for the past 50 years, has been the translation of your excellent textbooks, which we distribute yearly to our 450 extension campuses, reaching approximately 20,000 students in six nations in Africa, Asia, and Europe. Praise God for your faithfulness as a role model of ministry with integrity, dignity, and excellence. You are highly esteemed and loved."

Melvin Johnson, Asia Pacific Theological Seminary faculty member
"Hebrew did not come easily to me. But through your loving persistence, words of encouragement, and excellent instruction I succeeded. Your teaching has enabled me through 50 plus years of pastoring and teaching. . . .'Thank you' seems a very small expression of gratitude for all you have meant and done for me and multitudes of others. But it comes from deep within my heart."

Bill Kirsch, Managing Director, Africa's Hope (CBC, mid-1970s, AGTS, late 1980s)
"I felt honored to sit under the teaching of one whom many considered to be a legend [in] Assemblies of God education. Thank you for giving your life to training. I believe there is no other area of ministry that has greater impact. That is why I have focused my life on training the multitudes across Africa that have

much less opportunity for training than we do here in America. Thank you for your positive influence on my life."
Byron D. Klaus, President, AGTS

"It is with great joy that I congratulate you on your 90th birthday! The name Stanley Horton in the Assemblies of God and biblical scholarship are synonymous. Your books and writing have been part of my entire lifetime. Growing up in an Assemblies of God Sunday School, studying at an Assemblies of God Bible College, and then teaching . . . in an Assemblies of God college/university and seminary have given me ample opportunity to receive the influence of your biblical scholarship. I am one of those who has enjoyed, been enriched, and been proud of my association with you. On this milestone in your ministry, may God grant you great grace, great health, and continued ministry in His Kingdom."
Barbara Klein, Missionary to Austria

"When I came to CBC in 1975, I had been saved only a year. It was a blessing of the Lord that I had then your Pentateuch course and then all the other Old Testament courses you taught me at AGTS. . . . It was not only your academic expertise, but your personal love for the Word of God and for our Lord that made a deep and lasting impression on my life. I could see that you really knew the Lord of Scripture and lived a life in the Holy Spirit. One memory I have from an AGTS chapel service was when we were singing 'Learning to Lean' and I happened to notice you worshipping the Lord with your hands raised. It touched my heart to see my professor, whose wealth of Biblical knowledge I deeply respected, expressing his personal trust and reliance on Jesus. . . .When I applied in 1979 for a MAPS appointment to teach at Continental Bible College in Brussels . . . you wrote an excellent letter of recommendation for me. I will always be grateful to you for that. It helped me embark on a missionary career in Europe. Over the years, I have taught many times the truths and insights in the Word that you taught me. Many of my students are now teaching them in Bible schools and churches, so you have many 'grand students' around the world."
Robert Krist, Springfield, MO

"I have wonderful memories of Brother Horton . . . at CBI . . . in the early fifties. . . . [He] shared such wisdom with us as students and always came across as a very warm person. His knowledge of the scriptures was incredible and for us he seemed to be a 'Walking Bible'."
Gene and Norma Kummerer, Missionaries to Burkina Faso, Togo, and Belgium (1970–2006)

"Thank you for being the man of God that you have been before the thousands of students who have sat under your teaching. . . . Your work and life have helped to equip us [for] 50 years of ministry."
Rimantas Kupstys and Ivanas Shkulis, Bishop of the Union of Pentecostal Churches of Lithuania and President of Vilnius Theological College

"Please accept the warmest greetings from Lithuania. It would be difficult to overvalue the input the Lord has made [through] your ministry in theological education. [Great numbers] of books [have been] written by you, which also reached our country, bless[ing] our ministers in Pentecostal and other evangelical churches. Also we want to express our appreciation and thanks for your ministry in our Vilnius Theological College in March 1988. It's been a privilege to have you with us and learn from your experience. We saw how through your ministry to the Lord, His compassion was shown through your hands, how His truth was shared through your voice, and His love—through your heart."

David Lantz, Republic, MO

"Through you the Lord has greatly enriched . . . my life. Thank you for taking time out to come to our home to share. . . . You have been a wonderful inspiration to me of Christ's love. . . .We love you and treasure our friendship."

Edgar R. Lee, Vice President for Academic Affairs (Retired), Senior Professor of Spiritual Formation and Pastoral Theology—AGTS

"My first memories of your work flow from the Sunday School quarterlies of the 50s when, as a young Christian and fledgling minister in southeastern Georgia, I faithfully studied for my Sunday school classes. Then, as my own theological education commenced, I followed your career and writings through your books and various church media. Your academic accomplishments and example blazed a trail for so many of us younger colleagues to follow. Finally, in the providence of God, it became my privilege to become personally acquainted with you as I came to be Dean of Assemblies of God Theological Seminary in 1988. We have continued to be associated in many other projects over the years, including especially the Pentecostal Textbooks Project Board and the Commission on Doctrinal Purity. Always, you have been a beloved, Spirit-filled colleague and a rich repository of biblical teaching and Pentecostal lore. How you have blessed me personally along with many millions around the world through your writing and teaching ministries—as well as through your friendship!"

Norman Lestarjette, Retired Missionary to the Spanish-Speaking World

"Your books of Doctrine and Theology over the years have been a tremendous blessing as we used them as textbooks for years in our Bible Schools in Latin America and Spanish-speaking Europe. Your studies and writings have been a major factor in the foundation-building years, helping to establish our pastors, leaders, and churches in the true Biblical doctrines. Only eternity will reveal the extent of your labors."

David A. Lewis, Springfield, MO

"In 1954, we sat together in the classroom where you were teaching Bible courses to eager young students who, day after day, drank from the fountain of your deep knowledge of the precious Word of God. It was here in Central Bible College that I set my course that brought me into a mode of teaching evangelism that I have shared with churches in the USA, Iceland, Canada, Mexico, Europe, Bermuda, Egypt, Jordan, Israel, etc. Ramona and I have feasted richly on your gentle spirit and have always been impressed that in spite of having so much credit being heaped upon you by the community of academia and the churches, you have always manifested a quiet spirit of humility and the grace of God. . . . You have blessed us in so many ways, including partnering with us in local prophecy conferences. . . . Israel is such a big part of prophecy and we learned that you had followed the call of God to go to Israel and lived there . . . doing research and furthering your own education. You are a true lover of Israel. . . . Men like you . . . stand in the gap and are staunchly true to the end time call that commissions every believer to hold forth the Word of Life, which in these last days is a challenge, to preach the Word of God to a lost and dying world that desperately needs the message of Christ's return. . . . You have blessed us by partnering with us in . . . the Springfield Regional Eschatology Club. . . . Thank you for your service to the Christian community . . .giving your time and effort to the office of chaplain. . . . All the members of [the] Eschatology Club . . . salute you with blessings from God and from all our hearts, on this occasion."

Steve and Yen Lim (Steve—2008: AGTS Academic Dean; Professor of Leadership and Ministry)

"I (Yen) came from . . . Bangladesh . . . and was a student of yours at Central Bible College in the 1960's. Your commitment to biblical scholarship and living greatly inspired me, even as I received the spiritual foundation I would need for future ministry. . . . I was also impressed by the interest you took in your students outside of the classroom, being personally blessed by this. I (Steve) first became acquainted with you through your book *What the Bible Says about the Holy Spirit*, which greatly influenced my understanding on this subject. In particular, your description of Spirit baptism as 'immersion into a relationship with a divine Person' has stayed with me through the years and strongly shaped my thinking on this topic. Since coming to teach at AGTS in 2000, I have had the privilege of meeting you several times in person."

Bill Little, CBC 1973–77

"As a student, I had asked Dr. Horton which reference set or book would be the best, given a student's budget. He mentioned several and mentioned the one he preferred. The next time I saw him, he handed me a copy of the one he had mentioned. I still have that copy on my shelf and am reminded of his thoughtfulness every time I see it."

Melissa (Lyle) Peters, CBC 1979–83

"I attended CBC from 1979 to 1983. I . . . grew up attending Bethel Assembly of God. . . . During my growing-up years, I was totally oblivious to the gem we had right in our own church. . . . After graduating from CBC, I went to Ireland and found that Christians there had read his books. . . . I spent some years in Iceland after my time in Ireland, and Brother Horton and his wife were kind enough to often send offerings to me there for the missionary work in which I was involved. Dr. Horton is a very humble man though very well known and esteemed highly by many. I wish to give him honor for his faithfulness through his many years and for his continued faithfulness and perseverance after the loss of his beloved wife."

Robert W. "Bob" Lyle; Melissa Lyle

"Doctor Horton was my Sunday School teacher for about 10 years at Bethel Assembly of God. . . . I even had the honor of substituting for him a few times when he was ministering elsewhere. Once, when I was to teach, he showed up due to a change of plans, and he insisted that I go ahead. I've always been glad about that because that particular lesson had cleared up a seeming contradiction of scripture for me. When I had explained this to the class and given his interpretation as I now understood it, I asked Doctor Horton if I'd gotten his explanation right. . . . He nodded and smiled. . . . His brother Donald visited Bethel, and I was remarking to him about how privileged we were to be able to ask our teacher anything about the scriptures and how he was always so humble and not just willing but enjoyed answering our questions in detail, being careful to see that we understood. Donald replied, 'Yes, the thing about Stanley is that not only is he a scholar, he has remained a student of the word.'"

Bob and Bette Sue MacIsaac, Vilnius Theological Bible College, Lithuania

"We remember with great fondness your trip to Lithuania and your blessing to the students. . . . One of our memories will always be of your humble spirit as you talked with the nationals here. It was a pleasure to have you in our home."

John T. Maempa, Director of the AG National Prayer Center; President of the International Pentecostal Press Association

"I well remember that when I first began employment with the adult curriculum section of the Church School Literature Department in 1975, you were writing the *Adult Teacher* commentary. It seemed presumptuous of me at the time, being a fresh seminary graduate and fledgling editor, to 'edit' your writing. It would still seem presumptuous now 30 years later. Your work always was done with such excellence and clarity. . . . Thank you for the rich and enduring resources you have provided. Thank you for the superb scholarly and spiritual integrity you have modeled for all of us. Thank you for holding high the supremacy of the Word of God through your teaching, writing, and living."

Dennis Marquardt, Northern New England District Superintendent (CBC class of 1974)

"I had the wonderful privilege of being in your classes while attending Central Bible College in the early 1970's, and who would ever have thought today I would be a district superintendent! I recall many times questioning in class some of the fine points of our doctrines, and you were always calm, consistent, and with clarity . . . presented a good defense of the faith once delivered to the saints. Clearly men like yourself have shaped an entire generation of leaders today who are now at the helm of our fellowship, and we thank you—I thank you! You have shown the greatest statesmanship, faith, and joy in Christian excellence. You also showed us that faith and knowledge are not elements divorced from one another, but complementary to the highest levels. You are a treasured gift to this church, and I hold dear my memories of your lectures and your teachings, your warmth in class. You have helped shape my life and ministry to this day."

Daniel Mercaldo, Sr. Pastor and Founder, Church at the Gateway, Staten Island, NY

"Dr. Stanley Horton gave his life to give us a love for God's Word, and a passion to study the truth therein. His pleasant mannerisms and willingness to explain great truths so we could understand them will ever be a part of the legacy he leaves in the wake of decades of ministry. . . . How grateful I am to be able to say that I sat under his ministry."

Greg Mundis, Europe Regional Director, AGWM

"Your knowledge was never pitted against your wisdom, but they worked hand in hand to provide for young and impressionable students a model of a godly lifestyle. Your keen intellect and academic prowess advocated not only tolerance for study (so that we could get to doing the work of the kingdom) but were an example of the blending of heart and mind for the good of the kingdom! Thank you for your passion for the Word, for your passion for Witness, and your passion for Worship. You are a great blessing to your generation and for generations to come."

Alice Murphy, Director of Technical Services for Pearlman Memorial Library, Central Bible College

"I was blessed to have Dr. Horton as my Sunday School teacher while I attended Bethel Assembly when I first came to Springfield. He made the lesson come alive. Later it was my delight to have him as a teacher at AGTS. I recall his Bible Study methods class as being very worthwhile. In Background of the Old Testament, I had the feeling he was being careful not to overload us with information, which he certainly could have. Excellent teacher and author. . . . his book on Revelation . . . [and] the one on Acts . . . are written in such a way as to be useful to laypeople as well as more biblically educated people."

Wayne Newcomb, Equippers Network, Englewood, CO

"I remember my first class with Dr. Horton. You see, I was saved in a jail awaiting trial, and they said I would never get out. But God had other plans. A year later I started classes at CBC where Dr. Horton was one of my first professors. I remember his humility and passion for God's word. Dr. Horton has inspired me to keep learning and growing in God. . . . His keen knowledge of God's word and his humility inspired me to be as passionate about God's word as he was."

Kirk Noonan, *Today's Pentecostal Evangel*

"Thanks for encouraging me with kind words since I have worked for *Today's Pentecostal Evangel*. When I came to work for the magazine in 1999 I was honored to have my work appear in the same issues as your columns. (My parents—Barry and Linda Noonan—are very proud of this too.) I admire your energy and willingness to continue to travel around the world doing what you do best: teaching. If I live to be 90 years old I pray that I will be as humble and motivated as you are. For now, I will strive to be that way at 35 years of age."

Lori O'Dea, AGTS D.Min. Program Coordinator (2006)

"Thank you for your investment in my life personally and in the Church as a whole. Your writing, scholarship, and teaching have strengthened the Assemblies of God around the world and far beyond the walls of our churches. While [I was] an M.Div. student at AGTS, you were my advisor and teacher. I was continuously amazed at the amount of knowledge you could easily access. But it was your spirit, more than your brilliance, that captivated us. Whether you were walking us through some intricacy of the Old Testament or teaching Aramaic, you did so with passion and humility. I'll never forget this story I once heard: When you were asked by a student whether you preferred to be called 'Doctor Horton' or 'Brother Horton,' you responded that it cost Jesus far more for you to be called 'Brother' than it did you to be called 'Doctor.' That gracious spirit has infused your life and ministry with enormous influence. I'm very grateful to have been shaped by it."

Paul D. Parks, Center for Ministry to Muslims

"Of the many teachers I have had over the years you have probably influenced my life more than most. If there ever was a professor I wanted to be like, it was you. I was one of your many students at CBC from 1967 through 1970. I took several courses from you. . . . The one that stands out in my memory is two years of Biblical Hebrew. My purpose was to learn Hebrew in order that I could learn Arabic, for God had called me to minister to the Muslims of the Middle East. I remember the first day of Hebrew class when you began by addressing the class in Hebrew. With that opening, you were telling us it was possible to learn Biblical Hebrew, and I think it gave us all courage. . . . I made it as a missionary, 30 years now, and as I remember, you were one of my references who told the DFM that I could learn another language, which was not obvious from the test I took for them. . . . Then you were at the funeral of my first wife . . . and you spoke words of encouragement. . . . Most recently, my new wife, Lucille, helped you several years ago when you went to teach in the former Soviet Union for Jerry Parsley. You have greatly influenced my life, and for this I am grateful."

Diane Peters, AGWM Missionary to Paraguay

"I have benefited greatly from your writing. . . . Thank you, for your commitment to provide us with countless articles on theology and, especially, on the Holy Spirit. I am teaching Global University courses in Paraguay, South America, and thank God for your textbooks translated into Spanish. Your writings have influenced Assemblies of God leaders worldwide. Thank you for the rich contribution you have made to students and pastors . . . impacting the next generation of leaders."

Nicholas Paul Pirolo, CBC class of 1957

"You helped to 'Solidify my confidence in the Bible.' I often catch myself sharing with others and with my children some Bible facts that I remember learning in your classes. . . . My father died when I was eleven, and although I had a Christian heritage, there were still questions that I was seeking answers to when I arrived at CBIS in 1955. One of the influences that drew me to Springfield was letters from friends who were students. They bragged about the intelligence of two special professors, Dr. Horton and Dr. Johns. . . . Maybe you remember encouraging me to continue studying both Greek and Hebrew at the same time. Maybe you remember discussing a question about the original sin. Maybe you remember your wife inviting me and another student into your home to develop our Bible memorization. . . . Thank God for her ministry, too. . . . These are some of the special experiences that I associate with my interactions with you and your family."

Clydene Reep

"I always enjoyed your Sunday School class at Bethel Assembly in Springfield. . . . My husband Jon thought so much of you and bragged about how you were one of the 7 leading Hebrew scholars in the world. For him you were the final word!"

Curtis W. Ringness (Palm Desert, CA), former Assistant General Superintendent and Home Missions Director for the Assemblies of God

"Often I think of the fellowship we have enjoyed through the years. When I was called to serve at the General Council headquarters, our family moved into a Norton Road house and we became 'back yard' neighbors. Having known and respected you as an outstanding minister and teacher it was good for us and our families to enjoy a closer relationship. It is something we have cherished for well over a half century. . . . You, your beloved wife, and family have been true examples of what a Christian family should be. . . . Congratulations on your 90th. I celebrated my 90th on March 22, 2006. God has been good to us."

Shirley Schultz, husband was a CBC student 1969–70

"We appreciate your many years of serving our Lord and the sacrifices that you made to do so. We know that you could have been a professor at a major university and earned high wages instead. We met you on the street in downtown Springfield at Christmas that year and it was snowing so beautifully, and we remember the pleasant way that you took time to speak with us. Also, the model Passover feast that you presented each year has always stayed with us and enlightened our understanding of the scriptures. Thank you again for your humility and servant attitude in the midst of genius and greatness. We are continuing to help spread the gospel as you taught us to do."

Donald Dean Smeeton, Lee University

"I will not recount here a moment in class when your insight clarified an abstract concept, but I want to mention a much more humble moment. . . . On one particular day, you were a couple of steps ahead of me as we walked along the sidewalk in front of Evans Hall, when you stopped, bent over, and retrieved a piece of paper that had been thoughtlessly dropped by some student. . . . You placed the trash in the proper receptacle located just a few feet away. Your action that day had no significance to you and I am sure you can not recall it, but it lodged in my memory as a clear picture of what ministry really means. You showed me humble service. . . . I am richer because of your example."

Jerry Spain, Africa's Hope – Director of Ministries

"It was 50 years ago this coming fall that I enrolled at CBI. I was fresh out of the sandhills of northern Nebraska. Everything was new. One of my classes was Old Testament Survey taught by Dr. Stanley Horton. The memory is vivid. I sat near the front of a large class. The instructor would place two Bibles on the desk along with some notes. There was an English Bible and a Hebrew version.

For someone who had seldom heard or seen a foreign language, I was touched by the manner in which the original language of the Bible was used for reference. Of course, that someone was you. The Old Testament and for that matter the entire Bible took on new meaning. It was during those days the Lord touched my life. I surrendered to His lordship and told Him he could send me anywhere in the world with the good news. Joy and I have spent the past 40 years as missionaries to Africa. It has been a marvelous journey. In fact, at one point you were able to visit us on the campus of the East Africa School of Theology in Nairobi, Kenya. The students and faculty were impacted by your ministry. Thanks for your faithfulness to the Lord, His Word, His Church, and His mission."

Russ and Bobbie Spittler, Vanguard University (2006); Provost Emeritus and Senior Professor of New Testament, Fuller Theological Seminary (2008)

"Well do we remember our children growing up on Williams Street when you and I were on the faculty of Central Bible College. Your daughter, Faith, taught our daughter, Cheri, how to swing. Cheri has never forgotten that. Those were wonderful days, when you, Bob Cooley, Bill Menzies, Don Johns, and Zenas Bicket were among our closest friends and colleagues."

Chaplain (Major) Lane Stockeland, U.S. Army

"It was a blessing having Dr. Horton as an AGTS instructor. He was a true scholar, mentor, professional, and most of all approachable friend. I still recall his message from an AGTS chapel service entitled 'Seek Not Bethel' from Amos chapters 4 and 5."

David A. Swafford, Academic Dean CT, Republic of Georgia (2006); Global University; Caribbean School of Theology, (2008); Student of Dr. Horton's at CBC and AGTS. Was a pastor then became a missionary in the Republic of Georgia.

"We . . . have started the first Pentecostal Bible Institute in the history of this country. . . . Shirley has started the first . . .Women's Ministry Center in this country. . . . We believe God is going to use the graduates from our Institute to reach into the Muslim world with the Gospel."

Willard Teague, Global University

"Dr. Horton was my professor at AGTS. His humble spirit and scholarship were always evident both in the classroom and in personal conversations with him. He has inspired thousands to be faithful in their service to the Master and will continue to live on in his numerous writings. We spent 27 years in West Africa serving as missionaries, and we are presently continuing our missionary service through Global University. What he taught us has been a part of our ministry."

Esther Steelberg Pearlman Tisdalle, cousin (missionary to southern Africa) (Juanita's sister, daughter of Wesley and Ruth Steelberg, granddaughter of Elmer Kirk Fisher)

"My first memories of Stanley were when my folks would go back to California and the family would get together. Because he was 16 years older than me, I was in awe of him and the fact that he was 'so smart.' When he went back east to go to college, we corresponded and I was so proud that he would take the time for this little female squirt of a cousin. He always talked to me as an adult, which was very flattering, and I found him, although somewhat serious, to have a wonderful sense of humor. Through the years, he has been a shining example of a spiritual guide, and I have proudly claimed him as 'my cousin.'"

Eldon and Twyla Tracy, Abundant Life Association, Missionaries to the Portuguese-Speaking World

"We were honored and blessed to have had you as one of our teachers and mentors. I remember classes with you quite well. . . . Your desire to see the moving of

the Holy Spirit marked my desires as well. That you always honored the leadership around you, while you focused on your ministry task and people, given by the Holy Spirit, marked my memory. . . . 54 semester hours in undergraduate hours at CBC and graduate school hours at AGTS we were together. I know I was blessed and my life was changed by the truths I learned. Thank you for pouring your life into me. I hope that my life and ministry will bring honor to your investment. I don't remember either of us missing a class for the 918 hours we were together. I still have the notes."
Ray Trask, AGWM, Bangkok, Thailand

"Every time I prepare for a class or a sermon, I am reminded of your admonition, 'Be Faithful to The Word!' You are loved by this Great Fellowship."
Thomas E. Trask, AG General Superintendent (2006)

"Your service unto the Lord and the Assemblies of God over these years will receive its just reward, but until that day, we thank you for your dedication to the work of Christ's kingdom."
Russell and Ruby Wisehart, AG General Council, Bible and Doctrine editor

"Our acquaintance goes back about 47 years (CBI 1959–63). . . . You were my professor. . . . Little did I ever dream at that time that I would one day be working with my [mentor]. . . . You wrote the Adult and Student lessons for 1st and 2nd Corinthians (Fall, 1982). I felt it such a privilege to be asked to do the Methodology for that quarter. When I pull out Volume 5 of that series it gives me a proud but humble feeling to see my name linked with yours in the list of writers. . . . It is hard to believe I have been doing the Bible and Doctrine editing for around 20 years now. I have been fortunate enough to accumulate every hardback *Adult Teacher* since they first came out in 1958. I have a few of the saddle-stitched ones before that. I cannot count the times I have referred back to your lessons when doing my editing. There were a lot of notes in the margins of writers' manuscripts that said in essence, 'The writer says this, but Dr. Horton says this.' The people in the churches that I have pastored and the thousands of Berean students whose doctrinal questions I have tried to answer have all benefited from your wisdom and knowledge of God and His Word."
James, Delrae, and Rebekah Wiseman, AGWM Missionaries to Guatemala

"Thank you so very much for your part in the publishing of The Complete Biblical Library. That set has been a great help to me in the ministry."
George O. Wood, General Secretary of the Assemblies of God (2006); General Superintendent of the Assemblies of God (2007–present)

4/24/06 "I don't think anyone this side of heaven could truly calculate the incredible contribution you have made to the Assemblies of God, the body of Christ, and the thousands of thousands of lives you have touched through your teaching, preaching, writing, and the sterling example of your personal life. As a child of the Azusa Street Revival and Mission, you have effectively lived out over these decades the splendor and the glory of this modern day outpouring of the Spirit. You have provided an intellectual and theological anchor to countless students and ministers and have taught us all that Pentecost not only warms the heart but energizes the mind also. Through your careful handling of the Biblical text, you have passed on the rich treasure of Pentecostal doctrine and praxis. Thank you for being a ground-breaker in the Assemblies of God who helped pave the way for all of us who followed after you in serious scholarly engagement." 5/6/06 "You have served the Lord and the Assemblies of God with such excellence. You began your teaching and writing ministry at a time when those with academic credentials were regarded with some suspicion in our Fellowship. But you showed that heart and mind could be equally warm and open to the

Holy Spirit. You paved the way for generations of Assemblies of God scholars to follow you, and you enriched our entire church with your copious writings—books, articles, responses to questions. You have been a bridge linking the Azusa revival to the present day. Through your writings—especially in Acts and on the Holy Spirit—you have helped the Assemblies of God stand within the stream of apostolic thought and action. We all owe you a great debt of gratitude. And we are grateful most to the Lord who gave you as a precious gift to us!"

Joy York, Africa's Hope

"Though John knew you much better than I, having had you for a teacher when he did his MA and then working with you on various writing projects, I know that he highly respected you and appreciated your friendship through the years. If he were still here I know he would have specific memories to share and would note specific contributions you have made to the Assemblies of God through the years through your teaching and writing—and his words would be much more eloquent than mine! But, let me thank you for being a friend as well as colleague in ministry and a servant who loves the Word. You have impacted thousands of lives and have been a wonderful example for those who have followed you."

Bibliography

A complete list of works authored, edited, contributed to, by, or about Dr. Stanley M. Horton (over 40 pages) is available at the Flower Pentecostal Heritage Center Web site (www.ifphc.org/horton).

"1910–1911." *The Upper Room*, Vol. 2, No. 4 (January 1911): 1.

"A Great Move Forward." *Pentecostal Evangel*, May 1, 1926, 2, 3.

"Aimee Semple McPherson: Our Founder." The Foursquare Church, http://www.foursquare.org/landing_pages/8,3.html (accessed September 4, 2008).

"A Little Girl's Vision of Heaven." In *Azusa Street Papers: A Reprint of The Apostolic Faith Mission Publication*, Los Angeles, CA, 1906–1909. Edited by William J. Seymour. (Foley, AL: Together in the Harvest Publications) (Public domain) Vol. 1 No. 5 (Jan. 1907): 28. Also available from: http://www.evanwiggs.com/revival/history/azusa.html (accessed April 25, 2008).

"A New Look in . . . Student Government." *The Centralite*, May 26, 1971, 1.

Arrington, F. L. "Dispensationalism." In *The New International Dictionary of Pentecostal and Charismatic Movements.*" Rev. and expanded edition. Edited by Stanley M. Burgess and Eduard M. Van Der Maas. 585, 586. Grand Rapids, MI: Zondervan, 2003.

"Athar-Quadeemi Holds First Meeting." *The Centralite*, October 22, 1965, 1.

"Assemblies Plan 2-1/2 Million Building," *The Centralite*, May 18, 1960, 3.

"Assemblies of God Superintendents." *Enrichment* journal, http://ag.org/enrichmentjournal/199904/021_ag_supts.cfm (accessed August 31, 2008).

Bartleman, Frank. *Azusa Street: The Roots of Modern-day Pentecost.* S. Plainfield, NJ: Bridge Publishing, Inc., 1980. (Originally published in Los Angeles in 1925).

———. *War and the Christian* (n.p., n.d.)

Beaman, Jay. *Pentecostal Pacifism: The Origin, Development, and Rejection of Pacific Belief Among the Pentecostals.* Hillsboro, KS: Center for Mennonite Brethren Studies, 1989.

Blumhofer, Edith L. *Aimee Semple McPherson: Everybody's Sister.* Grand Rapids: William B. Eerdmans Publishing Company, 1993.

———. *Pentecost in My Soul: Explorations in the Meaning of Pentecostal Experience in the Early Assemblies of God.* Springfield, MO: Gospel Publishing House, 1989.

———. *Pentecostal Currents in American Protestantism.* Urbana: University of Illinois Press, 1999.

Booth-Clibborn, Arthur Sydney. *Blood Against Blood.* New York: Charles C. Cook, n.d.

"CBC to Receive New Men's Dorm," *The Centralite*, November 18, 1976, 1.

Central Bible College, Springfield, Missouri: A Souvenir Album Commemorating Seventy Years of Excellence. Western Printing, 1992.

Conwell, Russell H. *Acres of Diamonds.* Temple University. http://www.temple.edu/about/Acres_of_Diamonds.htm (accessed July 5, 2008).

Crane, Beverly. "Miss Parry Librarian." *The Centralite*, September 20, 1955, 2.

"Dr. Menzies Takes Leave to Write History of A/G." *The Centralite*, November 7, 1969, 1.

"Dr. Robert E. Fisher's Ministry Touched Thousands." *Church of God News*, Church of God, http://churchofgod.org/articles.cfm?sid=6029 (accessed July 2, 2008).

Enrichment journal (entire Spring 2006 issue, "The Azusa Street Revival: 100 Years of Pentecostal Power and Passion").

"Fellowship Maintains Active Interest in Jewish People." *Pentecostal Evangel,* July 12, 1981, 21.

Fisher, Elmer Kirk. "How to Receive the Baptism of the Holy Ghost and Fire." In *The Upper Room*, June 1909.

Flower, J. Roswell. "The Plight of the Conscientious Objector in the Present World Conflict." *The Pentecostal Evangel*, July 3, 1943, 2, 3.

"Flower, Joseph James Roswell (1888–1970), and Alice Reynolds (1890–1991)." In *The New International Dictionary of Pentecostal and Charismatic Movements.* 2nd ed. Edited by Stanley M. Burgess and Eduard M. Van Der Maas, 642–644. Grand Rapids: Zondervan, 2003.

"Following the Shepherd: Testimony of Mrs. Virginia E. Moss." North Bergen, N.J., n.p. n.d.

Frodsham, Stanley ed. "The Budding Fig Tree." *Pentecostal Evangel,* April 15, 1922, 1.

Gannon, Ray. "The Shifting Romance with Israel: American Pentecostal Ideology of Zionism and the Jewish State." Ph.D. diss., Jerusalem: Hebrew University, 2003.

Gaston, William T. "Looking for the Blessed Hope," *Enrichment* journal, http://www.ag.org/enrichmentjournal/199904/gs_04_gaston.cfm (accessed August 9, 2008).

Gaston, W. T. (Picture) http://www.flickr.com/photos/ifphc/255039878.

Gee, Donald. "Conscientious Objection." *Pentecostal Evangel*. November 8, 1930; November 15, 1930; May 4, 1940.

"Gordon Faculty Online." Gordon College, http://faculty.gordon.edu/ns/by/craig_story/PhiAlphaChi.cfm (accessed September 6, 2008).

"Gordon To Speak On Jewish Theme." *The Centralite*, March 15, 1968, 1.

"Grad School Might Be for You." *The Centralite*, March 26, 1976, 3.

"Grad School . . . More Faculty. Dean Johns Named," *The Centralite*, February 26, 1973, 2, 3.

"Graduate School . . . Opening Set For Sept." *The Centralite*, December 15, 1972, 1, 2.

Hartwick, Reuben. "Pentecost Comes to the Northeast: A Survey of the Early Events and Influential Leaders." *Heritage* (Spring 1990): 3–5.

"Historic Earthquakes: Long Beach, California." U. S. Geological Survey, http://earthquake.usgs.gov/regional/states/events/1933_03_11.php (accessed July 22, 2008).

"How Did the ETS Begin?" Evangelical Theological Society, http://www.etsjets.org/?q=faq (accessed September 6, 2008).

"How to Receive the Baptism of The Holy Ghost and Fire." *The Upper Room*, Vol. 1, No. 1 (June, 1909): 4, 5.

"Instructor Nikoloff Reviews Past." *The Scroll*, September 27, 1952, 2.

Jacobsen, Douglas. "Knowing the Doctrines of Pentecostals: The Scholastic Theology of the Assemblies of God, 1930–55." In *Pentecostal Currents in American Protestantism*. Edited by Edith L. Blumhofer, Russell P. Spittler, and Grant A. Wacker, 90–107. Urbana and Chicago: University of Illinois Press, 1999.

"Jewish Conference Calls for Wider Fellowship Participation." *Pentecostal Evangel*, September 9, 1979, 10, 11.

"Jewish Rabbi Speaks on Jewish Concepts." *The Centralite*, March 19, 1966, 1.

Larson, Mel. *Gil Dodds: The Flying Parson*. Chicago: The Evangelical Beacon, 1945.

Lewis, Paul W. "Reflections of a Hundred Years of Pentecostal Theology." *Cyberjournal for Charismatic Pentecostal Research*; Pentecostal-Charismatic Theological Inquiry International, http://www.pctii.org/cyberj/cyberj12/lewis.html (accessed January 4, 2007).

"Long Lost Photograph Finds a Home." Flower Pentecostal Heritage Center Blog, http://ifphc.wordpress.com/2008/07/29/long-lost-photograph-finds-a-home/#more-182 (accessed August 5, 2008).

"Looking at the A/G Graduate School." *The Centralite*, May 17, 1974, 2.

McGee, Gary B. *People of the Spirit: The Assemblies of God.* Springfield, MO: Gospel Publishing House, 2004.

———. "The Pentecostal Movement and Assemblies of God Theology: Exploring the Historical Background," Part 1, *AG Heritage* (Winter 1993–94): 10–12, 27, 28.

———. "The Pentecostal Movement and Assemblies of God Theology: Development and Preservation Since 1914." Part 2, *AG Heritage* (Spring 1994): 24–28, 31.

———. *This Gospel Shall Be Preached: A History and Theology of Assemblies of God Foreign Missions to 1959* (Vol. 1). 169, 170. Springfield, MO: Gospel Publishing House, 1986.

———. *This Gospel Shall Be Preached: A History and Theology of Assemblies of God Foreign Missions Since 1959* (Vol. 2). 101. Springfield, MO: Gospel Publishing House, 1989.

Mittelstadt, Martin William, and Matthew Paugh, "The Social Conscience of Stanley Horton," *Heritage*, 2009, 15–19.

"New Education Secretary Appointed." *Pentecostal Evangel*, May 4, 1958, 21.

"New York Rabbi To Speak Here." *The Centralite*, February 5, 1964, 1.

Nickel, Thomas R. "The Shakarian Story," 2nd ed. Los Angeles: Full Gospel Businessmen's Fellowship International, 3–14, also available at http://fgbmfi.org/who.htm (accessed July 11, 2008).

Olena, Lois E. "Pentecostals and the New Anti-Semitism: Walking in the Fruit and Fullness of the Spirit for the Sake of the Jewish People." D.Min. project, Assemblies of God Theological Seminary, 2006.

"Papers of Victor Guy Plymire." Billy Graham Center Archives of Wheaton College, http://www.wheaton.edu/bgc/archives/GUIDES/341.htm (accessed October 27, 2008).

"Peterson Becomes School President." *The Scroll*, October 22, 1948, 1, 4.

"Pillars of the Faith." Assemblies of God Theological Seminary, http://www.agts.edu/partners/pillars_of_faith.html (accessed September 6, 2008).

"Preacher's Comeback." *Time*, February 3, 1947; http://www.time.com/time/magazine/article/0,9171,886330,00.html (accessed August 30, 2008).

"Rabbi Bernard Visits Campus." *The Centralite*, March 6, 1964, 1.

"Registration Reveals Largest Enrollment in School History." *The Scroll*, October 22, 1948, 1.

Robeck, Cecil M. ("Mel"), Jr. *Azusa Street Mission and Revival: The Birth of the Global Pentecostal Movement.* Nashville: Thomas Nelson, 2006.

———"Azusa Street Revival." In *The New International Dictionary of Pentecostal and Charismatic Movements.* 2nd ed. Edited by Stanley M. Burgess and Eduard M. Van Der Maas, 344–50. Grand Rapids: Zondervan, 2003.

Shakarian, Demos. *The Happiest People on Earth*. Old Tappan, NJ: Fleming H. Revell Company, 1975.

"Spencer Jones Pastors Tampa St. Assembly." *The Centralite*, January 23, 1970, 1.

Studd, George P. "Chronology," a brief overview of his life from 1906–1943, FPHC Archive.

———. "Diary." January 19, 1908–December 7, 1908 (FPHC Archive).

———. "Los Angeles." *Confidence*, August 15, 1908, 10.

"The Evans Story . . .Dedicated in Memoriam to William Irvin Evans." *The Cup*. 16–29. Springfield, MO: Central Bible Institute, 1955.

"The New Nearly-Completed Bible School." *Pentecostal Evangel*, August 9, 1924, 1.

"Timeline of the Dust Bowl." PBS. http://www.pbs.org/wgbh/amex/dust-bowl/timeline/ (accessed July 5, 2008).

"To Hold Golden Anniversary Celebration at Gospel Tabernacle in North Bergen." *Hudson Dispatch*, September 15, 1961, 8.

Wacker, Grant. *Heaven Below: Early Pentecostals and American Culture*. Cambridge: Harvard University Press, 2001.

Warner, Wayne. "The Pentecostal Methodist: J. Narver Gortner—Pastor, Writer, Teacher, Executive Presbyter." *A/G Heritage*, Vol. 8 no. 2 (Summer 1988): 12–14.

"What is a Good Teacher?" *The Centralite*, May 9, 1962, 3.

"W. I. Evans With Jesus." *The Scroll*. May 20, 1954, 1–3.

Williams, E. S. " . . .In the Case of War . . ." *The Pentecostal Evangel*, March 19, 1938.

Wood, George O. "Resolve to Persevere." *Pentecostal Evangel*, May 23, 2004, 20. Also available at: http://www.ag.org/pentecostal-evangel/Articles2004/4698_wood.cfm.

Index